Child Welfare Services
for Minority Ethnic Families

of related interest

Supporting Parents
Messages from Research
David Quinton
ISBN 1 84310 210 2

Meeting the Needs of Ethnic Minority Children – Including Refugee, Black and Mixed Parentage Children
A Handbook for Professionals
Second Edition
Edited by Kedar Nath Dwivedi
ISBN 1 85302 959 9

Mental Health Services for Minority Ethnic Children and Adolescents
Edited by Mhemooda Malek and Carol Joughin
Child and Adolescent Mental Health Series
ISBN 1 84310 236 6

The Developing World of the Child
Edited by Jane Aldgate, David Jones, Wendy Rose and Carole Jeffery
ISBN 1 84310 244 7

The Child's World
Assessing Children in Need
Edited by Jan Horwath
ISBN 1 85302 957 2

Parenting in Poor Environments
Stress, Support and Coping
Deborah Ghate and Neal Hazel
ISBN 1 84310 069 X

Foster Placements
Why They Succeed and Why They Fail
Ian Sinclair, Kate Wilson and Ian Gibbs
ISBN 1 84310 173 4

Permanent Family Placement for Children of Minority Ethnic Origin
June Thoburn, Liz Norford and Stephen Parvez Rashid
ISBN 1 85302 875 4

Child Welfare Services for Minority Ethnic Families

The Research Reviewed

June Thoburn
Ashok Chand
Joanne Procter

Introduction by
Beverley Prevatt Goldstein

Jessica Kingsley Publishers
London and Philadelphia

The right of June Thoburn, Ashok Chand and Joanne Procter to be identified as authors of this work has been asserted by them in accordance with the Copyright, Designs and Patents Act 1988.

First published in 2005
by Jessica Kingsley Publishers
116 Pentonville Road
London N1 9JB, UK
and
400 Market Street, Suite 400
Philadelphia, PA 19106, USA
www.jkp.com

Copyright © June Thoburn, Ashok Chand and Joanne Procter 2005
Introduction copyright © Beverley Prevatt Goldstein 2005

Library of Congress Cataloging in Publication Data
Thoburn, June.
  Child welfare services for minority ethnic families : the research reviewed / June Thoburn, Ashok Chand, and Joanne Procter ; introduction by Beverley Prevatt Goldstein.
      p. cm.
  Includes bibliographical references and index.
  ISBN 1-84310-269-2 (pbk.)
  1. Child welfare--Research--Great Britain. 2. Children of minorities--Services for--Great Britain. 3. Social work with minorities--Great Britain. 4. Family social work--Great Britain. I. Chand, Ashok, 1968- II. Procter, Joanne, 1974- III. Title.
  HV751.A6T45 2005
  362.7--dc22

                                                    2004014818

British Library Cataloguing in Publication Data
A CIP catalogue record for this book is available from the British Library

ISBN-13: 978 184310 269 4
ISBN-10: 1 84310 269 2

Printed and Bound in Great Britain by
Athenaeum Press, Gateshead, Tyne and Wear

Contents

List of Tables

Preface

The format of this book is somewhat unusual so we take the somewhat unusual step of providing an authors' preface. Parts I and II take different approaches to reporting the results of a project to scope and summarise research findings on child welfare services for children and parents of minority ethnic origin that will be explained in more detail here. Although this book is a resource for educators and researchers, we anticipate that our main readership will be child welfare practitioners, managers and service planners themselves. We hope that it will also prove useful to individuals and groups in the community who currently make use of child welfare services, or would do so if they were more widely publicised or were more appropriate to the needs of the different ethnic groups that make up the UK's diverse population.

Part I is written as four extended commentaries on different aspects of child welfare work with introductory and concluding chapters setting the scene and pointing towards a future research agenda, referring to the research but not obscuring the main messages with too much detail. It is a summary of our interpretation of what research in the broad and overlapping areas of family support, child protection, child placement and social work practice has to say, where the ambiguities and contested areas lie and where there are major gaps. In undertaking this task we were greatly assisted by researchers who provided summaries of their own studies, took part in workshops and looked at earlier drafts. However, with such a broad area to cover, the emphasis chosen and the interpretation of the messages from the research are ours.

Part two, comprising more detailed summaries of the most relevant research, is therefore an essential companion to Part I, giving the opportunity to learn more about the aims, methods and findings of the studies referred to in the overview. Some will turn to these summaries for more information about the relevance of a particular study to their own work and interests; others will find it a useful indicator of the studies they need to read in full. Most of these have been provided by the researchers specifically for this project and edited by us to a common format or have been edited to that format from published summaries. We have not attempted to undertake a critical review of the 'quality' of these studies. Some provide very detailed information and insights from a very small number of children or parents; some involve large numbers and give evidence of associations between particular family characteristics and particular outcomes, but leave the reader with many 'but why might that be so' questions still up in the air. All those included are here because they had something to say, about the families needing services, the providers of services, the helping processes or the outcomes for parents or children. The extensive reference list points the way to other relevant literature mentioned in the text, including more general writing on 'race', ethnicity and religion from the fields of cultural studies, anthropology, sociology and demography on the one hand, and on child welfare policy, values and practice on the other hand.

As we went further into our project it became increasingly clear that, in concentrating on empirical research focusing on child welfare services, we were leaving out a great deal of scholarly writing, analysis and debate on the context in which they are provided. This work, emanating from the USA and more recently strengthened (in the English language literature) by significant contributions by writers in the UK, Australia, Canada and New Zealand, could not be squeezed in as an 'add-on' to this already lengthy publication, but should not be ignored. Beverley Prevatt Goldstein's introductory chapter stands in its own right as a reflective essay on some of the most important questions confronting anyone planning, providing or researching child welfare services for minority ethnic families in our diverse society. It provides essential context for what follows, offers a way into the literature on 'race', racism and diversity listed in the references and suggests some questions for readers to keep in mind as they contemplate the adequacy and relevance for their own work of what follows.

One clear message from the research is that it is not possible to 'unpick' what it tells us about child placement or leaving care services from what it tells us about approaches to the provision of family support. Tempting though it may be for the busy practitioner or researcher to turn to the sections that appear most relevant to their own work setting or research interest, we hope that most will read Part I as a 'story' of child welfare interventions that parallels the 'journey' that some parents and children take (some more and some less willingly) through the child welfare processes and systems. An inadequately publicised or inappropriately delivered service at the start of the journey could lead to families becoming unnecessarily caught up in more coercive interventions further down the line. The response to a particular research finding on court services, for example, may be not a change to the court service but a change to services provided to families when problems first become apparent. We have tried to keep the story told by the research as 'readable' as possible, but we would not have done what we set out to do if we had over-simplified an essentially complex picture.

Finally, we want to say something about the voices of children and parents. We have not included in this review the many moving and highly informative biographical accounts of what it feels like to be visibly or culturally 'different' from the majority and to be on the receiving end of child welfare interventions. However, many of the researchers provide detailed quotes and a small number have been included to illustrate some of the main points. In all cases names used by the authors whose work we cite have been changed to preserve anonymity. We thank these unknown contributors and the many more who have lent their voices to the review by sharing with researchers their own critiques of the services they hoped for or received. We hope that some of you will read this and will recognise yourselves and the contribution you have made.

Acknowledgements

We would like to thank all the researchers who attended the workshops, answered our questions about their research methods and findings, and completed the templates that formed the basis of some of the research summaries in Part II. Our thanks go especially to those researchers who were willing to provide stage one findings and as yet unpublished research, to allow this book to be as comprehensive as possible. We are particularly grateful to Beverley Prevatt Goldstein for her wise and thought-provoking introductory chapter and to Beverley, Julia Brophy and Jabeer Butt, who opened the workshops and the practitioners' conference with reflective critiques of the draft research overviews. Special thanks go to Sharon Witherspoon who, from out first approach to the Nuffield Foundation to these final stages, has been a source of advice and encouragement. Celia Atherton and Michael Little of the Nuffield Foundation Child Protection, Family Law and Justice Committee have also been there when needed to provide detailed comments on drafts and contributions to the workshops, and point us towards contacts to help fill in gaps. Our colleagues at the Universities of East Anglia and Nottingham have been generous with their time in pointing us towards studies we had missed or reflecting with us on the underlying issues. We are most grateful to all these colleagues for their time and support but we alone are responsible for the final shape and contents of this publication.

An indirect thankyou must be given to the children, parents and carers whose words bring meaning to our attempts to sift through the percentages, analyses and conclusions of so many and such varied studies. As Beverley Prevatt Goldstein reminds us in Chapter 1, none of this is worth anything if it does not bring improvements to the lives of a new generation of child welfare service users. Their willingness to let researchers enter their lives, and to share both their sadnesses and their triumphs, has greatly contributed to the value of the studies that do exist, and pointed the way towards a future research and practice agenda in which those who follow them will almost certainly have a greater part to play.

Last but not least we thank our partners and children (those old enough to do so) for understanding how important it was for us to do justice to this vitally important subject.

Chapter 1

Introduction: A Context to the Review

Beverley Prevatt Goldstein

This chapter complements the review by offering a context both to the research process and the research subjects. The context to the research process highlights some of the complexities that are embedded in any research review on 'minority ethnic children and their families', thus assisting the reader in appreciating the strengths of this particular review while questioning some of its assumptions. The context to the research subjects provides data, particularly from the 2001 census, that is pertinent to understanding their child welfare. This chapter draws on the views expressed by the other two discussants, Julia Brophy and Jabeer Butt, who commented on the review while it was in progress and the questions and comments shared by the participants in the workshops held during the compilation of the review. Nevertheless the views expressed are those of the author, a black community worker and former academic, who uses a 'radical perspective shaped and formed by [her] marginality' (hooks 1991, p.150) vis-à-vis the academic research community to offer alternative ways of interpreting this research review.

This review of research on child welfare services for children of minority ethnic origin and their families presents a host of studies. It is the first comprehensive review on this topic since that by Butt and Mirza, *Social Care and Black Communities* (1996). During the period 1991–2001 the black minority ethnic population has grown by 53 per cent to 9 per cent of the population of England, though some of this is due to the explicit inclusion, for the first time, of the black mixed parentage population (15 per cent of the total black population). This is a population with a high proportion of under-16s particularly in some ethnic groups (almost 50 per cent of those of mixed parentage in the UK population were aged 0–16 as were 38 per cent and 36 per cent respectively of those of Bangladeshi and Pakistani origin). It is therefore timely to reconsider and update our understanding of the child welfare of this growing population. Additionally, there are gaps in our knowledge, such as the level of over-representation in the care and child protection systems of some within this group (Butt and Mirza 1996), uncertainty in our policies, such as in the appropriate placement of black children with one white parent (Barn, Sinclair and Ferdinand 1997), and failures in our practice, such as the gross failure of the multiple public agencies involved to protect Victoria Climbié, an African child from the Ivory Coast (Laming 2003). A research review that can lead to improved knowledge and practice is therefore much needed.

A research review on black minority ethnic children and their families gives a clear message that this is a group worthy of study, worthy of being the exclusive focus of research. This is a challenge to the sometime invisibility of black people in policy documents and research. But there are other messages. The title of this review suggests that it is this minority ethnic status that is the determining factor in the experience of this group. There are limitations with this assumption. These limitations need to be considered as they affect not only our understanding of the research but also the practice to which the research may lead.

The title of this research review suggests that this is a group principally identified because they form the minority ethnic population of the UK. But this is not the case, as the review specifically focuses on African, South Asian and Caribbean children and families, omitting those of white minority ethnic status such as the Irish, one of the largest minority ethnic groups in Britain. This inaccuracy in terminology is common. Nevertheless, the use of the term 'minority ethnic children' as a synonym for black ethnicities can render invisible the experiences of those of white minority ethnicities such as Irish, Jewish and the travelling communities.

A further complexity is that despite the focus on black ethnicities and ethnic categorisation this review does refer to asylum seekers and refugees. This is, in one sense, understandable as asylum seekers and refugees, while from both black and white ethnicities, are currently subject to discrimination as if 'black'. Nevertheless, there needs to be an awareness that there may be many ethnicities and cultures subsumed in the term 'asylum seekers and refugees' and that for white asylum seekers and refugees the location within 'black' may be a temporary location.

The term 'minority ethnic' and the ethnic categorisation in many of the research studies need to be understood in the context of an academic and political debate on whether ethnicity or racialised grouping is the most helpful focus. There is a value to the focus on ethnicity. The disaggregation of 'black' into its historical, geographical and cultural components, where possible, enables the different outcomes of different groups of children within 'black' to be tracked. This has the benefits of recognising differences, avoiding stereotyping and enabling, if practice follows research, resources to be appropriately targeted. But this focus also normalises divisions by ethnicity rather than the solidarity of racialised groupings and experiences. Yet National Statistics Online of 2004 reveals that while the black ethnic groups have a broad range of experiences in employment, income and education, it is in the experience of racism that there is the most common ground (the risk of experiencing a racially motivated incident is 4.6% for Pakistani and Bangladeshi, 3.6% for Indian, 2.2% for African and Caribbean compared to 0.3% for white). This does not mean that the collective 'black' is unproblematic, and Brah, while endorsing it, warns that 'there will be a need to remain vigilant of the circumstances under which affirmation of a particular collective experience becomes an essentialist assertion of difference' (1992, p.143). There are implications for training and practice in whether the focus is on ethnicised or racialised groupings. The components of ethnicity – religion, culture, language – are fundamental to the identity and lifestyle of some within each ethnic group and it is essential that services acknowledge this, enhance it and reflect in their functioning the diversity of cultures (Parekh 2000). A focus on ethnicity may encourage cultural awareness training and separate and 'culturally appropriate' provision for ethnic groups while a focus on racialised groupings may encourage anti-racist training and a scrutiny of organisational processes. In the child welfare of black minority ethnic children and their families both have a place but it is essential that those reading the review are aware of the assumptions and consequences of the different approaches in research (Razarch 1998).

A focus on ethnicity can not only disaggregate a political collective but also prioritise ethnic divisions above divisions within and across ethnicities of class, gender, age, education, disability and location. This focus on ethnicity has been contested by Brah (1992) and by Wimmer in his article 'Does Ethnicity Matter?' (2004). The focus on ethnicity as the significant variable in research can lead to cultural explanations for different experiences and foster a static, homogenous view of culture rather than the reality of culture as nuanced, individualised and changing (Werner and Modood 1999). Dutt and Phillips' (1996) challenge to cultural explanations for child abuse has been widely accepted. However, there still remains a danger that we may rely on other people's culture to explain the use of services, and that in seeking to make services 'culturally sensitive' we apply stereotypical notions of culture without interrogating them for age, class, gender, etc. This is not intended to promote 'culturally blind services'. Rather it is to suggest that all services should be sensitive to the changing needs and culture of all individuals. Ethnicised groupings may provide some research accuracy but this is only one type of accuracy and it is noteworthy that research on white groups focuses less on ethnic divisions than on other categories such as age, gender and experience.

Ethnic and racial categorisation can facilitate the assumption that outcomes are a result of the innate nature of that ethnicity or racialised grouping rather than the result of underlying factors experienced by many in that group or of the particular circumstances of, and particular treatment accorded to, that specific research cohort. While each research study may seek to avoid ethnic or racial essentialism, the combined effect may be to encourage both this ethnic essentialism and generalisations within ethnic groups. This tendency to generalise is more likely the greater our distance from the subjects of the research (Strachan and Patel 1996).

Lewis (2000) highlights the 'othering' entailed in both racialisation and ethnicisation. There have been research reviews such as *Child Protection: Messages from Research* (Department of Health (DH) 1995); *Adoption Now: Messages from Research* (DH 1999b); *The Children Act Now: Messages from Research* (DH 2001) and *Supporting Parents: Messages from Research* (Quinton 2004). A specific review on the messages from research for minority ethnic children, despite some cross-referencing, may contribute to the 'othering' of this group. Perhaps one of the reasons for the specific focus is the concern that black minority ethnic children are not doing well in the child welfare system and that for this group, unlike white minority or majority ethnic children, discrimination may be a contributory factor. If this is an implicit part of the rationale, and a similar concern appears to be the reason behind the kind of ethnic monitoring that has been institutionalised, it may offer an important context for this review on children and families of black ethnicities.

But the explicit rationale for this review is also important. The review has been supported by the Nuffield Foundation in order to identify gaps in the research in this area. It therefore seems that an important purpose of the review might be to assist those funding research and those undertaking research to identify areas that have not been previously explored and areas where research might be both productive and constructive. The review might be said to have three interlinked aims: to identify gaps in knowledge, to promulgate knowledge and to further good practice.

The aim of identifying gaps in the research suggests a subject and object relationship whereby the researchers (and the funders) have the power to determine the type and area of research and those researched are 'done to'. Participatory styles of research may reduce the power imbalance while not fundamentally altering it. As the racialised power balance in universities replicates that of society (Fenton, Carter and Modood 2000), this is likely to play out, for the most part, as white academics and funders making the decisions on researching black families and communities, giving a racialised dimension to the research process. As bel hooks asks of 'the unprecedented support among scholars and intellectuals for the inclusion of the Other...who is controlling the new discourse? Who is getting hired to teach it, and where? Who is getting paid to write about it?' (hooks 1991, p.54). In 1991, Cross, speaking of research and action, stated that 'there are many articulate voices [of the minorities] pressing the claim of a myriad of new concerns' (1991, p.311). Do these research studies reflect the new concerns? Are the new concerns those of minority researchers and how far do they include the priorities of the families or of the children and young people?

The knowledge promulgated in this review needs to be set in the context of the wider situation of black minority ethnic families. Black minority ethnic families are of diverse ethnicities with the 2001 census recording the black minority ethnic population of the UK as Indian (1.8%), Pakistani (1.3%), Black Mixed Parentage (1.2%), Caribbean (1%), African (0.8%), Bangladeshi (0.5%), Chinese (0.4%), Other Asian (0.4%), Other Ethnic Groups (0.4%), and Black Other (0.2%). Is this range reflected in the research studies which identify ethnicity? Should it be? Is it possible to identify research on Chinese children with one or two Chinese parents? The 1991 census indicated that Chinese women were the group with the highest number of relationships with white people (Owen 1996) and therefore there is likely to be a significant group of Chinese mixed parentage children in the population. What does the paucity of research on Chinese children indicate? Is this a population that is not an object of political concern, apart from immigration? Is its under-representation in family support, child protection and family placement so great as to render it invisible? Is there an absence of Chinese child welfare professionals or researchers to put this on the agenda? Research by Parker (1995) on Chinese youth suggests that this is a population managing culture and identity in similarly complex ways as other black youth and its apparent resilience in terms of child welfare merits attention.

Black minority ethnic families have a long history in Britain, starting in the sixteenth century, with the communities being reinvigorated periodically: in the eighteenth and nineteenth century with slaves and freed slaves, in the early twentieth century with students and the sailors; in the mid twentieth century with those coming to meet the needs in Britain for soldiers in the Second World War, for workers in the hospitals, on the buses and in the textile factories and to gain a better life; and again in the twenty-first century with the refugee population. The black minority population of England is now 9 per cent with over 50 per cent being born in England and with some families, particularly Black Mixed Parentage and Caribbean, having been here for three generations or more. Therefore the mixed experience of these groups of service delivery, as outlined in some of the research studies, cannot be explained by service users' or providers' lack of opportunity to become familiar with each other or by differences in language and religion.

The black minority ethnic population is located mainly in London (45%) and in the West Midlands (13%) with under 4 per cent in the north-east or south-west. The density of this population in each research study may influence its findings. For example, in areas with low numbers of people of black ethnicities, the overall level of service received by them is likely to be less extensive and appropriate (Social Exclusion Unit 2003) and the level of isolation and racism experienced higher (MacLeod and Morris 1996). Isolation may be an important variable in increasing the vulnerability of black families to other stresses and this isolation may be exacerbated by the lone parenting found in 54 per cent of Caribbean families and 61 per cent of black mixed parentage families with dependant children.

The stresses experienced by many black families are varied but often include racism and economic deprivation. Racism ranges from everyday racist harassment to racist incidents (recorded at 215,000 in 2000–01 and estimated to be double this figure (London Research Centre 1993) to murders with a suspected or known racist motive (25 since 1991). Virdee found in his research that 'racial harassment contributes to a continual climate of insecurity' (1997, p.264) that is deeply hurtful and disruptive and Fitzgerald and Hale (1996) that a racist incident had a much greater negative impact on the victim than a non-racist incident. All the evidence suggests that racist harassment and racist incidents affect the health and lifestyle of not just the victim but also their family and associates (Nazroo 1997).

> Two of us went shopping together, always. Two of us had to be in the house to defend the others. We used to be scared going home. We used to phone Mum and say 'Mum, I am coming round the corner. Please look out of the window.' We always had to carry change for the phone in case something happened. We had to let the family know what shops we were going to so if we were late they could go and check. Everything was really organised. (Chahal and Julienne 1999)

Racism and racist harassment is not only mediated through the family but has a direct impact on children. Webster notes 'what was striking among the young people we spoke to was the pervasiveness and normality of racism and the possibility of violent racism as a routine aspect of everyday life' (1995, p.17). MacLeod and Morris (1996) found a high incidence of racial bullying particularly amongst children isolated from others in their racialised or ethnicized grouping, and NCH Action for Children (1997) found that children gave a higher priority to the reduction of racist incidents than adults. After studying indicators in health, poverty and education, Barter testifies to the 'detrimental effect racism has on the lives and life chances of ethnic minority children' (1999, p.14).

Black minority ethnic children and their families are affected not only by interpersonal racism but also by institutional racism, as evidenced in The Stephen Lawrence Inquiry (2000) on the police force and in the Bennett Inquiry (Blofield 2004) on the National Health Service. In 1997 Heath and McMahon spoke of the 'ethnic penalty' to be paid by all in the black minority ethnic communities, regardless of their qualifications and position in the job hierarchy, and in 2003 the Cabinet Office Strategy Unit Report stated that ethnicity is a determining factor in employment. The unemployment rate for black minority ethnic groups is two to three times higher than for the white population, with that of Bangladeshi men, at 20 per cent, being four times higher than that of white men, and that of Bangladeshi women, at 24 per cent, six times higher than that of white women. Forty-one per cent of African Caribbean, 45 per cent of Indian, 82 per cent of Pakstani and 84 per cent of Bangladeshi people have incomes of less than half the national average compared with 28 per cent of white people. Racism, unemployment and poverty have a cumulative effect on health and general well-being with Pakistani and Bangladeshi men and women having the highest rate of self-reported ill health.

Garbarino (1982) found that 'children from stigmatised racial and ethnic groups are particularly likely to experience multiple interconnected sources of stress' and the results of these stresses on well-being are well recorded (Bebbington and Miles 1989; Smith and Carlson, 1997). It is essential that we look carefully at all the research studies because these stresses of poverty, isolation and racism not only impact on the need for family support but may also provide a context for our understanding of child protection issues where physical abuse and lack of supervision is involved. The existence and impact of racism is one of the reasons for placing black children with families who can empathise and support them with this abusive experience. But while the overall knowledge of the extent of racism, of the socio-economic experiences of black minority ethnic people overall, or of South Asians or of Bangladeshis can give us a context and can help in planning, it cannot tell us the situation of the particular families researched. Every black child and family does not experience an identical level of stress or the same combination of multiple stresses nor experience the stress in the same way. We need to interrogate each research study for information on the racism experienced, the socio-economic factors and the ethnic composition of the population in the location of the research subjects. The recommendations and action plans might also be scrutinised for the attention they pay to reducing negative socio-economic factors for as Rutter (1987) wrote, 'to understand and encourage resilience and protective mechanisms we need to attend to the interplay between what occurs in families and what occurs in the political, economic, social and racial climates in which individuals perish or thrive'.

The broad contextual framework of black minority ethnic groups is often conveyed as solely negative. Yet the economic contribution overall has been tremendous; for example, the Bank of England estimated that in 1996 the contribution of black and Asian people to gross domestic product was around £37 billion (Parekh 2000, p.202) and the resilience maintained in difficult circumstances is considerable (Prevatt Goldstein 2003). Hylton (1997) outlines some of the strengths of black minority ethnic groups such as spirituality, religious and cultural boundaries, renewal and development of cultural identities and adaptation of practices and a reliance on friends, religion and prayer rather than statutory or voluntary services. Goodman and Richards (1995) found, from their research on African Caribbean families, high academic self-esteem among the girls until puberty, more family warmth and less dysfunction in spite of social disadvantage and a lower incidence of school refusals and a high value placed on education by African-Caribbean parents.

The 2001 census has confirmed the greater identification with religion of the South Asian groups and successful outcomes in education for Indian, Chinese, Black African and the 'other Asian' group. Many of these characteristics, for example, religious practice, education, strong cultural identification, have been linked with resilience (Fonagy *et al.* 1994). This strengths-focused data, like the deficit-focused data, will not apply to all within any ethnic group or across all the ethnic groups and, as Rutter (1987) has suggested, the way these factors are integrated may be very significant to the outcome. Yet strengths-focused data may enable us to question the overwhelmingly problem-focused approach that we may find in some of the research studies and perhaps contribute to an understanding of seeming anomalies, for example, the under-representation of some black minority ethnic groups in the care system, the capacity of some families to cope without visible support. But the finding of the panel in the Tyra Henry case that:

> There is a positive, but nevertheless false stereotype in white British society of the Afro-Caribbean mother figure as endlessly resourceful…essentially unsinkable. It may have been [that this] underlay the neglect of social services to make adequate provision for [Beatrice Henry] taking responsibility for Tyra (London Borough of Lambeth 1987, p.108)

is a reminder that positive stereotypes may be misused, perhaps when convenient to do so.

Research not only provides knowledge but structures knowledge and the problem-focused approach of some of the studies may encourage a deficit model of black minority ethnic children and their families. Positive findings need to be affirmed without generalising. Research studies which contradict this deficit approach by explicitly looking at organisational systems and their impact on the outcomes for the children and their families (see the review by Barnardos, forthcoming) and by focusing on the resilience and self help strategies of black minority ethnic children and their families should be welcomed. Rashid's article on 'The strengths of black families: appropriate placements for all' (2000) based on the research of Thoburn, Norford and Rashid (2000) illustrates that findings on strength and resilience may be obscured unless one is diligent in searching for them.

Research design may also limit our thinking as to what is a good outcome by the repetition of outcomes which are easily measurable, such as disruption or stability of placement. Tilbury (2004) suggests that 'case events or decisions such as "reunification", "adoption", or "case closure" may replace more meaningful case goals if they are elevated to become outcomes in themselves' (p. 232) and contests a simplistic reliance on indicators such as placement stability, permanency or re-abuse. These indicators are important but others such as cultural and religious continuity, interdependence, taking responsibility, educational achievement, showing respect, staying safe from racism, may also be rated as prime outcomes by some black minority ethnic families. Some of these are now being valued as contributing to resilience (Gilligan 1998) but many have not routinely been incorporated in the identification of satisfactory outcomes. Additionally, research studies may encourage us to focus on short-term outcomes but long-term outcomes, such as feelings of difference, alienation from adoptive family, an unsatisfied search for identity, identified by Kirton, Feast and Howe (2000) may be equally important.

A narrow range of outcomes may be the result of the concept and prioritisation of hard rather than soft data. The benefits and dangers of this have been much discussed (Sheldon 2001; Webb 2001). The search for 'hard' evidence is an attractive one in an 'evidence based climate' particularly as the sources of evidence are becoming more widely available with the ethnic monitoring of the Children in Need figures and wide data sets such as the Family Resource Survey. But the tools measuring this data may have been standardised on other populations and the responses to sensitive issues such as ethnic monitoring or identity may be unreliable. It is important that there is sufficient information for the reader to interrogate the methodology of the research studies. A focus on hard data, as well as missing some of the more difficult to quantify outcomes, can also exclude the practitioner knowledge and the voice of the researched. The findings of research can only take us so far without the voice of the children and their families, the complex and long term outcomes, the ethical issues, the political frameworks. As Parker, in his overview of research on adoption (DH 1999b, p.116) has also concluded:

> The fact that, judged against the particular outcome criteria and time scales that were applied, no significant difference was detectable between cross-cultural and convergent placements…is not in itself a conclusive argument for departing from the policy that children should be found ethnically compatible families with respect to new placements… There are other questions – identity, vulnerability to racism and the lifetime implications once people have left the adopted home to be considered as well.

Research can and must assist with practice but the burden of good practice cannot be borne by research devoid of context. The contribution of a review to good practice is particularly important to the black minority ethnic communities who largely consider that they have been research subjects for decades without noticeable benefit. Any research review will offer many messages with the inevitable inconsistencies in findings due to differences in perspectives, samples, methodology, etc., of the research studies. There is a danger that when faced with patchy, inconsistent data we do nothing or accept that which meets our own preconceptions (Strachan and Patel 1996). As well as considering our preconceptions, it may be helpful to focus on the findings of the individual study, scrutinise its methodology, place it in its socio-political and ethical context, add the voices of the young people, their families and practitioners from other sources, if they are absent, and take action within the context of that research study towards better practice. Additionally, some of the more common recommendations require care in implementation. Prevatt Goldstein (2002) identified from her research study that the use of black workers to contribute additional expertise above their stated role, in conditions of personal and institutional racism, had negative consequences for the workers, and Parekh (2000) that training, without organisational change, has severe limitations.

While it can be easier for a research review to be followed by more research than by improved practice, this is not inevitable. The evidence of black children being placed with white carers to their detriment sparked the move to recruit black carers (Small 1982); the evidence of poor practice with black parents/carers in the court system (Brophy, Jhutti-Johal and Owen 2003b) contributed to the Guidance enabling courts to make arrangements for interpreters in Family Court Proceedings (Court Service HQ 2003). But research evidence often needs to convey a simple message and requires a moral or political imperative to put it into practice. The tragedy of Victoria Climbié's death might act as a wake-up call to address properly the needs of black minority ethnic children across the board, but equally systems, which are blind to racism, may be put in place. The duty on all public bodies to be proactive on race equality; the inspections on equality processes such as those carried out by the Office of the Deputy Prime Minister and by the Audit Commission; the inclusion of outcomes for black minority ethnic children in the performance indicators of social services may all contribute to a driving force for positive change, even while structural reorganisations, or mergers between social services departments with health or education might divert from this focus.

This research review could have three outcomes, identifying gaps in the research, promulgating knowledge and promoting good practice. The first two are achievable through the review while the latter is dependent on the reader and the prevailing ethical, political and economic climate. None of these outcomes is unproblematic and the more convincingly the review achieves the first two outcomes and provides the information for the latter, the more aware we need to be of the pitfalls. These pitfalls centre on accepting the research data without placing it in the context of resilience and possible racism, poverty and isolation and being seduced into ethnic generalisations. There is also the issue pertaining to all research as to the extent to which the research is determined by the communities researched and to which it leads to improved outcomes for these communities. Nevertheless, this timely research review will contribute to our knowledge and has the potential to improve practice. Therefore, the message of this chapter is that because this review is so potentially useful we need to use it with care.

Part I

The Research
and the Messages

Chapter 2

Introduction to the Research Literature

The background to the research review

Over the past 20 years or so UK government departments, major research funders and some of the larger voluntary child care organisations have a commendable record in funding research on child welfare. Especially through its *Messages from Research* series (starting with *Social Work Decisions in Child Care*, (Department of Health and Social Services (DHSS) 1985) the Department of Health has published summaries and funded dissemination events on different groups of children 'in need' or in the public care. From this body of research some overarching themes (including the role of fathers and issues around sexual abuse) have been picked out as subjects for more detailed Department of Health (DH) commissioned research reviews (Jones and Ramchandani 1999; Ryan 2000). The particular issues relevant to children and families of minority ethnic origin were not included in this programme of work but the Department of Health commissioned separately a review, synthesis and critique of research and other data sources (mostly published between 1980 and 1996) relevant to people of African-Caribbean, African or Asian descent who receive a social work or social care service or would do so if an appropriate service were available (Butt and Mirza 1996). The Joseph Rowntree Foundation also funded a series of studies, initiated by a review of the contextual issues and the literature (Barn 2001).

In 1997 the Child Protection, Family Law and Justice Committee of the Nuffield Foundation called together a group of practitioners, policy makers and researchers to review the state of research on families of minority ethnic origin and to consider areas in which future research would be beneficial. The broad conclusion was that, although the literature on 'race', ethnicity, culture and child and family welfare might appear extensive, much of it was in the form of practice guidance or discussions of policy issues such as the question of same-race placements. The broader knowledge base and debates in these publications, which are outlined in Chapter 1, are essential companions to this book and are touched on in the chapters which follow.

One problem identified at the Nuffield workshop, and highlighted in all literature reviews, is that cohort studies tend to involve relatively few families of minority ethnic origin, and often, in analysis, do not differentiate between different ethnic groups, despite, as Berthoud (2000), Butt and Mirza (1996) and Modood and colleagues (1997) make clear, their differing strengths, problems, needs and responses to services.

When Dutt and Phillips (2000) were commissioned to write a section for the guidance to accompany the DH's *New Assessment Framework*, the lack of up-to-date research and research overviews on child welfare services to the different minority ethnic populations was again highlighted. It was at that point that discussions started with the Nuffield Foundation which led to the commissioning of this research review and synthesis. Its aim is to establish what research (broadly defined) tells us about children in the UK who are of minority ethnic origin and are in need of child welfare services. Our threshold for inclusion in the review is research on 'children in need' (Children Act 1989 Section 17). These are children who would be unlikely to achieve a 'reasonable standard of health or development' or whose health or development would be likely to be 'significantly impaired' without the provision of child welfare services to meet their identified needs. We have not included 'normative' studies of general populations of UK children, although these will be referred to where they have insights to offer, especially those that focus on 'needy' or 'potentially needy' groups of children in the population as a whole, or on questions such as 'normal' parenting behaviour, for example concerning the use of physical chastisement or parental responses to racial abuse or harassment.

Alongside research on those who actually receive a service, we include studies that provide information on children and families who, having sought and been assessed as meeting the threshold criteria, do not receive a service because no appropriate service is available or they are not defined as of sufficiently high priority. We also sought research evidence on those whose children would, if they sought assistance, be assessed as 'in need' but who do not seek a service from a statutory or voluntary sector child welfare agency, either through lack of awareness, anxiety about unwanted consequences, or because their additional needs are already being met by mainstream services or their families or communities:

- Who are these 'children in need'?

- Why do they need services additional to those provided on a 'universalist' basis?

- What do we know about the services provided to children, parents and carers, and how well do they fare?

At the outset, it is important to note that the threshold to inclusion in this review (as well as to the receipt of child welfare services) is not a clear line but rather a blurred area. Since we started planning this project four years ago, there have been many changes, not only in the characteristics of the children and families and the communities in which they live, but also in the services and especially in the settings in which these services are provided.

Children, families and ethnic groups

In terms of the children and families, it quickly became apparent that many familiar statements about children of 'minority ethnic origin' were based on out-of-date population figures. Terms in common usage to describe the different ethnic groups who are the subject of this study have changed over the years as has our understanding of concepts such as 'race', nationality, culture and ethnicity. The reader is referred to the work of Barn (2001), Beishon, Modood and Virdee (1998), Berthoud (2000), Brophy (2003), Butt (2000), Butt and Mirza (1996), Gilroy (1993), Jones and Butt (1995), Kirton (2000), Mama (1995), Prevatt Goldstein and Spencer (2000), Robinson (2001) and Rutter and Tienda (submitted). Other than when considering the impact of individual or institutional racism (a very important caveat), the term 'black' has become unhelpful in understanding the complex identities and needs of families who might be in receipt of a child welfare service.

When referring collectively to the subjects of this review, we have either used the language of the researcher whose work we are citing or the term 'minority ethnic group'. This is not entirely satisfactory. Although accurate when considering the UK population as a whole, the 2001 census establishes that in some whole local authorities white British children are in the minority, and in some wards, children from one of the other groups who make up our ethnically diverse population comprise the largest group of children. When we started the commission we had in mind principally children and families who were 'visibly different', mainly with one or both parents of African-Caribbean, African or South Asian heritage. Although many of their parents or grandparents would have been born overseas, the majority of the children would have been born in the UK. We were aware that an important minority would be recent immigrants (whether temporary residents, immigrants, refugees or asylum seeking families) and a small but growing group would be unaccompanied children seeking asylum. Children and families of white European, Middle Eastern or Central Asian heritage who have recently come to the UK as refugees in substantial numbers now figure amongst the vulnerable groups in need of child and family welfare services. In summary, the groups we are including in this review are those who, to use the Oxford English Dictionary (2002) definition, share 'a distinctive cultural and historical tradition, often associated with race, nationality or religion, by which the group identifies itself and others recognise it' and who differ 'physically or culturally from the rest of the community'. In the main, we are referring to those ethnic groups whose relatives settled in the UK within the last two or three generations and who, when completing a census or other form, may well identify themselves with the country from which their forebears migrated. There has been and still is much debate about whether and when 'black' or 'Black' and 'white' or 'White' should be used. Since we are mainly using these terms descriptively rather then in their political sense, we have not used capitals. However, when describing the research of others, or using direct quotes, we have used the form as it appears in the publications of these authors.

The period between 1991 and 2001 saw much debate about how census data on ethnicity and religion could be improved (Aspinall 2000; Ballard 1999; Halpern and Nazroo 2000; Haskey 1997; Nanton 1992). It is recognised that data based on self-completion check-lists collected for a range of different purposes cannot do justice to the complexity of identities already referred to. As it is, the check-list categories are based on different types of information including skin colour (black/white), country or region from which family members or forebears migrated (Indian or Caribbean for example); nationality/citizenship (e.g. British), sometimes in combination as with 'Black British' and parentage (as with 'mixed parentage'). The 'drop down' categories in the 2001 Census were arrived at after much debate so that those who opt to define themselves as 'Black British', 'Black' or 'mixed race parentage' can, if they choose (and not all do), provide more detailed information about heritage. Information on religion is now collected separately. Appendix 1 gives the data on ethnic groups and religion from the 2001 Census (National Statistics 2003). In summary, there have been major changes in the last decade, with increases in all ethnic groups but especially in each of the Asian ethnic groups, those of black African heritage, those in the 'mixed ethnic' group and those in the white 'other' group. Just under one English resident in ten was born outside the UK. The proportion born outside the EU had risen from 5.3 per cent in the 1991 Census to 6.9 per cent in 2001. As recorded by the 2001 Census, 87 per cent of the population of England is white British, 1.3 per cent white Irish; and 2.7 per cent 'other white'. Nine per cent in England and 2 per cent in Wales indicated on the census form that they were of an ethnic group other than white. These differences are even more apparent when the proportions of those aged 0 to 18 from the different ethnic groups are considered (Table 2.1). The largest increases in the child population over the decade have been in children of African, Pakistani and white/African-Caribbean heritage.

Table 2.1 Ethnic origin of children aged 0–17 in England (2001)

Ethnic group	Number	%
Total White	**9,623,899**	**86.5**
White British	9,379,596	84.0
White Irish	42,545	0.4
White Other	201,758	1.8
Total of South Asian heritage	**826,029**	**7.4**
If mixed ethnicity excluded	**730,615**	**6.6**
Indian	271,120	2.4
Pakistani	277,935	2.5
Bangladeshi	118,596	1.0
South Asian/White heritage	95,404	0.9
Other Asian background	62,974	0.6
Total Black or Black British	**513,158**	**4.6**
If mixed ethnicity excluded	**330,212**	**3.0**
Caribbean	130,046	1.2
Caribbean/White heritage	145,256	1.3
African	159,915	1.4
African/White heritage	37,690	0.3
Other Black heritage	40,251	0.4
Chinese	**49,252**	**0.4**
Other ethnic groups	**120,519**	**1.0**
Other mixed heritage	73,156	0.7
Any other ethnic group	47,363	0.4

Source: Data adapted from National Statistics (2003) Table S101

This is almost certainly an underestimate as it is known from qualitative research studies that some children of mixed race parentage will list themselves or be listed by the parent completing the Census form as 'White British'. This quote is from a boy of Pakistani and Scottish descent who told the researcher that he was English and explained: 'I was born in England, if I was born in Africa I would say that I am African' (Sinclair and Hai 2003, p.20). Others are listed under the country of origin or ethnic group of, for example, their Indian or African-Caribbean parent because they or their parent see this as an accurate description of their skin colour, nationality or ethnic group. (See, for example, Rutter and Tienda, submitted, for a fuller discussion on this point and Freeman and Hunt 1998, and Sinclair and Hai 2003 for examples from child welfare research).

The changing pattern of service provision

In terms of services, even in 2000 the major providers of child welfare services to children 'in need' were Local Authority Social Services Departments, in partnership with voluntary organisations most of whose work was funded by Social Services Departments. Health Trusts provided services to some of the children identified as having emotional and behavioural difficulties and were responsible for meeting some of the welfare as well as the health needs of children with disabilities. Schools and school psychological services were working with troubled children whose difficulties impeded their settling into school or making educational progress and local education authorities were responsible for vulnerable children needing subsidised day care alongside the general populations of families using child care services (Statham, Dillon and Moss 2001). The Youth Offending Teams (YOTs) were just beginning to take over from the Social Services Departments and Probation Service the provision and co-ordination of services to children in need who had committed offences, with some remit to concern themselves with those, including younger children, who were considered to be at risk of offending. There is now more diversity, especially amongst government or government 'arms-length' bodies who both provide and fund services, mainly in the area of family support to children who would come within our 'in need' definition. These, including Sure Start, On Track, Children's Fund, Connexions, New Deal for Communities, 'extended schools' and the pathfinder Children's Trusts) usually combine services for general populations with services for children 'in need'. The government green paper *Every Child Matters* (Department for Education and Skills (DfES) 2003) has accelerated these changes.

Some statistical data on these initiatives, including data on ethnicity, are beginning to emerge, alongside descriptive data from local evaluations, but the body of published research is still slight. This will be touched on but we concentrate on the services that fall within the remit of Social Services or Social

Care sections of what in 2004 are referred to as Councils with Social Services Responsibilities rather than their Education Departments, though recognising that these will be coming closer together.

Another recent change has been the performance assessment and target setting regime. This has had the very positive result of making available routinely collected statistics that, as data collection on ethnic groups becomes more accurate – and it has still some way to go – will enhance the reliability of our knowledge about under- and over-representation of ethnic groups amongst those using services. However, the problem with targets is that they imply that, for example, numbers starting to be looked after should come down and therefore that 'over-representation' of a particular ethnic group in the looked after statistics is a 'bad thing'. This may lead to the loss of a valued and needed service and may obscure the fact that some ethnic groups are losing out because they are not seeking assistance. In what follows we approach the question of under- and over-representation from a value-neutral stance and look, in the research, for data which explains why some children and families make more or less use of services.

The approach to the task of review and synthesis

A reading of the policy and practice literature in this area confirms that, quite appropriately, it arouses strong feelings, and that it is a field of research in which the evidence and its interpretation are contested. From the start we proposed to take a 'collegiate' approach to the review so that our conclusions would have broad consensus amongst researchers. An iterative approach to the task was therefore adopted. Rather than embarking on the 'traditional' literature search and systematic review, the authors asked the people who are most familiar with these studies (the researchers and statisticians themselves) to provide summaries and commentaries on the dimension of ethnicity and culture in their work. Researchers known to have published, or to be currently researching, in the three main areas of family support, child protection and the courts, and child placement, were invited to workshops for which preliminary papers were produced based on a trawl of the published research. To assist in the preparation of these papers and summaries, researchers were asked to complete a 'template' on their own studies so that broadly comparable information was available on each (see Appendix 2). These, and other relevant studies, were then summarised by the project team and comprise Part II of this book.

The emphasis in the workshops was on research methodology and the 'robustness' of the data currently available, with the aim of teasing out explanations for any inconsistencies and debating the validity and generalisability of the studies. Discrepancies of fact and differences of interpretation were explored. Areas of ambiguity and gaps in the research were identified, leading to suggestions for a future research agenda. At each workshop a 'discussant' with a research, policy and practice background provided a policy-based commentary on the introductory paper. The raw data for the next stage (following up more leads and writing the report) comprised the briefing papers that had been exposed to peer scrutiny, the papers provided by the discussants, the tapes of discussions during the workshops, and the research studies and summaries.

The penultimate stage was a national conference at which a summary of the draft conclusions (comprising a synthesis of all our sources) was discussed with policy makers, social work theorists and practitioners and the implications for policy and practice and priorities for filling the knowledge gaps were debated. Their comments have fed into our concluding chapter about the future research agenda.

Mapping the territory

We approached our task by viewing it as a complex jigsaw puzzle, from which a substantial number of pieces are missing and others are obscured, so that the picture is only partial or blurred. The division into family support, child protection and child placement was done to help to organise the material, but there is considerable overlap. The concluding chapters explore overarching questions around social work practice and service delivery and the future research agenda.

The term 'research' is broadly defined. We take the approach that the mark of a study that can offer something of value to the practitioner and policy maker is that it uses the research approach that best fits the populations and questions being considered. Some research provides descriptive and observational data and addresses the questions: which children and families are receiving services? what can we learn about whether services are available as needed? are the different ethnic minority groups over- or under-represented amongst service users? and what are their perceptions of service relevance, quality and availability? Descriptive studies greatly outnumber outcome studies – those that provide information about 'what works' for the different groups of minority ethnic children and parents. Included amongst outcome studies is a small number using more 'scientific' experimental or quasi-experimental designs; studies that combine analysis of quantitative and qualitative data (a hallmark of much UK research); studies that use a range of outcome measures including service user satisfaction. The research may be undertaken by social services agencies or teams themselves, including that which is part of the evaluation, audit or inspection processes; by researchers independent of the work being studied though sometimes joining with staff and using an action research approach; or by service user groups in partnership with agency staff or independent researchers. This 'broad brush' approach to research synthesis, rather than the more orthodox systematic research review addressing primarily 'what works' questions, was considered essential at this stage in the light of the broader questions being asked and the small numbers of child welfare outcome studies that include large numbers of ethnic minority children. The five broad groups of studies of child welfare interventions with minority ethnic families presently available are:

1. Cohort studies of populations of children and families in receipt of or referred for services, including minority ethnic families in the proportions in which they occur 'naturally' in the sample. These usually include data on service user populations and on outcomes but information on process usually lacks detail. Some deliberately 'over-sample' children from minority ethnic groups to increase statistical validity.

2. Smaller scale studies that provide more detailed data from interviews or focus groups but cannot claim to be representative since some families decline to be interviewed. Numbers of children of minority ethnic origin tend to be very small.

3. 'Mixed methods' research combining the first two and including an interview sample providing rich qualitative data on perceptions of services, satisfaction rates and sometimes outcomes against the background of quantitative data from the full cohort.

4. Surveys and other larger scale studies which specifically focus on children of minority ethnic origin, some of which involve a comparison group of white children.

5. Smaller scale qualitative studies that focus specifically on populations of minority ethnic families. They provide detailed descriptions of services provided and information on the satisfaction or otherwise of parents and children with the services. Some recruit and train young people as peer researchers, though as yet this is more common with research on public health and education services than on child welfare services (Khalique and Skidmore 2000).

Other sources providing data of a mainly descriptive nature include Social Services Inspectorate reports and the SSI/Audit Commission's joint reviews; the National Statistics/Department of Health *Children Looked After by Local Authorities* and other series (since 2004 produced by the Department for Education and Skills) and Census, Labour Force and General Household survey data. Where government statistics are used, these are usually for England, although sometimes for England and Wales and sometimes the UK. Attempts to identify descriptive and evaluative studies conducted by local authorities and voluntary agencies have met with limited success, providing a small amount of very interesting information on evaluations and statistical analysis on recent developments.

Research from outside the UK (especially of a descriptive or observational nature) has been consulted and is referred to for background and contextual purposes but not reported in detail. Where outcome studies from overseas are included, we have attempted to make clear to what extent the findings can reasonably be applied to the UK context. (Appendix 3 summarises the approach to seeking out the research.)

Finally, it is important to keep in mind that children 'in need' who are of minority ethnic origin are, first and foremost, children, with the same requirements for quality services as all children who have special needs or disabilities or live in difficult circumstances. Whilst this report focuses on what is known about any differences in needs and services for the different ethnic groups in the UK population, it does so against a background of the growing body of knowledge about 'children in need' more generally. Since the research that specifically focuses on how ethnic minority families make use of child welfare services is still sparse, findings from some of these more general child welfare studies are included alongside comments on their relevance to minority ethnic children and families.

Chapter 3

Family Support Services

Lots of people want to bring up their children in a better way but they can't afford it. We need better employment prospects in the area for sound financial support for the families. (Asian father, Qureshi, Berridge and Wenman 2000, p.16)

I'm more confident, and after I've left here [family centre] and I go home, I feel like I've been out for the day...I'm more relaxed, I can do anything. Wow, I'm super girl when I get home. (Black mother of mixed parentage, Butt and Box 1998, p.84)

The starting point for inclusion of studies in this review is the Children Act 1989 (Section 17.3) provision that any family support service 'may be provided for a particular child in need or for any member of his [or her] family, if it is provided with a view to safeguarding or promoting the child's welfare'. Data were sought on services directed at parents, carers, children or whole families, and those provided for groups or for individuals in service centres or their own homes.

Hardiker's 'grid' has provided a framework for mapping the literature (Hardiker, Exton and Barker 1991). We have not included references to 'universalist' services – those available to all children such as mainstream education in schools and colleges or child care facilities for working parents, or mainstream GP and other health service such as the health visitor service provided to all families during the early years. However, some services, such as those provided by Sure Start (DfEE 1999a) aim to include 'targeted populations' of children likely to be in need amongst the general populations of children and families living in socially disadvantaged areas. Most of the recent research and writing about family support has been either in respect of a cross-section of families, sometimes analysing the data in respect of the different ethnic groups, or has focused on British Asian families.

An important source of information on family support services is the report by the National Family and Parenting Institute (Henricson *et al.* 2001). These authors report a mapping exercise designed to provide policy makers, practitioners, researchers and parents with an overview of the range, scale and distribution of family services in England and Wales. They included, in their more detailed survey of services in ten areas, questions about strategies for making services more accessible to and appropriate for families who were harder to reach, including ethnic minority families. Many respondents, whether in rural or urban areas, reported that they were dissatisfied by the lack of success in making their services accessible to minority ethnic parents, especially if their first language was not English.

Who needs and who uses community-based family support services?

A small but growing number of studies has explored what ethnic minority community members might be looking for from child welfare services. Two important recent studies are the Ghate and Hazel (2002) nationally representative survey of 1754 families in poor environments, 198 of whom (11%) were of minority ethnic origin, and the Adelman, Middleton and Ashworth (2003) research. This study of 848 children under 16 in 'severe and persistent poverty and social exclusion' found that over a quarter of the children in the 'severe poverty group' (compared to 13% in the general population) were of minority ethnic origin. Interim findings are also available from a survey of parents in two materially deprived areas (one urban, one rural) by Axford, Little and Morpeth (in preparation). The study provides detailed information about the needs and service take-up of children and their families, using the child as the unit of analysis. In the urban area only 19 per cent of the children (392 or 464) were described by their parents as white British. These data provide evidence that many families from all ethnic groups live in the most materially deprived areas, and that children of minority ethnic origin, if they were to seek or be referred for services, would be as likely as white children, if not more so, to cross the 'Section 17' threshold. Oxfam and the Refugee Council (2002) and Dennis (2002) provide detailed evidence of the extent of poverty and multiple deprivations amongst refugee families.

There is confirmation from other sources such as the National Evaluation of Sure Start (Barnes and the National Evaluation of Sure Start (NESS) Research Team 2003; NESS 2003) which reports on the large proportions of ethnic minority families in Sure Start areas (selected because they are in areas of social disadvantage). Detailed area level data on ethnic minority children from the 2001 Census confirm this pattern of deprivation amongst some minority ethnic groups. For example, 41.7 per cent of Muslims compared with 12.3 per cent in the general population are overcrowded and one in eight compared to one in sixteen in the general population did not have central heating in their homes (National Statistics 2003). However, all the researchers cited above urge caution in reading their findings on ethnicity, especially in terms of representation amongst those seeking or receiving services, as their numbers are too small for analysis when the different ethnic groups are considered separately. Because of their very different family patterns (see Modood *et al.* 1997) and differing attitudes towards seeking help, the differences between ethnic groups may 'cancel each other out'. A finding that there is no difference between the use made of a service by white and ethnic minority families may conceal the fact that one group is over-represented amongst users of that service and another group under-represented. Another point worth noting is that research that uses the child rather than the parent as the unit of analysis is likely to give a more accurate picture of patterns of service use amongst the different ethnic groups since family size varies amongst the different ethnic groups.

The Ghate and Hazel (2002) study explored the differences between parents who are 'coping well' (46% of the sample) and 'coping less well' (2% coping badly and 52% sometimes coping and sometimes not). Taking the ethnic minority families together, there were no differences between whether the parents would describe themselves as 'coping' or 'not coping' according to ethnicity but the authors point out that this may conceal differences within ethnic groups. Unsurprisingly, parents with a mental health problem and those experiencing inter-partner conflict and violence were more likely to be in the 'non-coper' group. As we shall see, there is some evidence that these have been identified as particularly stressful aspects of the lives of some women in South Asian communities. Amongst child-related factors, having a child with emotional or behavioural problems or a disabled child and having a larger number of children were associated with families describing themselves as not coping at least some of the time. (For each additional dependent child in the family the odds of not coping rose by a fifth.) Lone parents were more likely than those in two-parent families to describe themselves as 'not coping', a characteristic of more African-Caribbean, mixed heritage and white British families than of African and Asian families.

The data from the Axford *et al.* study are not yet fully analysed but the descriptive and demographic data on the use of services is available. A quarter of the families in the London area described themselves as black African so the study is particularly helpful in understanding the stresses and help-seeking behaviour of this group. Just under a quarter of the ethnic minority children were born outside the UK – another important difference that often goes unreported when data on ethnic minority children are analysed as an undifferentiated group. Just over a third of the whole sample met the 'in need' threshold and only 19 per cent were rated by the researchers as having few or no unmet needs. The study analysed the needs of the children using cluster analysis to group together children with similar profiles of risk and protective factors. Children from ethnic minorities were no more likely than other children to be in particular groups.

These studies were not specifically designed to focus on child welfare services, but rather on the poverty and poor environments that characterise the lives of many families in all ethnic groups. However, a combination of these general population studies and the studies focusing specifically on (to date) smaller and less random samples of families from particular ethnic groups has the potential to increase understanding of why some ethnic minority families in difficult circumstances might manage well enough without additional help whilst others make use of family support services and yet others struggle but do not seek help.

Qureshi *et al.* (2000) used focus groups to seek the views of 53 South Asian families in Luton about the family support services offered by social care agencies. Topics covered included the kinds of family problems parents faced and their awareness of, and attitudes towards, family support services provided by the local authority or in partnership with voluntary agencies. The study also included the views of some social workers and managers. The researchers reported that participants felt that family stress and breakdown were more common in their communities than was often perceived by professionals and the public. Paradoxically, there was also the opinion that living in close-knit communities could generate social isolation, and that this was increased by living in stressful circumstances. Unemployment leading to economic hardship, poor housing and a lack of affordable day care were significant obstacles to combating social exclusion for the parents and for their children.

> Some people would not tell their extended family because of the shame and humiliation. They could turn to Social Services if they will keep it confidential. (Asian father, Qureshi *et al.* 2000, p.19)

Hylton (1997) evaluated the Moyenda Black Families project. He interviewed 230 people of African, African-Caribbean or South Asian descent in London and Luton to explore what strategies ethnic minority families employed to cope with some of the difficulties they experienced. This study identified a strong sense of spirituality amongst the family members interviewed and highlights the role of religious observance in helping families directly and also in framing the strategies they used to combat difficulties. Some interviewees expressed concern that officials, including teachers and social workers, had taken away or undermined their parental authority. This is echoed in the comments on services to assist in cases of domestic violence.

> My religion kept me going. We believe that your time on earth is full of tests. If you survive, your patience and strength will end your suffering. These are my tests. I had to stand by my mum because she was not in the wrong. That pulled us through and has made us stronger and better. (14-year-old South Asian boy, Mullender *et al.* 2002, p.149)

Racism, racial harassment and racial violence

I don't let them out of the house too often. It isn't safe, especially where I live. There are some white youths that start trouble because they don't like Asians. So I keep them in the house and they say, 'Mummy, let us go out to play – please'. (Asian mother, Qureshi *et al.* 2000, p.16)

Most researchers who focus on support services to black and Asian families consider the impact of racism and the extent to which services make efforts to confront and combat it, through both their own management systems and the sorts of services they provide. In many of the interview-based research studies, the impact of racism and discrimination for minority ethnic families is reported to be a significant feature of their lives. However, few studies of child welfare interventions *quantify* the extent and impact of institutional racism, racist harassment and racial abuse on the lives of parents and children who turn to or are referred to child welfare services. The quantitative research on discrimination, racism and racial abuse is to be found in the general population studies of employment, education, health and exposure to crime, summarised in the reports and research reviews of Barter (1999), British Crime Survey (2000), Cabinet Office Strategy Unit (2003), Commission for Racial Equality (1998) Modood *et al.* (1997) and the other research reviews referred to in the introduction to this section, as well as in the major inquiry reports such as the MacPherson report on racism within the police service and Bennet Inquiry on the mental health services (Blofield 2004). Discrimination and racism that impact on parents will also increase the stress on children. It is likely (though as yet a clear causal link has not been evidenced and it would be methodologically difficult to do so) that the cumulative experience of discrimination and racial abuse by generations of communities long resident in the UK (most notably those of African-Caribbean heritage) has contributed to the over-representation of black children amongst those referred for family support or child protection services and in care. For this reason reports from the DfES (Bhattacharya, Ison and Blair 2003; Cline *et al.* 2002; Swann Report 1985), documenting the high rates of school exclusion of black pupils, their lower levels of academic achievement and the extent of racial harassment and bullying in school and on the way to school, are highly relevant to an understanding of ethnicity and child welfare. These reports show that all minority groups suffer discrimination, though they may be discriminated against in different ways. For example, those whose first language is not English may fail to receive information about the services that are available. The assumption can then be made that these groups are not in need of services because they are not coming forward to request them. Derbyshire (1994) highlights the special characteristics of racism and racial discrimination in the rural areas and small towns in Norfolk, where numbers of minority ethnic children and families are small. Radford (2004) describes a quantitative and qualitative study involving interviews with 50 young people and full-day workshops with 12 of the participants from 8 ethnic and 4 non-Christian faith based communities in Northern Ireland. Families could also be more vulnerable if they stepped outside the norms and expectations of the ethnic group they were seen to 'belong' to, including by choosing a partner from a different race or culture.

> Mixed race kids have to expect abuse from both white and black communities
> – only mixed race couples can understand their experience. (Foster parent
> cited in Barn et al. 1997, p.72)

Sinclair and Hai (2003, p.23) quote a Jamaican mother whose partner was white:

> It is mostly black people not white people. They will make little comments
> behind my back like you [have] sold out…I was born in Jamaica. I have been
> brought up in England and I was the only black girl in the class. I lost my
> accent years ago so I am not going to put on anything else for anyone else.

Amongst the smaller-scale studies that have considered the prevalence and impact of racial harassment on minority ethnic communities are those of Chahal and Julienne (1999), Gray (2002a and 2002b) and McLeod (1996). McLeod reported that there was an element of racism (including name-calling, teasing and harassment) in all reports of bullying made to ChildLine by ethnic minority children. Chahal and Julienne (1999) convened focus groups and carried out in-depth interviews with families who had experienced racist abuse and harassment in Belfast, Cardiff, Glasgow and London. The research participants could all recount at least one experience of racial harassment. Racism was found to affect all family members but not to the same extent. For example, parents who went out to work (mainly men in this research) did not have to endure the daily racist harassment experienced by other family members. This could lead to conflict between the parents because the parent out at work did not always understand the extent of the problems for the family. Individuals and families were also seen to be very selective about whom they told about their experiences, because of feelings of shame and inadequacy. This selective disclosure of racial harassment could increase isolation from friends, wider family and community. In some instances, where families did disclose their troubles to family or neighbours, the responses were unhelpful or led to a withdrawal of support because others were not prepared to become involved. Children and young people were both the perpetrators of racist harassment and the victims of it. Some were pressured to adapt their lifestyle, for example, by having their freedom to play curtailed because parents felt unsure about their safety. Children were particularly vulnerable if they experienced racial harassment at school, and also on the journey to and from school.

This study identifies strategies adopted by families to deal with racist abuse, some successful and some less so. The researchers found that reporting racial harassment to the relevant authority was rarely the first response. Instead, parents first monitored the extent of the problem. The step to involve authorities was only taken when the pressures became intolerable or there was a fear of serious violence. Almost one quarter of the respondents did not report racially motivated assaults or harassment to any official agency until eighteen months after the first incident was noted, and this increased to four years in some cases. The local general practitioner was the most popular choice for disclosure because she or he could act as a confidante and was often asked to help by writing a letter to the housing department or with medication.

Gray (2002 a and b) found discrimination to be a significant feature in the lives of the minority ethnic families in Tower Hamlets. Elderly Bangladeshis and young children from all minority ethnic groups were particularly prone to bullying and racism. The finding about elders is relevant to this review since in some communities they play an important role in providing child care. The issue of the impact of racism and discrimination on the lives of children and parents is returned to when the different research studies and services are considered.

> Sometimes people tease me and call me names, especially white people in the area… It makes me feel unsafe. Mum is trying to get me a transfer to another school. I am just worried about being teased by white people – they do it because they don't like black people and can cause problems and be violent so you can feel really unsafe. (10-year-old Asian boy quoted by Mullender *et al.* 2002, p.139)

Some of the research studies evidence the extent and impact of institutional and workplace racism on social care workers and the ways in which this affects the services they are able to provide to children and families on their caseloads and in the communities in which they work. Prevatt Goldstein (2002) describes a qualitative study involving interviews with 28 black social care workers and analyses the important issues that arise when racism is not recognised and strategies to deal with it are not in place or are ineffective.

Services targeted at vulnerable families and communities

'Level 2' services and programmes are those that are targeted at families going through the sorts of stressful periods experienced by many families. Whole communities may be recognised as vulnerable to the ill-effects of living in potentially socially excluding circumstances. These may be 'neighbourhood' communities, or 'communities of interest' such as parents or children who have a particular disability. Amongst 'communities of interest' are families from particular ethnic groups who may not live within the same neighbourhood or ward but may be in need of or provided with services appropriate to their specific needs, for example as asylum seekers, or people of a particular faith or having particular needs because English is not their first language. Becher and Husain (2003) provide an overview of policies, practice and research on family support for South Asian families. These services are touched on even though many of those who make use of them do not come within our narrower definition of 'children in need'.

There are some descriptive accounts of neighbourhood projects resulting from government initiatives such as Sure Start, On Track or the Children's Fund, including data on ethnicity of staff, volunteers and service users. However, it is still too early for outcome data to be available. The Sure Start 'local context' report (NESS 2003) demonstrates that the first four rounds of funding led to the setting up of Sure Start projects in 'areas experiencing some of the worst deprivation in England'. About a third of the programmes are sited in ethnically diverse areas and one in ten is in an area with an ethnic minority population greater than 40 per cent. Eighteen per cent of the project areas had a large community from the Indian sub-continent, 10 per cent had a large black community and 4 per cent served large ethnically mixed communities. The report on implementation indicates that the strong policy steer to seek to ensure that minority ethnic families are fully involved and able to take advantage of these additional services is having some impact. In areas where there are large populations of minority ethnic families, parents from the different ethnic groups tend to be represented in appropriate proportions on management committees and amongst staff members. There was evidence of materials being translated. In just over a third of all projects a members of staff was designated to have special responsibility for services to minority ethnic families, including asylum seekers.

Another type of service, offering support to parents and children on a 'universal', open access basis but including service provision to some very vulnerable families, is provided by the growing number of telephone helplines. The best known of these are ChildLine for children (see MacLeod 1996 and Morris and Wheatley 1994) and ParentlinePlus for parents, but there are also more specialist services such as the National Drugs Helpline and a helpline for Young Runaways. The commitment of these services to go at the pace of the callers has meant that information on ethnicity is often not collected, although it is sometimes clear from the content, as when advice is sought about racism and racist bullying, that the caller is of a culture other than white British. Parentline Plus Nottingham (2002) undertook a small project to monitor the ethnicity of callers, both to gain information and to understand more about the feasibility of training volunteers to ask routinely for information about the ethnic group of the caller. A survey of other helplines indicated that only nine sought to monitor the ethnic group of callers (all for only a sample period each year). It is clear that some black and Asian families use helplines but there is no information on the extent to which children and parents from the different ethnic groups in the national or local populations do so. ParentlinePlus (2003) reports that, encouraged by the pilot project, diversity training for call takers was undertaken with the result that in a six-month period in 2003 they obtained information about the ethnic group of 77 per cent of the over 19,000 callers from across the UK.

These data demonstrate that minority ethnic families are making use of these services, possibly to about the same extent as white families although the missing data in respect of 23 per cent of callers make this difficult to calculate. Seventy-one per cent of all callers were white (including 2% Irish and 2% other white background); 1% were black Caribbean; 1% were black African; 1% were Indian; 1% 'other Asian background' and 1% 'other ethnic background'. Only 1 per cent of callers were recorded as of 'other mixed background' although it is not known whether the caller was living with a partner of a different ethnic group and their children were of mixed heritage. Call takers also recorded information on the ethnicity of those causing concern in 57 per cent of cases and 3 per cent of these were recorded as of mixed white and Caribbean heritage (1%), mixed white and Asian heritage (1%) and 'other mixed background' (1%). The further analysis of these data from a large number of callers according to ethnicity and the types of problems they are experiencing will become possible as the problems with 'missing data' are overcome.

Services targeted at vulnerable populations that also provide services to referred families

Some of the services that come into this category are those identified by Ghate and Hazel (2002) as 'semi-formal'. They may be provided directly by child and family teams of social services departments but are most likely to be funded by local authorities but provided by the voluntary sector. Increasingly they form part of Sure Start projects or are funded by the Children's Fund. The services that come under this category about which most has been written are neighbourhood family centres. Also included are services such as 'community parents' and volunteer visiting schemes, the best known of which is Home Start (Frost et al. 2000). Gibbons' (1992) edited book contains evaluations of some of these and there are small-scale evaluations of local schemes. Some provide services for particular times of stress or in particular circumstances, as with supported and supervised child contact centres. Although there is now a fairly substantial body of descriptive and, to a lesser extent, evaluative research on these services, little of it refers to the ethnicity of service users or considers whether services are appropriate to the ethnic composition of the neighbourhood in which they are sited. When they do, numbers in the different minority ethnic groups are too small for conclusions to be drawn.

An important exception is the Butt and Box (1998) research which focuses on the use made of family centres in the mid-1990s by African, African-Caribbean and South Asian families. Managers of 35 of the 84 centres either said that participation by ethnic minority families was representative of the community, or that black parents and children were over-represented (attributed to making services particularly relevant for these communities). In 26 of the centres black families were under-represented. Explanations for this under-representation related to the small numbers of black people in the local area, or reluctance of black families to take up the services. One finding was that Caribbean family members were more likely to use the services than Asian or African parents and children. The researchers reported a number of particular needs for black service users concerning health (including mental health), financial problems, housing problems (including harassment), and difficulties with child care.

Although there were several ways in which family centres advertised their services, some of the family members interviewed considered that the level of information and publicity was insufficient. Only six centres translated publicity materials as a matter of course. Twenty-three family centres had services specifically for black families, ranging from child protection risk assessments through to services around education. Managers of centres identified economic problems, crime problems including racial harassment, and housing problems as the main concerns for the black parents and children who attended the centres.

Those services which specifically catered for black communities had the highest proportion of ethnic minority families using them; day-care and after-school clubs were also popular. A high proportion of the ethnic minority families using the centres (86%) had been referred because of child protection concerns – though this was the case also with white families. Services working specifically with children and young people were less well used by ethnic minority families, as were those that specifically focused on parenting. The researchers also looked at user participation in family centres and found that, perhaps not surprisingly, services with a child protection focus were least likely to have any user involvement with regard to both management and delivery of services.

Many respondents were positive about the services and particularly mentioned the accepting and non-blaming atmosphere in the centres. They singled out the lessening of isolation and loneliness, through making friends with others taking part in centre activities.

> You never feel you are being listened to; we listen to each other don't we? We listen to each other's problems and relationships develop and we trust each other. We talk to each other and we go to each other's houses…we can have friendships as well. (Asian father, Butt and Box 1998, p.79)

Having more time for themselves and having a break while their children are in day-care or after-school activities; and practical help and advice, for example, on social security matters were also mentioned positively.

Everyone's equal…[at family centre] there are some people that are less fortunate than others but we don't put them in their own corners and say 'oh well
I'm not talking to that one'…everyone's a human being, we've all got feelings
whether dressed in designer clothes or jumble sale clothes (p.85).

The reason I like this centre is 'cause nobody points a finger at you; they are
there for you and that's what I like. (White mother of black child, p.78).

Parents reported that the centres offered a safe place for their children to play
and develop their social skills in contrast to the unsafe or limiting areas where
they lived. They valued support for their children in times of crisis, for example
by helping children who had been abused.

The worker used to sit here for hours and talk: what to do, where to go, who to
see, which Doctor if he needed an examination. They got him a social worker
and she came round and gave him counselling at home – we didn't have to go,
they came to the home and did it. (Mother of abused son, p.83)

The family centres were also seen by many parents as places which fostered an
improvement in their relationships (between parents and their children, and
between partners and/or family members).

A similar picture emerges from three studies of general populations of
children and families using family centres. Gardner (2003) sets a description
and evaluation of six NSPCC family centres in the context of a discussion of
family support services in the areas served by the centres. She comments on the
generally poor quality of ethnic monitoring. Smith (1996) researched the
views of parents and children who took part in activities at six Children's
Society family centres, four of which had 'open access' policies and were neighbourhood based. The report gives a detailed account of how one of these (an
open access centre in Leicester) had engaged ethnic minority families in its
work. The Tunstill et al. research (2004) focused particularly on the role of
family centres in co-ordinating formal and informal support and complements
the work of Ghate and Hazel (2002). Although not specifically focusing on
services to minority ethnic families, many of the centres were in areas with substantial populations of black and Asian families. Of the 83 parents interviewed
17 per cent were of minority ethnic origin.

The detailed picture of family centres that emerges from all these studies
provides helpful pointers to those looking for research studies that will help
them to make their services more appropriate to minority ethnic families. These
studies also look at barriers to take-up of services. The conclusions echo those
of other studies and are summarised in the concluding comments to this
chapter.

There is evidence from these studies, as from earlier research on the work of
family centres, that the 'mixed model' of referral and service provision is most
likely to reach the families most in need of help, whilst minimising the risk of

stigma and community disapproval. However, the most recent survey by Tunstill *et el.* (2004) found a trend towards either closure or a reduced role for family centres. Changes of referral systems had occurred towards more 'referral only' models. There was less variety and more 'homogenisation' of the services available, which were more likely to be problem focused and focused on parenting issues than on more general support to parents or children and practical services to help to reduce stress in daily living and environmental stress. This move to limit the availability and the range of services is not supported by the research and, looking again at the Butt and Box (1998) conclusions, may serve to reduce further their acceptability and relevance to parents and children from minority communities. This quote indicates the value of the neighbourhood, open-access approach:

> I heard off friends that if you got any problems with social security to bills or whatever, there's people that can sort them out, like do phone calls for you... I wanted help with the bills – it was all getting on top of me – and social, I was in a right state and (worker) helped me out. (African-Caribbean mother, Butt and Box 1998, p.74)

Turning to welfare outcomes for parents and children, there are no 'robust' outcome studies that can point positively to whether family centres as an entity 'work' and whether some models are more effective than others for the generality of families, let alone those of the different minority ethnic groups. There is some limited data on the effectiveness of some of the specific services provided by family centres such as parenting education. However, the interviewees in all studies generally express strong support for the family centre approach to service provision, especially when self-referral is encouraged and there are 'drop-in' facilities. Centres appear to be well-targeted at those most in need and a large majority of those interviewed considered that the family centre helped with problems arising from social exclusion. Tunstill *et al.* (2004) conclude that funders' pressure to concentrate on late intervention/crisis work could result in carefully developed strategies to include families from diverse backgrounds and cultures being undermined.

Moving on to a broader community approach to family support, a study by Gray (2002a, 2002b) describes and gives feedback from, mainly Bangladeshi, community members about three outreach projects providing a range of services to children and parents in their own homes. The nine families interviewed reported that family support services had helped to give them social support, and played a part in improved psychological and emotional well-being. They also commented positively on assistance in household and financial matters. There is congruence between these areas of improvement and the 'needs clusters' identified by other researchers, indicating that these services had been relevant to the areas of stress most likely to be experienced by ethnic minority families. The researchers concluded that family support workers recruited from local communities had a key role in strengthening families under stress, including those experiencing difficulties through depression, domestic violence, child–parent relationship difficulties and social isolation.

> We're from the same country. My Family Support Worker speaks the same language and she knows about my religion. She knows all about the difficulties of being a mother in England when you're from a Bangladeshi family... My Family Support Worker talked to my children about Islam and encouraged my children to attend the mosque and say their prayers. I have the chance now to sit and talk with my children. I feel that they have a better understanding and respect for me and Bangladeshi culture and Islam now. (Bangladeshi mother, Gray 2002a, p.17)

The family support worker could be seen as a helpful link between the family and statutory services and thus contributed to family members being more positive about longer-term involvement with the various professionals and services associated with the projects.

> By talking things over with my Family Support Worker it has been a lot of help to us all. Before, he was beating me and my kids had physical abuse. My worker gave advice to me and my husband... So, when she said, 'What's the children's future if they see their parents fighting, what future do they get?' I think that was a straightforward way that really got into him to make him understand about the kids. (Bangladeshi mother, Gray 2002a, p.18)

Thoburn, Wilding and Watson (2000) explored the extent to which minority ethnic families with children under eight who were referred for a family support or child protection service knew about and made use of what Ghate and Hazel (2002) refer to as 'semi-formal' services. Despite a substantial proportion of the families being aware of specific resources, few used them. Only a minority of families had not heard of any of the local resources listed by the researcher as available in their areas. For example 13 out of the 15 Asian parents interviewed were aware of at least one of the 8 community resources available specifically for South Asian families, yet only 2 families had used them in the past year. Only 7 of the 16 parents interviewed (from all ethnic groups) who had a child with a chronic illness/disability had made use of support groups that catered for their child. The most frequent reasons for not using resources were: long waiting lists; shortage of places; cost/distance/lack of transport. Some parents reported that they found the facilities to be of poor quality.

As with family centres, the UK 'what works' literature on the approaches to family support work and methods used is sparse for all groups, and even more so when it comes to a consideration of the approaches that are most effective for minority ethnic families. This question is returned to in Chapter 7 but mention is made here of research on parenting education, an approach that is becoming firmly established as a way of providing family support for a wide range of families and types of difficulty. Henricson *et al.* (2001) found that parenting courses were most likely to be provided in the voluntary sector and the health sector but more recently there has been interest in extending the approach to families where children have committed offences or are beyond parental control or children with mental health problems. Lloyd (1999) reviews the evidence on parenting programmes to help parents who are experiencing difficulty in managing their children's behaviour. Although researchers (mainly American) report positive outcomes for parents and children, not all parents and children benefit and the research is in its infancy.

Barlow, Shaw and Stewart-Brown (2003) review the (mainly north American) research that has set out to evaluate the effectiveness of parenting programmes in meeting the needs of minority ethnic parents and children. They note that most programmes ignore racial and ethnic diversity but that some 'culturally sensitive' programmes have been developed. The authors report that there are examples of mainstream programmes adapted or translated for use with minority ethnic parents (culturally sensitive programmes) and some designed specifically to fit with different cultural approaches to parenting (culturally specific programmes). None has yet been evaluated in terms of welfare outcomes though accounts of parental satisfaction are beginning to appear, as with Hylton's (1997) account of the group-based Moyenda project referred to earlier. The report concludes that there are many problems with research methodology which require caution when interpreting results of these studies. The biggest problem is that a high proportion of those invited to attend a group decide not to take part, and there is a high drop-out rate. In both the USA and the UK there is a higher likelihood that minority ethnic families will decide against attending and they are more likely to drop out of those programmes (the majority) that are not adapted or culturally specific (see also Butt and Box 1998). Even when programmes are designed around the needs of minority ethnic families, those who decide to attend and then attend regularly have different characteristics from those who never arrive or drop out, making research results on effectiveness unreliable. The report concludes that 'the evidence to support the effectiveness of culturally specific parenting programmes is not strong' (Barlow *et al.* 2003, p.48) but attributes this to the inadequacy of the research rather than the inadequacy of the programmes. The researchers also find evidence in their detailed studies of the research in the USA that providing a choice of programmes is important, which implies that a range of programmes with different approaches to parenting support, including culturally specific programmes, should be available.

Children 'in need' assessed for and/or provided with a service under the provisions of section 17 of the Children Act 1989

The chapters by Little and by Frost in Parton's (1997) edited book on family support and child protection are helpful introductions to some of the issues raised in this section.

Looking first at published statistics, in 2003 data on all referrals and assessments by councils with social services responsibilities started to be published alongside the annual child protection statistics, but this publication did not, for 2002, include data on the ethnic group of those referred (National Statistics and DH 2003a). Data on ethnicity were given only with respect to children whose names are entered on the Child Protection Registers (CPRs) see Chapter 4. During the year ending 31 March 2002, over 260,000 initial assessments were carried out in England to ascertain whether children were 'in need' and whether a service should be provided, a mean rate of 505 children per 10,000 under 18. The range for individual authorities was between less than 200 and over 1000 per 10,000.

Information on ethnic groups is, however, available from the National Statistics (2001, 2004) 'children in need' (CiN) census report. This data set also includes separate data on unaccompanied asylum-seeking children. The CiN statistics record that, in 2003, 319,200 children were on allocated caseloads as 'children in need' receiving a service in their own homes and that 164,400 of these (58%) had had time or resources spent on them during the census week. Fewer than 8 per cent were children on child protection registers, so the vast majority were, to some extent at least, willing recipients of support and services. It should be borne in mind that the ethnic group of 11 per cent was not recorded. With this caveat, it appears that children of minority ethnic origin as a combined group are more likely than white children to be receiving an 'in need' service. Twenty per cent of all those in need for whom ethnicity was known (and 18 per cent of all those in need if the 'unknowns' are included) were of minority ethnic origin compared to around 13 per cent of the population of children and young people aged 0 to 18.

Whilst some researchers working on services to families of minority ethnic origin have concluded that they are less likely than white children to receive a family support service, this appears not to be the case with respect to a local authority children in need service. However, when the different ethnic minority groups reported in the CiN census are considered, a more complex picture emerges. Children of Chinese and Indian heritage were far less likely than would be expected from their numbers in the child population as a whole to be receiving an 'in need' service. Pakistani children were also under-represented but not to the same extent as Indian children. Bangladeshi children and those of mixed Asian/white heritage children were represented in the 'in need' group in the same proportions as their numbers in the community. African-Caribbean children and those in the African-Caribbean/white, African/white, and 'other Asian' groups were about twice as likely to receive an 'in need' service as would be expected by their numbers in the population. The groups most likely to be over-represented were those of black African heritage and those in the 'other black' and 'other ethnic' groups. It seems likely that the over-representation of black African children results in part from the fact that African parents and children are likely to have additional problems owing to more of them being refugees or asylum seekers. African children comprise 1.37 per cent of the child population but 3 per cent of the child 'in need' population. (See Okitikpi and Aymer 2003 for a discussion of the issues arising from a small-scale study of the views of refugee parents of African origin and immigration officers.) To illustrate the differences between groups, Indian children comprise 2.2 per cent of the child population but only 1 per cent of the 'in need' population. This is likely to be in part explained by the fact that a smaller proportion of Indian children than is the case with most other ethnic minority groups are being brought up in poor economic and environmental circumstances.

Because the distribution of different ethnic groups across the UK is so different, it is useful to look at the figures for an area where there are larger minority ethnic communities. Here we are using Labour Force figures for the child population as the detailed 2001 Census breakdown on age, locality and ethnicity was not yet available (National Statistics 2002). Only broad groupings of 'white', 'mixed ethnic origin', 'black', 'Asian' and 'other' are available for both the general population and for children in need. With the above caveats about 'missing data' it is interesting to note that, where a particular minority ethnic group is present in large numbers, the pattern is different. In Birmingham, for example, where around 33 per cent of the child population is of Asian heritage and white children comprise less than half of the child population, the under-representation of Asian children is more marked than for England as a whole (comprising only 9% of those receiving an 'in need' service). White children are slightly over-represented amongst children recorded as 'in need' (49% of the child population and 51% of the 'in need' population). In contrast to the position for England as a whole, the combined group of 'black' children are only slightly over-represented amongst children in need (10% of the child population and around 12% of the 'in need' population.) The pattern is similar in other West Midlands authorities with large ethnic minority populations but reverts to the general England pattern where there is a large majority of white families.

Key questions posed by the statistics are: are the families who are receiving services those who most need them, and are those not receiving services doing well enough without them? Is it broadly a 'good' or a 'bad' thing to be in a group that is over- or under-represented? It is to detailed studies of family support services (those referred to above and those specifically about services to children 'in need') that we have to turn for possible explanations. As with the more informal support services, research studies specifically focusing on ethnic minorities are few. Shortly after the implementation of the Children Act 1989, Aldgate and Tunstill (1996) sent a postal survey to the 109 English local authorities to ascertain whether, as the Act encourages, social services departments were providing services to 'predetermined groups' where there was a high likelihood that those in the group would be 'in need'. Only 21 per cent indicated that 'black and ethnic minority children' were a predetermined group and only 9 per cent indicated that this applied to children whose first language was not English. Given the higher incidence of HIV/Aids amongst African families, some families of African descent may have become eligible for help in the 40 per cent of authorities that listed 'children at risk of HIV/Aids' as a predetermined group. Eleven per cent listed refugee children as a high priority group for receipt of services.

Turning first to research that has focused on services to children 'in need' in minority ethnic communities, two studies look at formal family support services for specific ethnic groups. These are the Qureshi et al. (2000) research and Husain and O'Brien's (1999) EU funded study which compares statutory agency approaches to family support in England, Belgium and Denmark. This report provides contextual information on the circumstances of Muslim families in the three countries and on the statutory services available to support them if problems develop. The research team interviewed social services staff and a small number of families in order to identify best practice initiatives in the non-profit and statutory sectors. They draw attention to the need for improvement in interpretation services and the training and vetting of all interpreters. The importance of better training for social workers, managers and reception staff on issues affecting Muslim families was also highlighted as was the importance of recruiting social workers and social work students from religious and ethnic minority communities.

Key themes emerging from focus group discussions with South Asian families reported by Qureshi et al. (2000) fed into a study of a purposive sample of twenty cases open to a social worker in family support, looked after or leaving care teams (eleven families originally from Pakistan/Kashmir; six from Bangladesh; two from Bengal, and one was a mixed heritage Pakistani/white family). Social workers were interviewed about their work with Asian families. Two were from Asian communities, two were of African or African-Caribbean ethnic origin and seven were white. Four cases were analysed in more detail and in these cases one or both parents were interviewed in their preferred language. Despite the large number of South Asian families in the community very few services were provided specifically with South Asian families in mind. There was a low level of self-referrals, with parents in only two of the twenty cases seeking help themselves and sixteen being referred by others because of child protection concerns. Social workers considered that about half of the twenty families 'did not comprehend the nature of state and local authority responsibility for children's welfare' (p.54). This is not surprising since the Social Services Department employed few Asian staff and no South Asian managers; there were no specific policies concerning South Asian families and no specific training for staff. The researchers concluded that professionals' misunderstandings about family circumstances sometimes led to negative assumptions about caring. In three of the sixteen child protection cases initial concerns were not substantiated and the case closed quickly. The social workers and managers interviewed recognised the importance of their having an understanding of the meaning to the family of being a member of a particular minority community and the research had been commissioned so that improvements could be made.

In a study including all ethnic groups Thoburn, Wilding and Watson (2000) focused on referral patterns, services and interim outcomes (12 months after referral) in parts of three authorities. The majority of the 386 children under eight referred to child and family teams in the two urban authorities were of minority ethnic origin (61% and 77% respectively). The largest groups were of South Asian and African heritage. The researchers estimate that ethnic minority children were over-represented amongst those considered by their parents or others to be in need of a service. A partial explanation is that this was an area of settlement for recent arrivals in the UK including refugees and asylum seekers. Twenty-eight of the parents in the interview sample came to England as adults, in nineteen cases as immigrants and in nine cases as refugees or asylum seekers. For 25 per cent of the ethnic minority parents interviewed (in their language of choice) in one city area and 45 per cent in the other the first language was not English. Although 50 per cent of the referrals were in respect of child protection concerns (and discussed in the next section), around half were of children referred for family support services. Ethnic minority families were more likely than white British families to be referred for a family support service and correspondingly less likely to be referred because of child protection concerns. Ethnic minority children were more likely than white children to be referred when under the age of 12 months.

When comparisons were made on indicators of economic and social disadvantage, few differences were found between those referred for family support services and those referred because of child protection concerns. In this respect white families and those of minority ethnic origin were similar. Overall levels of informal social and emotional support were similar for ethnic minority families and white families. However, white parents were more likely to have access to support from extended family members, including their own parents, whereas ethnic minority mothers were more likely to get support from their husbands or male partners. White families were more likely to be in the 'families with long-standing and multiple problems' group and ethnic minority families were more likely to be in 'acute distress' or to have a 'short-term problem'. Although slightly different 'needs groups' are used, there is congruence between these areas of need and those identified in the community samples of Axford *et al.* (in preparation) and Ghate and Hazel (2002).

Turning to services received, it is interesting to note that roughly equal proportions (around a quarter) of ethnic minority and white families in the Thoburn *et al.* (2000) study referred themselves for assistance. This is a different pattern to that found in some other studies but fits with Ghate and Hazel's (2002) conclusion that families in greater need in all ethnic groups are less likely to be inhibited from seeking support from statutory agencies. These findings, and the 'in need' statistics referred to above suggest that when needs are greater, barriers to seeking help or accepting a referral from a GP, teacher or health visitor may be as likely to be overcome by at least some ethnic minority families as white families.

There was a trend towards white families being more likely than those of minority ethnic origin to receive a long-term service and for the service to ethnic minority families to have ended within four weeks of referral. This is related to the fact that more of the white families had long-standing and multiple problems and these families were more likely to receive a long-term service. There was a trend for more of the white than the ethnic minority families to be provided with a service rated by the researchers as 'generally good' and for more of the services to ethnic minority families being rated as 'inappropriate to their needs'.

This study provides some data on interim outcomes 12 months after referral as well as data on the satisfaction of parents with the services provided. Overall, less progress was made by parents and children referred for a service (more of the ethnic minority families) than those where child protection issues were the reason for referral (more of the white families). There was a trend towards more of the white families showing either overall improvement or deterioration and more of the ethnic minority families experiencing little change or mixed outcomes. The same proportion of ethnic minority and white families interviewed expressed general satisfaction with the service provided (40%). It is important to note that families in all ethnic groups who received a social casework service combining practical help and emotional support from an allocated social worker were more likely to be satisfied (a 'satisfaction rate' of over 70 per cent for those who actually received a social work service). A small minority were dissatisfied with the quality or relevance of a service actually provided, but a greater number were unsatisfied in that they did not receive a service, or enough of the service that they thought could have helped. This applied especially to parents whose child had a disability, or who themselves had a disability or health problem. This point is also made by parents cited in other studies, as by this South Asian mother quoted by Mullender *et al.* 2002, p.138.

Workers should ask mothers how they are feeling if there are problems. Instead, workers label the women as a problem rather than providing more comprehensive support. Some of the problems are because the services are inadequate and insensitive – sometimes they are inappropriate too.

Reporting on another of the DH The Children Act Now research studies, Tunstill and Aldgate (2000) provide a detailed account and interim evaluation of family support services to 93 'middle years' children 'in need'. Twelve (13%) were of minority ethnic origin. As with similar studies including small numbers of children from diverse backgrounds, the authors did not consider it appropriate to analyse the data in terms of ethnic groups. However they conclude that 'the qualitative data suggested that their [ethnic minority families] needs in relation to services for their children were similar to those of other families. For example, many families were concerned about their children's behaviour' (p.36). A wide range of practical, advocacy and social casework services was provided to these parents and children, sometimes in family centres and sometimes in their own homes. As with the research cited above, the response of the parents and children interviewed who actually received a support service was generally positive. The number feeling stigmatised as a result of receiving services had dropped when the family members were re-interviewed. The finding that professionally referred families were more likely to feel stigmatised than those who sought help on their own behalf is congruent with the research on family centres that points towards more partnership-based models of assessment for the provision of support services to families under stress.

An approach to both assessment and helping, initially developed in New Zealand in order to take account of the culture and approach to family and community life of the Maori people, is the Family Group Conference (FGC). Brown (2003) provides an account of its adaptation for use in the UK child welfare system and notes that its availability as a family-centred approach to assessment and service planning is patchy. There has been very little research on the extent to which family group conferences have been used with minority ethnic families. Marsh and Crow (1998) reported that 13 per cent of families involved in the FGCs they surveyed were of minority ethnic origin; that black families were as likely as white families to take up the suggestion of becoming involved in conferences but that Asian families may find it more difficult to take part. Smith (1998) and Simmonds, Bull and Martin (1998) found that, in areas of population diversity, minority ethnic families appeared to be taking part in conferences as would be expected by their representation amongst those receiving child welfare services. Other studies have found an under-representation of ethnic minority families amongst those taking part in FGCs, and this applies especially in areas where there are fewer minority ethnic families in the community (Lupton and Stevens 1997; Thomas 1994).

Research on family support for ethnic minority children and families in particular circumstances

A small number of detailed studies has provided data on services to children in need from particular ethnic groups or with particular stress factors such a child or parent with a disability. Some of these form part of a research programme on ethnicity and disability funded by the Joseph Rowntree Foundation and available in summary on the JRF website (www.jrf.org.uk/knowledge/findings).

Children with physical and/or learning disabilities

The children in need census (National Statistics and Department of Health 2001) indicated that 21 per cent of 1,700 Asian children receiving a 'child in need' service were disabled (compared to 14% of the white children and 9% each of the black children and those of mixed heritage). Ali *et al.* (2001) collate and analyse research studies that provide information on the views of minority ethnic children and adults on being disabled and on the services available to them. Chamba *et al.* (1999) carried out a large national survey in 1997 focusing on the needs and circumstances of minority ethnic families caring for a severely disabled child. The study provides information on the daily lives of parents and children; on their particular needs arising from the disability; how these were being met; and on the views of minority ethnic families about their experiences as service users. Twenty-three per cent of the 647 survey respondents (a 60% response rate) indicated that they were African or African-Caribbean, 38 per cent Indian, 27 per cent Pakistani and 12 per cent Bangladeshi.

Most of the families (and especially those of Bangladeshi and Pakistani origin) were living on low incomes. Seventy-five per cent of the mothers in the survey were looking after their family full-time. Problems with housing and getting out and about were also identified. This profile is shared with white parents of children with severe disabilities. However, many of these families had additional difficulties concerning language. Parents who understood English well were more likely to be in receipt of disability benefits to help meet the needs of their children. The researchers noted that it may appear that Bangladeshi families have low levels of unmet needs, but suggest that this may simply reflect their lower expectations of services. It is also of note that almost half of the Asian parents and 26 per cent of the combined group of African and African-Caribbean families wanted help with their children's learning and understanding of their own culture and religion. Parents' needs were most often concerned with the need for more money, help during school holidays, help with finding out about services, learning about the best way to support their children, taking a break from child care and planning for their children's future independence. With regard to differences across ethnic groups, African and African-Caribbean parents reported the greatest levels of unmet need. This study is particularly important since it identifies similarities and differences between groups and points the way towards services that are designed around the wishes and needs of particular ethnic minority groups, rather than assuming that their needs are all the same.

Data from this research is complemented by a study by Hatton *et al.* (2004). These researchers reviewed available demographic data and concluded that the prevalence of severe learning difficulties amongst South Asian communities may be up to three times greater than in the general population. They provide detailed information from interviews with 136 South Asian parents of children with severe learning disabilities. Seventy per cent were Pakistani; 17 per cent Indian and 11 per cent Bangladeshi. Most main carers were born outside the UK but had spent many years in the UK and most were not employed outside the home. A major focus of the study is the inappropriateness of methods of communication in light of the fact that very few of the mothers could speak, read or write English. The extent and range of unmet needs was higher than reported in similar studies based on general populations. Less than half the respondents described collaborative relationships with professionals. As in other studies, problems reported were concerned with communication barriers and a constant fight to get appropriate and timely services. Special schools, on the other hand, were highly rated, with the important exception that few were considered to make adequate provision for the cultural and religious needs of the children. Only 28 per cent of parents had an identified key worker – usually either a social worker or a health visitor. Their role in raising awareness of benefits, co-ordinating packages of care and providing emotional support was viewed very positively. Factors associated with a positive outcome in terms of family functioning and general well-being were identified. A well-conducted process of disclosing to the parents the nature of the disability, thus facilitating parental acceptance, was associated with mobilising packages of care and take-up of benefits. The availability of informal support and information from parent support groups helped parents to mobilise formal support. Language support and a key worker were associated with the availability of appropriate informal support. Culturally sensitive services were associated with collabora- tive relationships with professionals and care workers and helped to reduce unmet needs and parental health problems. Appropriate support led to an active social life and reduced depression.

Flynn's (2002a) detailed study of short break services comes to broadly similar conclusions to those of other researchers on the question of how services can be made more accessible and appropriate for minority ethnic parents and children. She particularly points out that most families want short-term break services to provide care for their children in their own homes as well as (or instead of) overnight or longer stays in foster or residential care. (This study is returned to in Chapter 5.) A study by Jones, Atkin and Ahmad (2001) considered the needs of young Asian deaf people and their families and develops some of the issues raised by Chamba *et al.* (1999). The research was qualitative and focused specifically on how Asian deaf people and their families engage with welfare provisions. Both parents and young people highlighted the practical difficulties faced by deaf people in accessing services. The lack of British Sign Language (BSL) interpreters caused particular problems. Confidentiality and lack of privacy emerged as specific problems especially when older children had to rely on their hearing parents to communicate for them. The researchers concluded that statutory sector workers exerted a form of social control over Asian deaf people by privileging 'oralism' over sign language. Other parental concerns were that their children's deafness limited their ability to socialise them around their cultural and religious values, as well as reducing their ability to manage effectively their children's excursions into what many considered to be a potentially 'dangerous' white/deaf world. Many parents objected to their children attending deaf social clubs.

Another small-scale research study that provides additional detail and reaches similar conclusions is that of Fazil *et al.* (2002). The authors interviewed Pakistani and Bangladeshi parents of children with severe disabilities in Birmingham. They conclude that many national surveys may have underestimated the extent of material disadvantage of Pakistani and Bangladeshi families and overestimated the availability of extended family support. The researchers conclude that the situation for ethnic minority families with a disabled child may be particularly acute given the additional dimension of negative stereotyping and institutional racism.

Children and adolescents with mental health problems

The research on the incidence of mental illness and emotional and behavioural problems amongst ethnic minority children has been summarised in an edited book by Malek and Joughin (2004) which also has chapters exploring some of the challenges confronting researchers in this field. Some of the practice, policy and service issues are discussed by Kurtz, Thornes and Wolkind (1994) and, especially in relation to child abuse, by Maitra (1996). Meltzer *et al.* (2000) undertook a survey of the prevalence of mental health problems amongst children and adults in the UK in 2002 and were able to follow up 88 per cent of the young people in 2002 (Meltzer *et al.* 2003). They found that nearly 10 per cent of white children and 12 per cent of black children (mainly African-Caribbean and African) were assessed as having a mental health problem. As with other areas of need and service provision, South Asian children and adolescents were less likely than white or black children to be referred for a mental health service (8% of the combined Pakistani and Bangladeshi child population and 4% of those of Indian heritage were receiving a service). When other variables were considered the ethnic origin of the child was not related to whether the mental ill health persisted over the three-year period.

Turning to the services, Malek and Joughin (2004) report on a survey of health commissioners and Child and Adolescent Mental Health (CAMH) teams in areas selected to include high, medium and low proportions of minority ethnic families. They found that none of the eleven commissioners of services regularly reviewed service provision for minority ethnic families; that only one provided guidelines to service providers about assessing the needs of minority ethnic children and families and that only four included specific requirements about meeting the needs of local minority ethnic groups in contracts and service specifications. Only two of the CAMH service managers said that staff regularly received training on meeting the diverse needs of the ethnic minority children and families in their areas, and only five took steps to evaluate the impact of their services on the different ethnic groups.

The Department of Health funded the evaluation of 'pathfinder' development projects and has provided additional resources to improve the CAMH services to children in the community as well as those looked after. Some of these are located in communities with large populations of minority ethnic children. Reports of individual projects that discuss ethnicity in any detail are largely accounts of process rather than outcome. Anane-Agyei, Lobatto and Messent (2002) and Messent and Murrell (2003) report on the pattern of referral and service provision to the different ethnic groups in Tower Hamlets. Although the majority group in the community served by the team is Bangladeshi (54% of the child population) they represented only 19 per cent of referrals whilst white children (28% of the child population) were over-represented amongst referrals. African and Black British/Caribbean children were also under-represented amongst referrals for a service (in contrast to the position in respect of other family support services). However, caution is urged since the ethnicity of 30 per cent of the children was not known. Bangladeshi parents were less likely than other groups to refer themselves and were likely to wait longer for the first appointment. African-Caribbean families were the group most likely to refer themselves and their children were more likely to be referred in an emergency and to be seen quickly. African and African-Caribbean children were more likely than South Asian children to be assessed by a psychiatrist. When interviewed by the researchers, Bangladeshi parents all agreed that the low rate of referral was not due to Bangladeshi children having fewer problems, but rather resulted from the low level of awareness of the service and how it might help.

Family Support services to teenagers including young asylum seekers and young people who are offenders

The Children Act 1989 (Section 20 (4) and Schedule 2) lays a duty on local authorities to provide accommodation for young people over 16 if their health or development would be 'seriously prejudiced' without such a service. As a minimum this required local authorities to respond to young people referred or referring themselves by checking that the 'seriously prejudiced' duty does not apply. In the main, this duty is met by using family support (Section 17) powers rather than (Section 20) accommodation, and often by referral to a voluntary agency or housing association. However, several studies of adolescents in vulnerable circumstances note that social services departments are often reluctant to listen to young people who seek their help. Lees (2002, p.920) quotes an African-Caribbean young woman who eventually had a positive experience in residential care but only after having been exposed to serious risk.

> I went to the police station and they called up Social Services and they said I had a perfectly good home and what was I doing at the police station. I told them my father had been emotionally and physically abusing me. I didn't disclose the sexual abuse at that time because I wasn't ready to, but I just wasn't believed. As far as they were concerned my dad had said I could go back so I ended up living on the streets for about two months.

Over the last ten years, young unaccompanied refugees and asylum seekers have become a significant group of young people receiving child welfare services. Most of those claiming asylum when under the age of 16 are 'looked after' by the local authority, but those over 16 and some under 16 are provided with services as children in need. The research on young asylum seekers who are looked after by the local authority will be discussed in Chapter 4. There is very little research on young asylum seekers who are looked after and even less on those who are not looked after. Mitchell (2003) reviews the available statistics, research and legal position as the first part of a research study. The Refugee Council and British Agencies for Adoption and Fostering (2001) provide an overview of the different sources of information and statistics on young people seeking asylum on their own behalf. There were 2735 in 2000 with applications being considered by the Home Office, the largest number (over 600) from former Yugoslavia, and the next largest number (300) from Afghanistan. Hamilton, Daly and Fiddy (2003) mapped the provision for refugee and asylum-seeking children in Essex. The children in need (CiN) census report for 2003 (National Statistics and DfES 2004) records that the 12,500 'active asylum seeking children' comprised 6 per cent of all children in need. Of these, 10,400 were supported in their families or independently and 2,100 were looked after. Forty-five per cent of these were white European and 55 per cent of other minority ethnic origin. Jones (2001) places her study of the variability of social services department responses to a cohort of young asylum seekers in the context of a discussion about the conflict between the Children Act 1989 and immigration legislation and policy, especially the use of detention centres.

Looking at adolescents in the general population, African-Caribbean young men are particularly vulnerable because they are over-represented amongst those excluded from school (see Bhattacharya *et al.* 2003) and those referred for help with mental health problems (see earlier section). There is a cross-over between the duties of local authority social services departments, the Connexions and CAMH services and youth offending teams in respect of adolescents who offend. Some will already be provided with 'child in need' services and others will be looked after or provided with a service as a formerly 'looked after' child. The Connexions service is too new for any evaluations of their work with vulnerable children from minority ethnic groups, but some descriptive information is provided by Aymer and Okitikpi (2001).

Phillips and Bowling (2002) provide a detailed analysis of the response of the criminal justice system to young black people who become involved in crime. Rutter, Giller and Hagell (1998) review the research on ethnic minority young people who become involved in antisocial behaviour. They report that, at the end of the 1990s, black and Asian young people were over-represented amongst those who were the victims of crime. At that time, on the basis of self-report, white and black young people were more likely than Asian young people to be the perpetrators of property crime and black young people were more likely than other ethnic groups to report that they had committed a crime involving violence. However, the authors note that the statistics are complex since ethnicity interacts with other variables associated both with offending behaviour and being a member of a minority ethnic group (such as poverty, living in a deprived area and school exclusion).

Although descriptive data on ethnicity are available from the reports of the Youth Justice Board and from local evaluations, there are as yet few outcome studies of the impact of the welfare aspects of services provided by the YOTs to ethnic minority children and their parents. Many of the programmes are new and more time will be needed to evaluate them systematically. This is an important issue, especially for African-Caribbean young people who are over-represented in the criminal statistics. The Youth Justice Annual Statistics for 2002–3 (Youth Justice Board (YJB) 2003) report that 5.6 per cent of young people found guilty or admitting to an offence were African-Caribbean though only 1.1 per cent of the under-19 population in England is of African-Caribbean origin. This over-representation holds true when young people themselves are the respondents to surveys about offending behaviour (YJB 2003). In this large self-report survey (comparing the responses of 4963 pupils aged 11 to 16 with 586 who were excluded and attending special units) 33 per cent of young black people compared to 26 per cent of the white young people and 23 per cent of those of Asian heritage in mainstream schooling answered 'yes' to the question 'have you committed any criminal offence in the last 12 months'. The numbers of survey respondents in the different ethnic groups who were excluded from school were too small for any differences to be statistically significant, but the pattern here is reversed with 61 per cent of the white excluded young people saying they had committed an offence in the last year compared with 58 per cent of the black young people and 53 per cent of the Asian young people. The survey also shows that excluded young people from white ethnic backgrounds are three times more likely to drink alcohol regularly than black or Asian excluded young people.

Some information on ethnicity and welfare outcomes is available from leaving care studies and from small-scale studies of services to young people abused or at risk of abuse through prostitution and young runaways. The Safe on the Streets Research Team (1999) and Wade *et al.* (2002, 2003) undertook a series of surveys of schoolchildren asking about their experience of running away from home. They conclude that around 11 per cent of young people run away or are forced to leave home before the age of 16 owing to difficulties in their lives including family conflict and instability, abuse and neglect. The researchers found that white young people were most likely to have run away (10% of white children had done so) followed by 7.5 per cent of young people of African-Caribbean origin and 5.5 per cent of young people of South Asian origin. From their interviews the researchers concluded that young people from ethnic minority communities run away for broadly the same reasons as their white peers but they may be less likely to access city-centre-based services and thus remain more vulnerable whilst sleeping rough. Research on children abused through prostitution is discussed in Chapter 4.

Parents with mental health problems or physical or learning disabilities

Most studies of children in need have found a high incidence of physical and mental health problems amongst parents and consider the impact of the experience of racial harassment and discrimination on mental health.

> I'm trying to get out of here because of abuse. I'm getting harassment from the neighbours, I'm not heading for a breakdown but I'm getting there. (Butt and Box 1998, p.76)

Using a standardised instrument to indicate depression in mothers receiving a family support service, Sheppard and Kelly (2001) concluded that 43 per cent were depressed. The sample included African-Caribbean, Asian and European mothers (a third of the sample in one of the authorities studied) as part of the general population but data were not analysed according to ethnicity. Studies of South Asian women who have mental health problems indicate that there is a higher incidence of suicide and self-harming behaviour amongst Asian young women than is found in other ethnic groups. Some of these will be parents and some will be young people under the age of 18. The normative study of Sonuga-Barke and Mistry (2000) explores the impact of nuclear and extended family living on the mental health of three generations of Asian Hindu and Muslim women and children living in East London. Mothers and grandparents in the sample, contacted through letters sent via the children's schools, reported high levels of depression and anxiety. Children and grandparents were found to be better adjusted in extended families, but mothers were better adjusted in nuclear families. Bhardwaj (2001) describes how some Asian women have to find ways of incorporating into their family lives and parenting practices social and religious pressures that can arise if matrimonial roles and the duty of women to maintain the family honour are rigidly defined. She also found inequalities between men and women as well as domestic violence from husbands, parents or relatives as a community-sanctioned way of exercising control and discouraging independence.

Jones, Jeyasingham and Rajasooriya (2002) provide information on the special issues arising for young people of minority ethnic origin who take on caring roles in respect of an ill or disabled parent. The findings are similar to those from other studies of young carers and point to the negative impact on the children's education and peer relationships of carrying out caring tasks and responsibilities. The researchers found that social care agencies often lacked information about black young people with caring responsibilities and were therefore uninformed about the extent of the potential problems. None of the families in the study reported that they were in receipt of family support services such as home care, counselling, social activities for families, educational support or health-based services. Where young black boys had caring responsibilities, this was reported to affect their behaviour and progress at school and was more likely to result in school exclusion than any other response. Along with similar studies of all ethnic groups, the researchers found that some parents were reluctant to approach the social care agencies, for fear that they may be seen as inadequate parents, and that their children might be removed from them. The study also considered the perspectives of family members in terms of how they felt their experiences were affected by their ethnicity and culture. Amongst the issues raised, language was significant to the extent that children were often required to act as interpreters if their parents did not speak English. There were also issues related to accessing places of worship, stereotyping black and Asian families, and differences in perception of the parenting role between professionals and parents.

Parents who misuse drugs and alcohol

Another area where parental difficulties impact on children is substance misuse by a parent. Harwin and Forrester (2002) studied services to children and parents where drug or alcohol misuse was a major reason for assessment that the child was 'in need'. Concern about substance misuse was raised in respect of 34 per cent of newly allocated cases. It was less likely that parental substance misuse would be a feature of the lives of the 247 children in the sample who were of minority ethnic origin than was the case with the white children. However, alongside the white children, those of mixed heritage were more likely to be included in this group (48% of the 73 children of mixed heritage compared with 33% of the 75 Black British/Caribbean children; 33% of the Asian children and none of the African children were in the substance misuse group). First generation immigrants were half as likely as other parents to be in the substance misuse group. Since most of the cases where there was concern about substance misuse involved an element of child protection, the findings are returned to in the next chapter.

Children in need as a consequence of separation and divorce, parental conflict and domestic violence

The research of Modood, Beishon and Virdee (1994) and Modood *et al.* (1997) has demonstrated that patterns of marriage and family formation are very different across the ethnic groups. However, the research on the impact on children of trauma, separation and loss, which for most children accompany marriage breakdown, suggests that a family support service for all ethnic groups should pay attention to the special needs of children at the point when the relationships between their parents are starting to unravel. In terms of generally available open access services, Pankaj (2000) found that ethnic minority families were under-represented amongst those who use family mediation services in Scotland. This community-based qualitative study was commissioned by the Scottish Executive to explore (through community associations) the views of the African-Caribbean, Chinese, Indian and Pakistani families about the stresses that might lead to marriage breakdown and the service that may reduce any negative impact on parents and children.

Most studies of general populations of children receiving an 'in need', child protection or mental health service have identified inter-parental conflict including inter-partner violence as having a negative impact on the emotional health of the children (see Brandon *et al.* 1999; Cleaver and Freeman 1995; Ghate and Hazel 2002; Meltzer *et al.* 2003; Owen and Farmer 1996). Indeed it is recognised as one of the major contributors to emotional neglect. The Thoburn, Wilding and Watson (2000) study found that problems in relationships with partners were less frequently mentioned by the combined group of ethnic minority families, but that 'extreme spouse abuse' was a cause for concern in respect of 15 per cent of white children and 12 per cent of the ethnic minority children.

Studies by Mullender *et al.* (2002) provide more detailed information on how children make sense of male violence towards their female partners. The survey found no difference between the attitudes of the different ethnic groups towards domestic violence, nor on their reports of knowing someone who had experienced domestic violence. From their interviews with a sub-sample of Asian young people whose mothers had been abused by their fathers (only half of whose mothers were UK born), the researchers found that confidentiality emerged as a distinctive theme for Asian women and children when compared to the wider sample. There were many similarities in the understanding between all the children, irrespective of gender or ethnic differences. However, one notable difference identified in the South Asian sample was the potential contribution of other members of the extended family to their mother's abuse. Researchers also found that there was an awareness by the Asian children that outside help may lead to isolation from their community, compounded by a fear of unsympathetic treatment from white people or organisations, which further restricted the likelihood of seeking help. Some of the Asian young people inter-viewed were influenced by considerations of family honour ('izzat') and referred to cultural expectations that they must continue to show respect to their fathers irrespective of their behaviour towards their mothers.

> He is OK with us, Dad. I have to respect him, not for the violence [but] because he is my dad. (14-year-old South Asian boy, Mullender et al. 2002, p.148)

> He wanted to keep us under his control – that is why he terrorized us. Mum stayed so long because of us and because of izzat, you know. 'What will people say?' She hid it from her family – wouldn't tell them how bad things were for such a long time. (16-year-old South Asian girl, Mullender et al. 2002, p.141)

For all the children in the study, moving away from their familiar surroundings, friends and family, was very difficult, but for South Asian children the problem was compounded by a greater vulnerability and exposure to racism in new communities and schools. The researchers conclude that, to enable a greater understanding of domestic violence in South Asian communities, there needs to be greater understanding of the significance of marriage as a union between families as well as between individuals.

> If you speak to adults, make sure they understand about your family and religion and they don't take things the wrong way. Like, sometimes, goray [white people] will not know about izzat and shame and they can make you do things which bring shame to the family. You are left without any help or support from the community, if they feel that you have gone against the religion. I don't say it is always right, but sometimes we have to sort things out our own way – white people can never really do things in the same way if they don't understand. (16-year-old South Asian girl, Mullender et al. 2002, p.138)

Recent years have seen a growth in supported and supervised child contact services to help children to stay in touch with the non-resident parent. Many of these are known to provide services to minority ethnic parents and children and provide practice guidance notes including advice on the special issues that may be relevant to the different ethnic groups. However, we have not identified any research that analyses descriptive and outcome data in terms of the ethnicity of families using these services.

Overview of research on family support services and barriers to their use

There is much overlap in the findings and conclusions of researchers about the social work and social care services provided to minority ethnic families, across the areas of family support, child protection and child placement. Cross-cutting questions include those on the ethnicity of the workers, the use of interpreters and the provision of information in the languages used by residents in the different parts of the UK. These points will therefore be taken up in Chapter 6.

In this chapter we have done little more than map the complexity of the issues for children and families who may need family support services. Despite the number of references, it will be clear that a start has barely been made on providing descriptive data on the use made of family support services by the different minority ethnic groups. There are very few studies that give the service planner and practitioner unambiguous messages about what works for which sorts of families, in which ethnic groups, in which circumstances.

However, progress has been made between the publication of the DH *Child Protection: Messages from Research* studies in 1995 and more recently completed studies, in that most now include larger populations of minority ethnic families. Research is also beginning to appear on families and children with particular needs (especially those with disabilities). Most importantly, researchers are now more specific about which minority ethnic groups are included in the research. In this respect, it is noteworthy that, although the groups most likely to be in receipt of general family support services are black African and African-Caribbean families and mixed heritage families, very little research has specifically focused on the ways in which services can be made more appropriate to their needs. These three groups are very different. Caribbean and mixed white and Caribbean families have in the main been in the UK for longer so it is important to understand why they are over-represented amongst those needing additional assistance beyond what is available from mainstream services. A key question in respect of Bangladeshi, Pakistani, Indian and especially Chinese and other east Asian families is whether the children would benefit if more families sought assistance from the family support teams.

Ghate and Hazel (2002) provide an important reminder that many families in poor environments manage without the need for additional services or prefer not to use them and manage well enough. A finding from this study is that, despite the lower levels of use of all forms of support, ethnic minority families were no more likely than white families to be in the 'non-coping' or 'sometimes not coping' groups. Broadly, all families have the same sorts of needs and want the same range of good quality services for themselves and their children. It is inadequate incomes, living in run-down, unsafe and depressing environments, in poor and overcrowded housing that explain most of the difference between families who do well enough without additional help and those who need family support services. The rest of the difference is explained by personal and interpersonal characteristics either resulting in additional stresses or mitigating the effects of living in poor environmments. The availability of, and just as importantly willingness to use, informal support from partners, family members, friends and local or faith communities also make a difference to whether families will need, will seek out or will accept informal and formal family support services.

A pattern emerges from all studies about service usage, indicating that African and African-Caribbean families and mixed partnership families where one parent is African or African-Caribbean, are more likely to be referred, to refer themselves for and to take up family support services. There is, however, a difference between the use of semi-formal services (mainly run by community groups) and formal/ statutory services, with those in greater need in all ethnic groups being more likely to take up formal than semi-formal ones. In that context, we highlight the consistent finding that, although there is a relationship between severity of need and the receipt of services by families living in stressful environments (including the large numbers of minority ethnic families in these communities) significant numbers of children in need do not get social services help. Axford et al. (in preparation) found that the proportion 'in need' not in contact with social services was roughly 1.6 times the proportion who were benefiting from such assistance.

The research we have reviewed has pointed toward some possible answers on the question of under-representation of Asian families. Only in respect of severe learning disability, where there is growing evidence that prevalence is higher amongst South Asian families, is there any difference between the needs of Asian families and the other groups making up the UK population. There is some evidence that on average Asian families, and especially those of Chinese and Indian heritage, are experiencing fewer of the very serious problems such as drug and alcohol addictions and severe mental health and personality and relationship problems that lead to families being referred for services against their wishes, or becoming visible to professionals because of their inability to manage without additional services. In other words, it seems likely that much of the variance in terms of under-representation may be explained by, on average, greater coping capacity in families and communities. There is also evidence amongst all ethnic groups of the resilience of extended families as providers of help at times of crisis. To the extent that poverty is less marked, family members in some communities are more able to help each other out as in this case of severe spouse abuse.

My nani and nana have helped my mum the most. Her parents and brothers have always been there for her and for us. They bought this house for us – paid the deposit. [They] bought dad the taxi. (16-year-old South Asian girl, Mullender *et al.* 2002, p.142)

The risk is that these strengths that benefit the majority make it more difficult for the minority who cannot turn to family and friends to seek timely assistance from social services departments or other welfare agencies.

The consensus view expressed by focus group attenders in the Qureshi *et al.* (2000) study was that when help was needed, families would first seek help from other family members and friends. The use of social work services was considered less likely, owing to a mixture of embarrassment, stigma about the organisation, and parents being unaware of what was on offer. Many group members in this study did not know what social services departments did or what supportive services were available. When asked whether they would be likely to use these services now that they were aware of them, there were gender differences in the responses, with South Asian women more positive about social work initiatives and programmes that can reduce family stress and break-down, and men being more suspicious of the motives for family intervention.

There is, however, evidence from some of the detailed studies we have reviewed about the barriers that reduce the willingness of ethnic minority parents, especially those of South and East Asian origin, to ask for support or be willing to be referred. This applies especially to informal support, where the barriers are highest for the families who need it most. Ghate and Hazel (2002) report that negative attitudes were widespread. The risks perceived by parents as potentially attached to seeking informal support were that it could under-mine authority and threaten family privacy since it often came with 'strings attached', and that it was not always reliable. Although reaching a higher pro-portion of the families in greatest need, problems with semi-formal and formal support were also identified, some of which may be especially important when considering the way in which these services are used, or not used, by families in different minority ethnic communities. Some of the research we have cited has identified, as barriers to the use of formal as well as neighbourhood or 'semi-formal' services by ethnic minority families, the lack of perceived rele-vance, linked to families feeling that the services are for 'other families but not us'. Other barriers to using formal (statutory agency) support concerned fear of loss of control of the way they organised their family lives; concerns that what they told professionals may not remain confidential; and fear of being labelled as a 'struggling parent'.

We would concur, from our overview of the research on family support services for vulnerable parents and children of minority ethnic origin, with the comment made by Henricson *et al.* (2001, p.72) from their large-scale mapping exercise of the full range of family support services: 'While constructive approaches are being adopted in some areas, it is evident that not enough is being done to provide members of minority ethnic groups with family services that are in their language and sensitive to cultural differences.'

A consistent picture emerges from the studies that, to increase their value to parents and children whose beliefs, languages or family cultures may differ from those of the majority white community, family support services will need to understand and find strategies to overcome the barriers identified by those interviewed or surveyed that include:

- inhibitions arising from cultural expectations, including the views of wider family members that it is shameful to admit to the existence of unmet needs or problems and to seek help outside the family

- difficulties resulting from lack of or poor quality interpreting services, including training of interpreters in the special issues that concern the needs of vulnerable children, neglect and abuse

- inadequate strategies for recruiting ethnic minority staff at all levels and in proportions that reflect the children and families in the community served by the services

- the dominance of white middle-class perceptions of parenting standards and practices which often prevail even when ethnic minority staff are recruited into the workforce.

Given the many gaps in prevalence and process studies, the paucity of information about what the different ethnic groups find helpful and the almost total absence of even interim outcome studies, the above conclusions must be highly tentative. We can say with confidence, because of the consistency with which researchers reach this conclusion, that, whilst families of all ethnicities have similar strengths and problems in bringing up children, different approaches to the provision of services are needed depending on the characteristics and preferences of the different groups. The studies we have cited, whilst not providing definitive answers, give many clues about how services might be designed around the needs of Asian communities, but tell us very little about how best to meet the needs of African and African-Caribbean parents and children. Given the findings that they are most likely to be over-represented amongst those whose children need long-term out-of-home care (see Chapter 5) as well as family support and mental health services, more research is needed on issues specific to the highly diverse groups of children of dual heritage. The availability of more detailed census data helps us to understand more of the complex identities of UK children, but detailed qualitative studies are needed, particularly of children growing up with a single parent and out of touch with the other part of their heritage. Finally, within ethnic groups, research is needed to differentiate between the needs of children of recent immigrants, including refugee and asylum-seeking families, and those born in the UK.

Chapter 4

Child Protection Services and the Family Courts

They should try to understand the cultural levels of shame experienced about a court appearance which can be the last straw in damaging someone's life. (Asian mother quoted in Freeman and Hunt 1998, p.31)

You receive us into your country but suddenly there is a family problem, the police are at your doorstep, the social workers arrive. In our country we don't have social workers. The police don't come for family problems... The first thing you should do is to get well-established families from my country when Africans arrive here. You should get them to say to them – if you do this, this will happen, if you do that, that will happen. (Brandon *et al.* 1999, p.114)

Child maltreatment and child protection – an overview

In this chapter we consider the research that focuses on the formal child protection systems as described in government guidance *Working Together to Safeguard Children* (DH 1999a) and including the public law work of the family courts. We noted in Chapter 3 that, for many of the children and families receiving family support services as children 'in need' there are issues concerning the need to protect them from 'significant impairment to their health and development' (Children Act 1989, Section 17 b). The majority of children and families referred or referring themselves for a service in which there is a protective element will be provided with services outside the formal child protection systems. An important minority of referrals will result in a formal inquiry as to whether the child is 'suffering or likely to suffer significant harm' under the provisions of Part V of the Children Act 1989 (a 'Section 47' inquiry). In most cases this will result in a child protection conference which may then lead to the child's name being placed on the child protection register (CPR) as in need of a formal, multi-disciplinary child protection plan. In a minority of cases referred for a child protection service, court action is taken which may lead to the making of a care order or a supervision order (Section 31) and an even smaller minority of all referrals result in the child being looked after under a care order. (The research on children in care will be considered in the next chapter.)

In some cases parents or carers suspected of being responsible for ill-treating a child will be prosecuted in the criminal courts and the police, probation and prison services become involved. The point being made here is that the reader of research should note that findings (including findings about the ethnic composition of the children receiving a child protection service) differ depending on the point in the protection process at which the research sample is identified. A sample of children drawn from the nearly 70,000 children subject each year to a 'Section 47' inquiry (for example the Gibbons, Conroy and Bell 1995 study) will contain a larger proportion of cases of inappropriate discipline or control strategies which are not assessed as amounting to physical assault or neglect leading to significant harm. A sample drawn from the 20,000 or so public law cases considered by the family courts in the course of a year (as with the Brophy, Jhutti-Johal and Owen 2003a, 2003b and Hunt and Macleod 1999 studies) will include a much higher proportion of cases of serious ill-treatment by parents and carers or serious failure to protect children from harm; and this will be even more the case if the sample includes only the 6000 or so cases each year in which a care order is made (as with the Harwin *et al.* 2003 study of care plans).

It will be clear from the research cited in Chapter 3 that children and parents of all ethnic groups have much to gain from the approach in the recent Green Paper, *Every Child Matters* (DfES 2003) that concerns itself with helping all children to 'achieve a reasonable standard of health and development' and preventing the impairment to children's development, whatever the cause (Children Act 1989 Section 17 a and b). The research on the formal child protection system (summarised in Child Protection: Messages from Research, DH 1995, and The Children Act Now: Messages from Research, DH 2001) gives many examples of children in need of services in order to protect them, for example, from the damaging impact of living in very adverse circumstances or being exposed to bullying and/or racial abuse, yet denied services because the abuse was not attributable to ill-treatment or neglect by a parent or carer (and thus not prioritised as a 'child protection case'). Broadly based family support services that include elements of protection have been discussed in Chapter 3. In this section we are concerned with children referred to the formal child protection systems we have just described. By considering minority ethnic children in particular, we explicitly raise the idea that child protection services might be responding to different needs, or might be provided in different ways, for children and parents who identify with different ethnic groups.

Before looking at statistics on incidence it is important to use the messages from a range of research studies and practice texts to define what, in writing this section, we mean by 'child ill-treatment' or 'child abuse and neglect'. The Children Act 1989 helpfully moved away from a definition of ill-treatment as specific parental acts, to one based on the harm to the child, harm being linked to impairment of health and development and to parenting behaviours. The underpinning philosophy, influenced by the *Child Protection: Messages from Research* studies, is that child maltreatment is a complex phenomenon. It includes specific acts of physical, sexual, verbal or psychological abuse, or failures to act to protect children from exposure to significant harm. However, other than in the cases of sexual assault or physical assault leading to serious injury, to define a piece of behaviour as ill-treatment causing or likely to cause the child to suffer significant harm (the threshold for statutory intervention) requires a consideration of some or all of: the intentions behind the act; the frequency of occurrence; whether it is likely to continue; whether it is accompanied by other harmful behaviours; and the emotional climate within the family. Is this particular child being brought up in a warm and loving family that is using a method of discipline that in UK society is regarded as psychologically harmful, degrading or a criminal assault but may be viewed as 'normal' within the family's ethnic or cultural group? Is this a generally warm and loving family whose standards of care have temporarily slipped in reaction to exceptional stress or trauma? Or is the pervasive emotional atmosphere in this family, as the *Child Protection: Messages from Research* introduction puts it, 'low on warmth and high on criticism' and likely to be causing significant harm? Is this particular child being exploited and abused for the gratification or financial gain of the parents or carers or being physically assaulted and exposed to risk of serious or even fatal injury?

This approach to an understanding of child maltreatment is taken in the Framework for the Assessment of Children and their Families (DH 2000) and especially, in respect of minority ethnic families, in the chapter in the guidance by Dutt and Phillips. It may help to explain why the proportion and actual numbers registered because of physical abuse have halved between 1998 and 2002. It may be that the incidence of physical abuse (including physical punishment) has gone down, but it is more likely to mean that some parental behaviours are being understood as potentially harmful acts to be discouraged by appropriate services to the parents and child, rather than as abusive behaviour leading to a child protection conference. This issue is explored and debated in several of the studies discussed in this chapter.

However, it is important first to consider what research studies of general populations of UK families can tell us about the ways in which mothers, fathers and other family members in the different ethnic, cultural and social class groups bring up their children, including how they control and discipline them. Smith *et al.* (1995) in one of the *Child Protection: Messages from Research* studies, used a survey instrument (administered in person) to ask about the ways in which UK parents disciplined their children, including the use of physical punishments. The sample, selected randomly from health authority records, was of parents of 'indigenous children' defined to include all children whose grandparents were born in the UK. It included a small number of African-Caribbean and South Asian children but data on these were not analysed separately in the published reports. A further analysis (Nobes *et al.* 1999) compared punishments used by 362 mothers and by 103 fathers in the 366 two-parent families. Although not analysed by ethnic group, this study can provide baseline data for other researchers when the relationship between physical punishment and significant harm is being discussed in respect of different patterns of family life in different cultural groups. In common with earlier researchers whose work they discuss, the authors found that physical punishment of children (usually by way of smacking, and spanking, pushing and shoving) was a common occurrence in UK family life. Fathers were more likely than mothers to use physical restraint (including pushing, throwing and holding). The forms of punishment categorised by researchers as 'more severe' were less common but still could not be viewed as rare. Sixteen per cent of mothers and 21 per cent of fathers had used punishments rated as 'severe'. For example, 10 per cent of mothers and 15 per cent of fathers said they had used an implement to smack a child – most usually a slipper or wooden spoon. It is clear from this, and from earlier community sample studies, that far more children experience 'severe punishment' than appear in the child protection statistics (on the basis of this study, around 2 million children at any point in time). However, it should be pointed out that the definitions used by researchers for 'severe' punishment are not necessarily those that would be used by family members.

> If my Dad or Mum hits me or my brother or sister it's because we have done something really bad but if you told the social worker that my Dad beat me they say it is abuse or something like that. But it's not – it's how we are brought up in our community, to respect our elders and to listen to them. White people don't understand this. My parents only discipline us the way they were brought up and I know that it is out of love. (Qureshi *et al.* 2000, p.17)

> Dad would punish me. He would pull my ears. Yes, I hated him. I remember once he hit me with a wooden ruler and it snapped in half, and I had a big gash at the back of my leg. My mum couldn't believe that my dad would do such a thing, but neither her nor me said anything to him. I really hated being smacked, it just built up into a hate thing. (African-Caribbean young man about a long-term foster placement cited in Thoburn, Norford and Rashid 2000, p.114)

A more recent community sample study by Cawson *et al.* (2000) also informs the important debate about the circumstances in which discipline and other parenting practices tip over into what is likely to be considered by UK child protection systems as ill-treatment or neglect. Interviewers spoke to 2,869 young people aged 18–24, all born in the UK, obtaining information about their family life as they grew up and about the ways in which their parents sought to ensure compliance with family expectations. Ninety-two per cent of respondents described their ethnicity as white and 229 (8%) as belonging to another ethnic group. Five per cent of the total sample described themselves as Asian and most of these identified themselves as Indian or Pakistani. Two per cent identified themselves as black and these mostly identified themselves as African-Caribbean or 'black other'. An additional 'top-up' sample (keeping to the same ethnic profile as the national population) was sought, bringing the number of young people of minority ethnic origin to 510. Preliminary examination of the results from the enhanced sample of minority ethnic young people gives a picture of family life and relationships, and of maltreatment, which is broadly similar for all ethnic groups, but where there are some specific differences between ethnic groups which tend to be masked when all are included together as 'minority ethnic' respondents. This analysis compared results between aggregated Asian (Indian, Pakistani and Bangladeshi) and black (African-Caribbean, African and 'black other') respondents, 'other ethnicity' and white respondents. The 'other ethnicity' group is likely to include some who were of mixed heritage, though some of mixed heritage will have included themselves with the black or Asian groups. Differences between groups are small (of the order of 5–10%) and could be explained to some extent by class, low income or family type. (Growing up in a single-parent family was more common among black respondents and the 'other ethnicity' group than among Asian or white respondents.)

The published report refers primarily to the base sample. In terms of discipline, methods such as reasoning, 'grounding' and withdrawal of pocket money or privileges were used by most parents, but 87 per cent of young people reported that they had experienced verbal treatment including being shouted and screamed at, sworn at, called names such as stupid or lazy, and threatened. Most had also experienced physical punishment. This was most commonly an occasional slap with an open hand on the bottom, arm or leg but 21 per cent had been slapped on the face, head or ears. A quarter of the sample reported more serious violence including being hit with implements, punched, kicked, burned or scalded, knocked down, and choked, with most of this occurring at the hands of parents, especially mothers. A detailed picture is also provided of the extent to which the young people were exposed to inappropriate sexual attentions from a family member or someone outside the family, were neglected or inadequately supervised or were psychologically maltreated. The survey shows that a sizeable minority (38%) grew up in families where there was 'a lot of stress' and this was broadly similar across ethnic groups. Respondents from all minority ethnic groups more often said that physical violence had occurred between their parents – approximately a third of all groups compared to a quarter of white respondents. Levels of domestic violence were highest for black young people, 13 per cent of whom said it was 'constant' or 'frequent' compared to 4 per cent of white and 7 per cent of Asian respondents.

Which minority ethnic children and families are referred for a child protection service?

Having reviewed the information about the extent of stress, harsh discipline and inappropriate control strategies in 'normal families' we turn to what is known about the children and parents who come to the attention of the formal child protection services. Until 2002 there were no nationally collected statistics giving details of referrals of different ethnic groups to social services departments which involved concern about possible maltreatment. The only sources of data on ethnicity have come from a small number of research studies or the reports of some Area Child Protection Committees (ACPC) and it is therefore not possible to provide reliable data on changes over time.

There are now three sources of official statistics on children 'in need' who are also referred to the formal child protection system. The CiN census data (National Statistics and DfES 2004) indicated that in 26 per cent of cases the major reason for the provision of family support to children living in their families or supported independently was abuse or neglect (almost 80,000 children). In a further 12 per cent of cases 'family dysfunction' was given as the main reason and it could be assumed that in some of these cases emotional and other forms of neglect or maltreatment may be present. As yet, this figure is not broken down by ethnic group. The other source is the Department of Health annual statistics on children and young people on child protection registers. For the year ending 2002 this was extended to include data on children and families referred for a service and those that led to initial and 'core' assessments as well as those where a Section 47 inquiry was undertaken and those on the child protection registers (National Statistics and DH 2003a). The only data as yet analysed by ethnic group are the data on children on the registers. It should be noted that these data do not give a picture of the number of children known to have been abused or maltreated, but only of those for whom there is a child protection plan monitored by the members of a multi-disciplinary core group. There are major variations between similar authorities in different parts of the country as to the extent to which they manage child protection work through the registration system or as part of their broader family support services. Thus, two boroughs with large ethnic minority populations and similar levels of problems within their communities have very different patterns of registration. Each had around 800 referrals per 10,000 children during the year and completed 'child in need' assessments at broadly the same rate. However, one of these conducted around 50 Section 47 enquiries per 10,000 children in the year whilst the other completed over a hundred. The first had around 20 children per 10,000 on the child protection register whilst the second had around 50. To further illustrate this point, 42,600 children were recorded on the CiN census as receiving a service whilst living at home because of concerns about abuse or neglect, but at the end of that year, only 25,700 were registered on a child protection register as having a formal child protection plan. Older children at risk of significant harm because their own behaviour was putting them at risk were least likely to be 'on the register'. This African-Caribbean teenager eventually came into care:

> Looking forward I would like to see things different by behaving myself and stop hanging around with bad companies and not putting my self at risk. I'll also stop smoking and drinking because I'm only young and it's not nice seeing a young girl smoking and drinking and also self harming. (Timms and Thoburn 2003, p.99)

With this caveat about data on child protection registration, looking at data for the whole country, the statistics show that 17 per cent of children registered as receiving a formal child protection service in March 2002 were of minority ethnic origin (compared to 13% ethnic minority children recorded in the Census). Six per cent of those on the registers (compared with 3% of children aged 0 to 17 recorded in the 2001 census) were of mixed race parentage; 4 per cent (6.4% of the child population) were Asian or Asian British; 4 per cent (4% of the child population) were Black or Black British, and 2 per cent (0.4% of the child population) were in the 'other ethnic groups'. In summary, white children and those of Asian origin are under-represented whilst those of mixed heritage and the 'other' group are over-represented amongst those registered as receiving a formal child protection service. The combined group of African-Caribbean and African children are neither over- nor under-represented amongst those on the child protection registers.

When compared to the statistics for children receiving a child protection service as part of a general 'in need' service in their own homes, a slightly different pattern emerges, though caution is advised as there are more 'child in need' cases in respect of which data on ethnicity are not available. (Also, some of those on the child protection register are looked after away from home, which may make some slight difference though probably not enough to change the overall pattern.) The 'in need' service received in their own homes by white children and by those of mixed race parentage was more likely to include a formal child protection service involving registration than was the case for the combined group of African and African-Caribbean children or those in the 'other ethnicity group'. The service received by the combined Asian group was as likely as not to be a formal child protection service. (4% of those on the child protection registers and slightly over 4% of those receiving a 'child in need' service were Asian.)

The third source of routinely collected statistics is the annual report on children who start to be looked after by local authorities each year. We shall explore these data in more detail in the next chapter, but it is relevant to note here that 10,900 (44%) of the 24,600 children who started to be looked after in 2002 were in this position primarily because of concerns about abuse or neglect. This was the case for 45 per cent of the white children, 48 per cent of the children of mixed heritage; 47 per cent of those of South Asian heritage, 30 per cent of the combined African and African-Caribbean group and 34 per cent of the 'other ethnicity' group. Thus, although (as we shall document later) children of South Asian heritage are much less likely to be looked after by local authorities than African-Caribbean children, those who are looked after are more likely to leave home because of concerns about abuse or neglect. Only around half of these 10,900 children (5,500 – not differentiated by ethnic group in either these or the Judicial Statistics, DCA 2003) initially left home through a care order or emergency protection order based on suspicion of significant harm, with the others leaving home with the consent of or at the request of a parent.

Thus, white children are under-represented amongst those whose children are the subject of a formal child protection plan and even more so amongst those who need out-of-home care, but when they do start to be looked after it is as likely as with other groups that this will be because of concerns about abuse or neglect. Children of mixed heritage are over-represented amongst those in respect of whom there is a formal child protection plan and over-represented amongst those who need out-of-home care. But, if they do need to be looked after, they are no more likely than others to start to be looked after because of concerns about abuse or neglect. South Asian children are less likely to be the subject of a formal child protection plan and less likely to be placed in out-of-home care. However, if they do need to be provided with care away from home there is a (non-significant) trend for this to be more likely than for other groups because of concerns about abuse or neglect. The pattern for the combined group of African and African-Caribbean children is different. They are neither more nor less likely than white or Asian children to be the subject of a formal child protection plan but are more likely to be amongst those who are placed in out-of-home care. However, for those who start to be looked after, it is far less likely than for the other main groups that this will be because of concerns about abuse or neglect.

Further clarification of what these statistics may mean for the different ethnic groups may be found in recent research studies. Two research studies designed specifically to explore the way in which the formal child protection system impacts on ethnic minority children and their families are those of Brophy et al. (2003a, b) which looked at various aspects of statutory interventions under Section 31 of the Act and the role of the family court, and the Barn et al. (1997) study of how social services departments have responded to section 22(5)(c) of the Children Act 1989. However, some earlier studies of general populations of children referred for a child protection service, and more of the more recent ones, have included ethnic minority families in their samples. The key ones are mentioned and their conclusions on ethnicity will be summarised. Numbers in some of these studies are too small to provide reliable statistical data on prevalence rates or on outcomes for the different ethnic groups but, as with the family support research, they can provide clues to understanding the statistics and also pointers to future research. We start with those that consider cases at the point of referral and move on to research on 'heavier end' cases.

Research studies that analyse data on reasons for referral by ethnic group go some way towards filling the gap in the national statistics on referral rates. From a national survey and detailed study of cases in eight authorities, Gibbons *et al.* (1995) found that the combined group of ethnic minority children in the sample of children referred for a child protection inquiry were over-represented in all of them. Barn *et al.* (1997) scrutinised 196 open child and family cases in three authorities all of which had large ethnic minority populations. There were roughly equal proportions of African-Caribbean (18%), Asian (14%) and mixed parentage children (16%) in their sample. Ten were African and four were Chinese. Most of the children of mixed parentage had white birth mothers (27 out of 30) and the majority of fathers were African-Caribbean (11 out of 22 where information was available). Seventy-three per cent of the ethnic minority children compared with 86 per cent of the white children were initially referred because of child protection concerns.

Three of the four areas in the Brandon *et al.* (1999) study of 105 newly identified cases of 'significant harm or likely significant harm' had large populations of minority ethnic families. Forty-six of the children (44%) were of minority ethnic origin, the largest group being African-Caribbean or having one African-Caribbean and one white parent. The children were followed through for a twelve-month period between 1993 and 1994 and an eight-year follow-up is now being completed. Reliable data on children in the different ethnic groups in the wards in which the study took place were not then available, but the researchers estimated that the combined group of minority ethnic families was over-represented when compared with white families.

Thoburn, Wilding and Watson (2000) compared services to children under eight referred for a family support service with those where child protection concerns had been raised at the time of referral. Two of the three authorities had large populations of minority ethnic families. Where data on ethnicity were available in these areas (386 children) well over half (263) were of minority ethnic origin. The largest group were of South Asian descent (114) followed by 68 of African descent. Unusually in research samples of social services referrals, only 38 (9%) were of mixed race parentage. The use of research interviewers from the same ethnic groups as the families led to a higher response rate than is often the case from minority ethnic families (67 of the 122 interviewed at least once). Although as a group ethnic minority families were over-represented, it was not possible to determine whether all minority ethnic groups were over-represented or just some. As with the Barn *et al.* (1997) study, minority ethnic children were more likely than white children to be in the youngest age group. They were less likely than the white children to be referred because of child protection concerns and more likely than the white children to be referred for a family support service. This was especially the case for those of mixed race parentage.

Differences between findings about the different ethnic groups are to some extent explained by the different years when the data were collected as well as different 'thresholds' for inclusion in the research samples as already discussed. Since the national statistics on the different ethnic groups are now collected annually and published in national and local statistical returns, it should in future years be possible to explore this question more fully and with greater accuracy.

Why are children and families referred to the formal child protection systems?

Some of these studies have included more detailed information on the types of referral for the different ethnic groups, as well as interview data from the family members giving their own perceptions of the reasons they sought or were referred for help. (See Chand 2000, for a review article discussing reasons for referral and the question of over-representation.) These small scale studies need to be read in the context of the general population studies of Smith *et al.* (1995) and Cawson *et al.* (2000) referred to earlier and also of the research in Chapter 3 that shows the extent of disadvantage and the resultant stress amongst families in the different ethnic groups. Although studies usually identify a main reason why a child comes to the attention of the formal child protection service, whether through the 'lower threshold' formal child protection system or the (higher threshold/smaller numbers) looked after and court systems, in most cases the concerns will be complex. Information about possible impairment to a child's development will usually be combined with concerns about deficits in the quality of parenting or serious relationship problems. The link between parental behaviour and impairment to a child's development has to be teased out in the assessment processes. The conclusion of the DH (1995) *Child Protection: Messages from Research* studies on children who are brought up for long periods in an atmosphere that is low on warmth and high on criticism finds echoes in the Meltzer *et al.* (2003) finding that one of the variables associated with child and adolescent mental health problems being more long-lasting was the prevalence of a pattern of discipline based on frequent and loud shouting at the child. The Cawson *et al.* (2000) finding that many children in all ethnic groups experienced being shouted and screamed at, sworn at and belittled takes on particular relevance. Combining these two, it can be deduced that inappropriate parenting patterns, including harsh discipline that stops short of physical assault, may lead to a deterioration in the child's behaviour and referral for a child protection service because of concerns about emotional neglect or emotional abuse. Conversely, a deterioration in the child's behaviour as a result of parenting which is emotionally neglectful may lead to harsh discipline in order to 'correct' the child's behaviour and a referral because of physical abuse when the underlying problem is emotional neglect. Brandon *et al.* (1999) note the 'blaming' of children (by teachers as well as parents) whose behavioural problems are the result of witnessing serious conflict and violence between their parents. On the other hand, some families may be judged to be harsh in their approaches to discipline and control strategies due to stereotyping and cultural biases in what constitutes good parenting. Smacking with an implement in a family where the children are shown affection and generally positive parenting may not lead to physical or emotional harm but could result in a referral to the formal child protection system.

Starting with the 'lower threshold' studies of children referred for a service Thoburn, Wilding and Watson (2000) found that, amongst the 50 per cent of the sample referred because of child protection concerns, white children were more likely than the combined ethnic minority group to be referred because of concerns about physical abuse (for 18% of the referrals of white children, this was the main concern compared to 11% of the ethnic minority children); sexual abuse (11% and 3% respectively); emotional maltreatment (9% and 2%) and neglect (excluding 'home alone') (20% compared with 11%). There was a statistically significant difference between the ethnic minority and white families with respect to referrals because of 'other child protection concerns' – that is, those that were complex and could not, without further exploration, be fitted into any one category of abuse (28% of the ethnic minority referrals and 17% of the referrals of white children). Having interviewed the families, the researchers explain this in terms of the great complexity and extent of material deprivation in the lives of many ethnic minority families, especially those seeking asylum. Communication problems, in part linguistic but in part the result of trauma, mental health problems and incomprehension of a very alien child welfare system, helped to explain the lack of clarity around the exact reasons for concern in the early stages of the case. In a substantial minority of these, and of the 'home alone' cases, it became clear that this was not a 'child abuse' case but one where practical help such as day care, or help to find more suitable accommodation or with welfare benefits, was needed (although there was often an element of emotional neglect stemming from the parents' distress). These families were usually channelled out of the formal child protection system, though not before some of them had become even more distressed and confused by the allegation of child abuse and, as some of them saw it, the incomprehensible 'ritual' of the child protection conference. (The impact of an allegation of maltreatment on parental behaviour is explored more fully by Cleaver and Freeman 1995, through their detailed interview with thirty parents, seven of whom were of minority ethnic origin). The trends (not significant) were considered for each minority ethnic group separately and it was found that Asian children and mixed heritage children were more likely to be referred because of concerns about neglect; 'black other' and white children were more likely to be referred for reasons of physical or sexual abuse; African-Caribbean children and African children were more likely to be referred because of non-specific child protection concerns.

The findings from the Barn *et al.* (1997) study are slightly different. Asian families were less likely than other groups to be referred because of concerns about neglect (in 11% of cases compared with 32% of those involving white children and 26% of the African-Caribbean children and those of mixed parentage). However concerns about physical abuse were raised in respect of 21 of the 28 Asian children (75%) compared with 29 per cent for African-Caribbean children, 38 per cent of mixed parentage children and 37 per cent of the white children. Concerns about sexual abuse were more common in respect of white children (16%), roughly twice as often as for each of the other groups. Seventy-one per cent of the Asian children and 64 per cent each of the African Caribbean and dual heritage children were registered under the category of physical abuse.

Gibbons *et al.* (1995) also found (in their sample comprising all cases in which concern about possible child maltreatment had been raised) that as a combined group, minority ethnic families were more likely to be referred for a Section 47 inquiry because of concerns about physical abuse. Fifty-eight per cent of minority ethnic families were referred for this reason compared with 42 per cent of white families. They were less likely to be referred because of concerns about possible sexual abuse (20% compared with 31% of the referrals of white children). They also found that minority ethnic families were often referred for using an implement to inflict physical punishment '...40 per cent of Asians and 43 per cent of black Africans had beaten their children with a stick or other implement compared to 30 per cent of African-Caribbeans and 16 per cent of whites' (p.40). In a pre-Children Act study focusing on family member involvement in child protection proceedings, Thoburn, Lewis and Shemmings (1995) concluded that data on physical punishment should be analysed separately as a sub-group of the 'physical abuse' category of referral. Whilst nine per cent of the 218 child protection referrals (18% of which concerned minority ethnic families) were categorised as 'serious physical assault', 11 per cent were in the 'excessive punishment' group. Numbers in each group were too small for separate analysis, but the authors note that 'disagreements [between parents and professionals or between one parent and the other] about the appropriateness of physical punishment featured in a disproportionate number of cases involving black families' (p.200).

Hunt and Macleod (1999) in a study of more serious cases that involved court proceedings, found that the type of harm did not differ between groups, except that, contrary to some 'lower threshold' studies, physical abuse was more prevalent amongst white families. They found that minority ethnic families were over-represented among cases primarily based on risk attributable to parental difficulties or circumstances. Brophy *et al.* (2003a), also from a study of care proceedings, emphasise that reasons for court action are complex and rarely result from a single act of ill-treatment. However, taking the main reason given, they found that allegations of physical maltreatment were highest in the white group (55%) followed by the South Asian group (41%) and were lowest for the black group (26%). There is a difference between this 'heavier end' court sample and 'point of referral' samples in respect of sexual abuse in that referrals with this as the main cited reason for court action (though usually one of a number of allegations of ill-treatment) were highest in the mixed parentage group (27%), followed up by the South Asian group (19%). Sexual abuse was one of a number of allegations resulting in care proceedings for only 6 per cent of the white children and 3 per cent of the black children in this study of 'heavy end' cases which were considered by the courts.

In summary, differences between types of maltreatment for the different ethnic groups being considered at the different stages of the child protection system, and for different age groups, need further study. It may be that there is less sexual abuse or emotional abuse amongst ethnic minority families; it may be that this sort of maltreatment remains hidden until the evidence can no longer be missed and the case is taken quickly to court. There is not enough evidence on which to reach a firm conclusion. Combining the evidence from Chapter 3 on the reasons why minority ethnic children and parents may need help, with this complex data on patterns of referral because of child protection concerns we conclude, as we did at the end of Chapter 3, that, in the main, minority ethnic parents want for their children what white parents want for their children, and that they fall short of acceptable standards of parenting for broadly similar reasons. However, researchers have identified some specific differences, mainly around conceptualisations of family roles and responsibilities and concerning communication patterns that are influenced by cultural, linguistic and religious differences. Research also demonstrates that these differences have an impact on the way in which the services and the child protection systems themselves are understood and responded to and this will be the subject of Chapter 6.

Physical and emotional neglect and inadequate supervision

Although most attention tends to be paid by the media and by researchers to physical and sexual abuse, the most frequent reasons for referral for all ethnic groups are actual or likely physical and/or emotional neglect, whereas emotional abuse is increasingly cited as a reason for initiating court proceedings (Brophy *et al.* 2003a). Thoburn, Wilding and Watson (2000, p.27) found that emotional *neglect*, which largely results from the unintended neglect of children's emotional needs because of acute distress, conflict, trauma or mental ill health in the lives of the parents, was often mis-categorised as emotional or psychological *abuse*, which usually contains an element of deliberate or 'out-of-control' cruelty. The underlying factors contributing to emotional neglect (which is often linked to physical neglect) are stresses from a range of sources including depressing and depriving environments, domestic conflict and violence, mental ill-health and, increasingly, substance misuse (Harwin and Forrester 2002; Iwaniec 1995; Stevenson 1998). To the extent that there are differences between the different ethnic groups in their vulnerability to these problems, and between those who have arrived only recently in the UK and those born here, the type and incidence of maltreatment may differ. The available research points to the need for more detailed information on the impact of migration, stress and trauma on the way parents from different ethnic groups and at different stages of settlement respond to their children's needs.

There are already some pointers in the research, mainly drawn from interviews with parents, children, community leaders and social workers, towards understanding differences that may have an impact on referral rates rather than, or as well as, on the incidence of maltreatment. Within the 'neglect' statistics, some ethnic minority children come to the attention of child protection agencies because of the lack of child care that pushes their parents into leaving them without supervision. This is more likely to occur with single parent families. For recent arrivals in the UK, there may be different views about the age at which a child may be left unsupervised, or may be left in charge of other children in the family. Thoburn, Wilding and Watson (2000) identified a trend for more minority ethnic families to be referred because of concerns about physical neglect (53%) than was the case for the white families (40%). Because they found a high incidence of neglect referrals concerned 'home alone' or 'lack of supervision', the researchers analysed this group separately and found a trend towards more ethnic minority children being referred for this reason (16% compared with 11% of the white children).

Discipline and control strategies and physical abuse

Researchers writing from the academic disciplines of anthropology and cultural studies, as well as those conducting general population surveys, report differences in the way in which discipline is understood and maintained and the forms of punishment used in different ethnic communities. It is clear from these studies that a majority of parents in all ethnic groups in the UK use physical punishments in order to control and discipline children. Indeed, our legislators have consistently failed to outlaw the justification of 'lawful chastisement'. The method of punishing children in white families tends more often to be a slap, a push, a pull or an angry shout (in 'high criticism, low warmth' families often repeated and potentially causing long term harm) and the use of implements that leave a physical rather than a psychological mark will often be judged to constitute an assault, though leading in only a minority of cases to a criminal prosecution. However, in the countries of origin of some of the ethnic groups that now make up the UK's diverse population, the use of an instrument to punish a child is more generally acceptable and, in moderation, may be considered a sign of good parenting. Barn (2001) found evidence to suggest that some minority ethnic parents may use more punitive parenting measures in Britain than they would if still in their countries of origin to try to curb some of the western influences on their children.

To summarise, literature from cultural studies and anthropology as well as the empirical studies described here suggests that, whilst the extent of physical punishment as a control strategy is likely to be no different between groups, the way in which it is inflicted has brought some ethnic minority parents into the formal child protection (conference and registration) system or the court arena. This may in part account for the higher incidence in the physical abuse category found by some, but not all, researchers, at some stages in the protection process and in respect of some ethnic groups. For example, although ethnographic studies indicate that use of physical chastisement may be an acceptable mode of discipline in the cultures from which Chinese, Korean and Vietnamese families migrated, the lower visibility of these families to the statutory services, and the fact that they barely feature amongst those receiving family support services, may explain why they do not appear as an over-represented group in the child protection statistics.

For those cases which resulted in care proceeding, Brophy et al. (2003a, p.41) found a lower incidence of physical abuse amongst black and Asian children as the main reason for care proceedings but added that '...the pictures behind the statistics for the South Asian and black groups...demonstrate that where physical ill-treatment underscored applications, this ill-treatment was usually severe and of some duration. In other words, it could not be conceived as culturally accepted "reasonable chastisement" which was misunderstood by white western professionals'. They conclude that it is essential for what in the American literature is termed 'culturally competent' professionals to be available to comment when parents or other professionals refer to values and parenting practices in countries of origin as an explanation for behaviours that are being considered as possible ill-treatment or neglect. They stress the importance of differentiating between 'normal' child care practices and deviant or idiosyncratic attitudes and behaviours that fall outside of acceptable norms and values in any community (Brophy 2003; Brophy *et al.* 2003a, 2003b).

Other types of abuse

> I have started feeling a bit scared recently because Dad has started to come into the house a lot to see Mum… I feel, sometimes, that they may get back together. I am really scared that this is because he wants to get me married off. That's why he is coming around. I want a job, I want to help Mum. He just wants to show his control by getting me married off. (16-year-old South Asian girl quoted in Mullender *et al.* 2002, p.142)

Though there is much concern about some types of abuse that affect sub-groups of children of minority ethnic origin, such as female genital mutilation and psychological and sometimes physical abuse contingent on 'forced marriages', the fact that the abuse itself often takes place out of the UK makes it difficult to acquire reliable statistics. There are also indications that some young people of mixed heritage are more vulnerable to abuse through prostitution because they are more likely to be in care and at risk of disrupted placements, homelessness and extreme vulnerability to exploitation (Barrett 1997, 2000; Kershaw 1999; Melrose, Barrett and Brodie 1999; Palmer and Stacey 2002). Concern is emerging about the abuse of a group of 'trafficked' child migrants who are brought to this country for exploitation, whether as servants or for the 'sex trade' (Africans Unite Against Child Abuse 2002; Anderson 1997; Barrett and Melrose 2003; Gallagher *et al.* 2003). Both involve abuse of a very serious nature to children who have already been traumatised by the loss of their family and may also be threatened that harm will come to their family back home if they do not comply. There are accounts of practice but we have not identified any research on child welfare outcomes from this work.

In summary, these studies and the more recent national statistics appear to indicate that, although there is some justification for the ongoing concern by policy makers, practitioners and social work writers and researchers about the possibility of minority ethnic families being over-represented in referrals to statutory agencies because of actual or suspected child maltreatment, the pattern of referral and service delivery is more complex. It has to be considered in respect of the different ethnic groups and has to be seen alongside the pattern of service provision more generally. As with families receiving an 'in need' service and, as we shall see, children looked after, Asian children are under-represented amongst those receiving a formal child protection service. However, once referred, the service they receive is more likely to be a formal child protection service than is the case with the (more frequent) referrals of African-Caribbean and African children. This may fit with what we learned earlier about the reluctance of Asian families to seek help at an earlier stage when problems are starting to develop. The challenge is for the family support service to find ways of improving this situation and thus more often to help without the need for the coercive elements of the formal system.

Stress factors amongst families referred to the formal child protection systems

> I've had pneumonia twice now, a couple of weeks ago and a few months back. That's when I applied for a loan for the carpet I've got on the stairs and the living room...and that's why I caught pneumonia – cause I couldn't afford to keep the heating on. (Butt and Box 1998, p.58)

The findings from research on families referred to the formal child protection system are similar to those from the family support studies. Farmer and Owen (1995) and Owen and Farmer (1996) considered the management of child protection cases over a two-year period. The main research was carried out in two local authorities, but a third large metropolitan local authority was used in the study to examine the detailed views of ten minority ethnic families. Six of the families were of Asian origin and the suspected abuse concerned physical abuse in seven cases, and sexual abuse in three cases. They reported that, especially in the ethnic minority cases, the alleged abuse or neglect usually took place against a background of multiple deprivation. Unemployment and financial difficulties were common and most parents were on income support. The kinship and friendship networks which might have been available in the families' countries of origin did not exist in some of the cases and were missing for many of the parents. Housing difficulties were also common. A high incidence of marital conflict and domestic violence was found in this and other studies amongst families referred to the formal child protection services. The prevalence of domestic violence with respect to some ethnic minority groups was referred to in Chapter 3 (Mullender et al. 2002). Looking backwards from the incidents that led on to court applications Brophy et al. (2003a) concluded that for some minority ethnic parents, when parenting difficulties are experienced, options for mothers in terms of acceptable help-seeking behaviour within their extended families were very limited. This was especially the case for mothers who suffered domestic violence, lived in closed communities, spoke little English and/or had no members of their birth family in the UK. In this study high levels of male violence were documented in respect of all groups. Although it was highest in the white group at 64 per cent, it also featured in almost half (48%) of cases concerning mothers of South Asian origin.

Humphreys, Atkar and Baldwin (1999) explored in detail the circumstances and perceptions of 20 Asian families referred to the formal child protection services. In 16 cases the mothers and/or fathers had problems with mental or physical ill-health. The researchers noted with some concern that, for the most part, these issues were not central to the child protection plan unless they were seen to impinge directly upon the child abuse incident.

In a sample of cases that resulted in care applications Brophy *et al.* (2003a) found that for 15 per cent of the black or Asian families and 6 per cent of the mixed parentage group, the parental difficulties leading to allegations of failures in parenting were compounded by the parent, carer or child having been subjected to racial abuse or harassment.

When Thoburn, Wilding and Watson (2000) compared those referred for a family support service with those referred because of concerns about emotional maltreatment or neglect they found few differences in terms of stressful material circumstances. If anything, those referred because of child protection concerns had more sources of support but there tended to be more concerns about personal and relationship problems. This study found that more of the white families had long-term social, environmental and emotional problems than the families of minority ethnic origin and more of the white parents had a physical, learning or psychiatric disability. However, the parents of minority ethnic origin were more likely than white parents to report high levels of emotional stress and to report more problems with parenting. This becomes even more marked when the research sample is of cases going to court. Brophy *et al.* (2003a) found that parental mental ill-health was a factor in 40 per cent of all the ethnic minority cases and a worrying 48 per cent of mothers in the South Asian group had at least one adult psychiatric report filed in proceedings.

The Thoburn, Wilding and Watson study found a statistically significant difference between minority ethnic families and white families in terms of the broad groupings originally used in the Cleaver and Freeman study (1995) that have now been adapted to collect national statistics. White families were more likely to be in the 'multiple and long-standing problem' group, whereas minority ethnic families were more likely to have characteristics associated with the following groups: 'acute distress' (in 16% of cases), 'specific issue' (46%), and 'short term problems' (19%).

The Brandon *et al.* study (1999) used the 'Cleaver and Freeman' broad groupings as a way of capturing the constellation of difficulties that brought families within the child protection system. There was a statistically significant difference when white families were compared with the combined group of minority ethnic families. As with the 'lower threshold' Thoburn, Wilding and Watson (2000) study, white families were more likely to be in the 'long standing and/or multiple problems' group (almost half compared with just over a third each for the mixed parentage group and those in which both parents were of minority ethnic origin). Those in this last group were far more likely than the white or mixed ethnicity families to be in the 'acutely distressed' group (47% compared with 14% of the white families and 18% of those of mixed parentage families). Mixed parentage families (almost half of them) were more likely to have a single issue, such as marital discord, a physical disability or a chronic health problem. If this problem could be reduced, the reduction in stress would be likely to remove the risk of child maltreatment.

Several cohort studies have pointed to the high incidence of substance misusing parents amongst those whose children are referred to the formal child protection system. Harwin and Forrester (2002) allocated cases to the parental substance misuse (PSM) category if any professional expressed concern about actual or suspected substance misuse. The PSM sample was broadly similar to the non-PSM sample but there were some important differences with respect to ethnicity. The two groups to be significantly over-represented in the PSM sample were white British (53% of the PSM sample compared with 43% of the non-PSM sample) and black mixed parentage (18% of the PSM sample compared with 11 per cent of the non-PSM sample). The researchers noted that this latter group were also over-represented in all care proceedings (comprising 21% of all children subject to care proceedings compared to 12% of all children worked with on any other basis).

The child protection and family support services received

Apart from the procedures required by government guidance when a referral is made that indicates that a child may be suffering or likely to suffer abuse or neglect, the protection element of services is provided as part of family support services or children looked after services. The impact on ethnic minority families of social work and other helping services will be covered in Chapter 16. Here we look specifically at the way in which the processes that are integral to the formal child protection system impact on minority ethnic families. Most research studies follow the process sequentially, from referral through to, in some cases, the child's placement for adoption.

The initial and re-referral processes

> I found the social worker and others involved to be treating me like a criminal – therefore why should I be honest? I held back a lot of information which I wouldn't have done had they allowed me a black worker (Thoburn, Wilding and Watson 1995, p.202).

It will be clear from the above section that different patterns of referral and the extent to which some ethnic groups are more visible than others to the child protection professional system may contribute to explaining the apparent differences between ethnic groups. Our chapter on children in need of family support services is also relevant here because most studies report that, across the ethnic groups, the majority of children referred because of child protection concerns had already had contact with a social services department.

The main sources of referrals in the Barn *et al.* (1997) research were professionals (police, 14%; schools, 18%; health service staff, 16%). Of the 20 per cent who referred themselves, the largest groups were white parents and parents of mixed heritage children (26% and 33% respectively). Fifteen per cent of those of African-Caribbean origin referred themselves but strikingly this applied to only 4 per cent of the Asian families, the corollary being that 71 per cent were referred by statutory agencies.

Thoburn, Wilding and Watson (2000) found that roughly equal proportions of white and the combined group of minority ethnic parents referred themselves, but this may be because any different patterns between Asian, African-Caribbean and African families cancelled each other out. There were trends towards more ethnic minority children being referred by a parent living outside the home or by a relative; and more of the black and Asian children being referred by health and school personnel. Broadly equal numbers of white and ethnic minority families were referred by the police. Referrals of white families were more likely to be re-referrals and white children were more likely to have been listed on the child protection register on a previous occasion.

Owen and Farmer (1996) found that the pattern of referral for the minority ethnic families was similar to that in the main study. First indications that the child might be at risk of significant harm came from family members in six out of the ten cases. In the other four cases the referrals came via schools. There were however, two differences in the sample of minority ethnic children in that none of the children had complained directly to the authorities about their abuse, and none of the families had had contact with social services at the time of referral.

Initial and child protection conference assessments

In those cases in the Thoburn, Wilding and Watson study (2000, p.125) where the possibility of maltreatment was mentioned at the time of referral, minority ethnic families were less likely to be subject to Section 47 enquiries and more likely to be provided with an assessment of need. This was most striking for referrals involving 'home alone' child safety issues. In terms of levels and types of assessment, those referrals that included concerns about 'inadequate supervision' were less likely to result in any contact with a social worker. Since a significant number of these families are known to be of minority ethnic origin as discussed earlier, this is an important issue. In some cases the responses '...were either a series of phone calls and case closure, or a letter to the parents warning of the dangers of not providing adequate supervision for their children'. This type of response which the researchers termed the 'deterrent model of prevention' often aroused anger and high anxiety in parents and some reported that it had deterred them from seeking the help they knew they and/or their children needed.

Owen and Farmer (1996) found that the ethnic minority parents they interviewed, like the white parents in the main study, complained about two particular issues at the child protection investigation stage. They were unhappy about child protection procedures being initiated if they had previously referred themselves for support; and they were angry if their children were referred to social services by another professional without them being informed or involved. This latter circumstance was experienced as an undermining of parental responsibility.

Brophy et al. (2003b) show how assessments continue to be revised in the light of new information and reports for some families as they move through the child protection, court and care systems. Physical harm resulting from chastisement, psychological abuse and sexual abuse are reported by researchers to be particularly contested areas, with family members disagreeing amongst themselves as well as with professionals about harmful parenting behaviours. Carstens (2001) describes a study undertaken in the USA (with potential for replication in the UK) comparing the conclusions reached by social workers with more or less 'conservative' attitudes as to whether parenting behaviours in different ethnic communities should be considered to be sexually abusive.

Child protection conferences and registration

Thoburn et al. (1995) examined the issues around the participation of different family members in the different aspects of child protection work, looking especially at attendance at child protection conferences before this practice was officially recommended. In 14 of the 40 ethnic minority families at least one parent was not fluent in English and an interpreter was needed, though not always provided. The researchers found that at least one parent in black and Asian families was likely to become involved, at least to some extent, in almost 80 per cent of cases – slightly more than for white or mixed heritage families and there was no difference in respect of attendance at formal child protection conferences. However Hunt and Macleod (1999), in a more recent study of 'heavier end' cases that eventually went before the courts, found that although minority ethnic adults had the highest invitation rate, only 50 per cent attended compared with 89 per cent of white parents.

When reading this section, our earlier comment on the variability of registration rates between authorities should be borne in mind, and also that many of the studies cited here concern practice prior to the tightening up of the registration categories and processes by the revised guidance in 1999. Barn et al. (1997) and Aldgate and Tunstill (1996) found that most authorities placed child protection at the top of their priority list when deciding whether a case should be allocated to a social worker. Several researchers have concluded that in some of their sample areas numbers on registers were artificially inflated because referrers (including family members themselves) considered than the mention of the possibility of abuse or neglect was the only way to ensure the provision of a service.

Almost a quarter of the 50 children in the Barn *et al.* (1997) sample were currently on the register and 87 children had been on the register at some point. A larger percentage (71%) of the 21 Asian children was or had been on the register because of concerns about physical abuse than was the case for the 11 African or African-Caribbean children (64%), the 14 mixed parentage children (also 64%) or the 41 white children (56%). Numbers are too small in respect of the other registration categories for analysis by ethnic group, but descriptively, more of the white children were registered under the sexual abuse category; more of the combined African-Caribbean and African group and the mixed parentage children under the neglect category.

Minority ethnic families and the courts

Hunt and her colleagues explored in detail the issues for a cohort of children who were at risk of significant harm, and whose interests required compulsory protection through the legal process (Freeman and Hunt 1998; Hunt and Macleod 1999, Hunt, Macleod and Thomas 1999). They followed up over a three-year period the 133 cases in respect of whom a care or supervision order had been made. The three areas involved each had fairly large populations of minority ethnic children resulting in a sample in which 52 (40%) were of minority ethnic origin. Thirty-eight (almost one in three) were of mixed heritage compared with fourteen 'single heritage' minority ethnic children. The children in all ethnic groups were generally young, fewer than half being aged five or more when the case came to court. However, the children of minority ethnic origin were more likely than the white children to be amongst the small number who were aged 11 or over. Children of minority ethnic backgrounds were more likely to have special educational needs but were less likely to have health problems or disabilities. The adults from minority ethnic families were less likely than white parents to have problems concerning drug and/or alcohol abuse (as with the Harwin and Forrester study) learning disabilities, and to a lesser extent a psychiatric disorder. They were almost three times as likely to have an adult in employment and the mothers tended to be older at the birth of the first child. Fewer of the parents were known to have experienced abuse; to have been in local authority care as children, or to have a criminal record. In short, '…on almost every one of a range of indicators of social morbidity it was the white UK families who presented the more troubled profile'. Minority ethnic families were also less likely than the white families to be known to a social services department at the time of the referral that led to court action.

The researchers found that the cases of half of the minority ethnic families reached court within three months of their involvement with social services, which is twice the rate noted in the rest of the sample. The researchers comment that '…despite their general shorter continuous involvement with the welfare system, these families were in receipt of around the *same level* of service provision as the rest of the sample. They were also much *more* likely to have refused services' (p.30). This study is also referred to in the next section on looked after children, since the plan for 27 per cent of the mixed heritage children and for 23 per cent of the ethnic minority single heritage children was adoption or long-term foster care (compared with 41% of the white British children). Initial plans were less likely to be carried through in respect of minority ethnic children than was the case for the white children. This may in part be because plans for younger children were more likely to be successful and more of the ethnic minority children were older.

The detailed accounts of the perceptions and experiences of the parents reported in the Freeman and Hunt (1998) study echo those interviewed in the Owen and Farmer (1996) study and the other qualitative studies that include minority ethnic families. Since most comments refer to services and social work, they will be reported in Chapter 6. However, a key point to be made here is the plea from all ethnic groups for parents whose children have been removed from home against their wishes to be shown respect and concern for their distress, and for social workers to be honest about plans and not 'fudge' issues. Some, especially parents of mixed heritage, made a strong plea for workers to talk with them and seek to understand how they themselves viewed their ethnicity, including discussing with them how they wished to be described in court reports.

> I was born in X country of mixed race, but am still white. They said I was black and even put it in the Children's Report. It really got up my nose because I have always been British and the social worker hadn't even seen me and told the foster parent I was black. (Freeman and Hunt 1998, p.64)

Other suggestions included the provision of information packs, which could be particularly helpful if provided in the first language of a parent, or for families who were newly arrived and had no understanding of the UK court processes.

The findings from a more recent study of care plans by Harwin *et al.* (2003) are broadly similar. This was an even 'heavier end' study of a cohort of 100 children from 57 families on whom care orders were made, followed up after around 21 months. As with the Hunt and Macleod (1999) study, around half the children were under five at the time of the care proceedings. The sample included five children of African-Caribbean heritage and nine children of dual heritage (four of whom were of African/white ethnicity; four with one white and one Asian parent). The findings are similar to those from the Hunt *et al.* (1999) study, and are reported more fully in the section on looked after children.

Both of these studies demonstrate the complexity of the different routes by which children leave home and the different purposes served by care proceedings, as does the Brandon *et al.* (1999) study in which 71 of the 105 children were living away from home at some point during the year after the identification of significant harm (with care proceedings taken in 25% of cases). Hunt and Macleod (1999) identified seven different routes to court, some involving prior emergency procedures and some involving the child first being accommodated under voluntary procedures. Children of minority ethnic origin were more likely to be amongst those unknown to the services until they became involved in crisis situations leading to emergency action and court within days (22% of ethnic minority children compared with 9% of the white children followed this route). Or the children were placed on a 'voluntary' basis (Section 20) for assessment in a supervised setting such as a hospital (11% compared with 7% of the white children). They were less likely than white children to be removed at birth because a previous child had been seriously maltreated (4% compared with 13%); or to be placed with both parents on a voluntary basis in a setting such as a mother and baby unit whilst assessments were carried out (4% compared with 9%). Thirty (73%) of the minority ethnic children were already believed to have suffered significant harm when proceedings started (as opposed to proceedings being started because there was a likelihood of harm in the future) compared to 62 per cent (26) of the other children. Care orders, rather than supervision orders or orders for 'no order', were also more likely to be made for families from minority ethnic backgrounds.

The only major UK research studies that have focused specifically on the impact of the courts on children and families of minority ethnic origin are those of Brophy (2000a, 2000b) and Brophy *et al.* (2003a, 2003b). The first of these was a secondary analysis of an earlier national survey (Brophy *et al.* 1999) of the role of guardians *ad litem* (now children's guardians) and of psychiatrists acting as expert witnesses in care cases. Data were sought on a nationally stratified random sample of 338 care cases, 16 per cent of which concerned children of minority ethnic origin. Black children and those of mixed parentage were over-represented in the sample, and South Asian children were under-represented, when compared with their presence in the England and Wales population of children aged 0–5 as reported in the 1991 census. However, the authors advise caution in interpreting these data, in part because of missing information on court application forms. Very few minority ethnic children had a guardian *ad litem* matched for ethnicity. This is particularly relevant when we consider that only about half (57%) of the guardians had undertaken equal opportunities training, though many wanted more training specifically looking at representing minority ethnic children. There was very little use of cultural advisers or advocates from the same ethnic groups as the families.

In their most recent study, Brophy *et al.* (2003a, 2003b) explored some of these issues at greater depth by examining a sample of 100 case files concerning section 31 (care or supervision order) applications in respect of 182 children. As with the previous studies in this stream of work, it focuses on children whose cases reach court and therefore where there are grounds for concluding that a child has suffered or is likely to suffer significant harm. The study aimed to provide information on whether reports, including those from experts, ensured that the courts had access to information on ethnic, cultural, religious and linguistic diversity within families at key stages in care proceedings. The report focuses on the applicability of the 'significant harm' definition and threshold criteria to minority ethnic families. Anonymised case material and quotes from reports, and interviews with judges, magistrates and court clerks illustrate the complexity of 'culture' and 'ethnicity' as well as the complex and troubled lives of the children and parents who come before the family courts.

Court hearings were observed and interviews undertaken with some of the judges, magistrates and legal advisers to seek their views on the availability and relevance of information on 'diversity' for assessments of significant harm and potential for change in parents. Thirty-four cases (61 children) involved black children; 25 cases were in respect of 42 South Asian children; 23 cases concerned 47 white children, and 18 cases concerned 32 children of mixed parentage. Information was analysed for aggregated groups (black, Asian and mixed-parentage) and, where sample size allowed, for the eight 2001 Census categories. Qualitative data are a rich source of information on the different ethnic groups, providing information on services that were provided or not provided prior to the application to court as well as on the court proceedings and reporting processes. Almost half (46%) were under five years at the date of application, with African-Caribbean and Indian children being most likely to be under five. Having explored the debates around notions of 'cultural conflicts' the authors note that, in the event, these cases of significant harm did not turn on issues of cultural conflicts about different values, patterns of childcare between professionals and parents. With regard to issues of physical ill-treatment, the researchers comment: '...the pictures behind the statistics for the South Asian and black groups...demonstrate that where physical ill-treatment underscored applications, this ill-treatment was usually severe and of some duration. In other words, it could not be conceived as culturally accepted "reasonable chastisement", which was misunderstood by White Western Professionals' (Brophy *et al.* 2003a, p.41). The researchers note that in all ethnic groups applications for care orders were based upon multiple allegations of child maltreatment and also multiple concerns about failures in parenting.

At the point of the application to court, children of South Asian origin were considerably less likely to be still living with a birth parent than those in the other ethnic groups. As with those in the Hunt and Macleod (1999) study, Brophy *et al.* found that minority ethnic children were more likely to be subject to emergency protection orders (EPO) than were white children and this was especially the case for South Asian children. In 10 of the 13 cases involving Indian families the children were subject to EPOs. However the findings differ from those of Hunt and Macleod in that 98 per cent were already known to social services departments and 73 per cent had been or were already on child protection registers when proceedings were initiated. This was least likely to be the case for the Indian children. A care order was ultimately made in respect of 115 (70%) of the 165 children subject to court applications but this was less likely in respect of Asian children. A care order was made in respect of 72 per cent of the combined group of black children, 77 per cent of the white children, 82 per cent of the mixed heritage children but only 49 per cent of the South Asian children. This, combined with studies reported earlier, suggests that court action could have been avoided in more of the cases involving Asian children than was the case with other groups and again puts the spotlight on the availability, visibility and acceptability of family support services that might have been able to help at an earlier stage.

The researchers note that little attention was paid to diversity in almost all paediatric reports and that the information on diversity was better in child and family centre assessments and reports from child and adolescent psychiatrists. However this varied according to ethnic groups, with, for example, more descriptive and substantive information in respect of Black African and South Asian families but very poor information with regard to reports for African Caribbean families. The reports to the court also provided information on the responses of parents to allegations. There were similarities across all ethnic groups (e.g. initially denying, minimising or justifying ill-treatment by reference to the child's behaviour), but there were also some appeals to diverse cultural or religious backgrounds in order to argue that ill-treatment could not have happened in their particular religious group or community. The researchers reported that change occurred in some families whose firmly held beliefs about appropriate parental actions had limited earlier attempts at intervention, and that these changes led to beneficial outcomes for children (in terms of the eventual return children to a birth parent/extended family).

Related to the issues concerning court applications is the question of the use of accommodation by 'voluntary' agreement in child protection cases, sometimes as an emergency protection measure, sometimes to allow for a period of assessment and sometimes as a precursor of care proceedings. This question is explored in some detail in the overview to the *Children Act Now: Messages from Research* studies because of the apparently different conclusions drawn by researchers. Packman and Hall (1998) found that Section 20 accommodation was increasingly used in child protection cases, following its introduction by the Children Act 1989. Their sample included two black children, one Asian child, and 11 children from mixed parentage backgrounds (9% of the 177 admissions studied). Although recognising that at times it can be used as, or at least be perceived by families as, a back door way into care proceedings without telling the families that this is its purpose, Packman and Hall (1998) and Brandon *et al.* (1999), looking at a sample of child protection referrals, concluded that in many cases it was a helpful response to an unclear situation or one where the risks to the child could be diminished by a short period of separation from the parents. However, researchers looking only at cases that reach court describe greater concerns about the extent to which this is 'forced' rather than 'voluntary' accommodation. Hunt and Macleod (1999, p.35) found that a third of the 21 ethnic minority children were accommodated prior to care proceedings compared with 21 per cent of the white children. Having looked at these cases in more detail, they concluded that these were less likely to be 'enforced accommodation' than was the case with the white families, 'enforced accommodation' being defined as '…agree accommodation or we go to court'.

Outcomes for minority ethnic parents and children referred to the formal child protection systems

The term 'outcome' is used in this review to refer to outcomes for parents and children and the term 'output' is used when providing data on what are sometime referred to as 'service outcomes' (for example whether a service was provided, or a care or supervision order made). (See Sellick, Thoburn and Philpot 2004 for a discussion on this point.) There is more output data in the research on child protection than there is information on outcomes. When we look at outcomes it is important to be aware of whose outcomes we are considering: the children's, the parents', or the outcome for the family as a group? Most of the studies that provide 'change over time' data do so for periods of between one and three years and can therefore only describe interim outcomes. Some of the studies listed do however provide detailed information about the views of the parents, and sometimes the children, on whether and in what respects their situation had improved or deteriorated. These 'change over time' studies sometimes indicate that although problems may not be solved, parents and professionals consider that the child protection process and the services and support provided have benefited them. Others report that the formal child protection process was so alienating that it detracted from any benefits they might have gained from the services. Brandon *et al.* (1999), Freeman and Hunt (1998), Harwin *et al.* (2003) and Humphreys *et al.* (1999) give case examples demonstrating this mixed response.

> I was so worried and unhappy. First it was my mother-in-law and all of that, and then the Social Services. I don't know the law and the language. I'm very worried about the court. I class it all as racism and that goes on. I only want to bring my children up. It's the only thing I can do. I can't fight with the government and the court. I am a mother and I am worried for my children. (Brandon *et al.* 1999, p.112)

Some studies analyse the service provided and look for associations between the different aspects of the service and the interim outcomes for children and/or parents. Thoburn, Wilding and Watson (2000) rated the outcomes for families at the end of the 12 months and found that more of the white families showed either an overall improvement or deterioration and that minority ethnic families were more likely to experience little change or mixed outcomes. In terms of the well-being of the parents, more of the white parents considered that their own well-being had improved (62% compared to 47% of the minority ethnic families). However, more of the white parents also referred to a deterioration in their overall well-being than the minority ethnic parents (29% compared to 19%). More of the white children in the study were rated as having improved outcomes (53% compared with 12% of the ethnic minority children) but that is largely explained by the finding that fewer of the black or Asian children had emotional or behavioural problems at the start of the study and therefore were more likely to be in the 'no change' group. However, the authors concluded that 'it is of concern that only four of the 19 children of minority ethnic origin who displayed problems at the start of the study had actually improved in their overall well-being', (p.172).

Brandon *et al.* (1999) concluded from their triangulation approach to the measurement of outcomes that the well-being of more of the black and Asian children improved than was the case for the white children. The researchers speculate that this may be due to more of the white families having multiple and long-standing problems which are harder to overcome in such a short period of time. The well-being of 94 per cent of the 17 children of mixed race parentage and 83 per cent of the 23 children with two black or Asian parents had improved compared to 56 per cent of the 54 white children. Where well-being had deteriorated, this was in respect of older children who, whether in care or at home, continued to put themselves at risk because of their behaviour and neither their parents, social workers, foster or residential carers had been able to engage them in bringing about change. Leaving aside the question of change over time, at the end of the study, whilst equal proportions of the white children and those of mixed race parentage children were rated as of average or good well-being (29%), this applied to 35 per cent of the children both of whose parents were of minority ethnic origin. The well-being of more of the white children (18%) was rated as poor whilst this applied to 12 per cent each of the other two groups. However there was also a trend, not statistically significant, for more of the parents of minority ethnic children to be rated as of poor well-being.

Conclusions on child protection

The above examples demonstrate that minority ethnic families, perhaps in particular those who have settled in Britain only recently, are likely to find the formal child protection and court systems confusing, anxiety-provoking and alienating unless strenuous efforts are made to help them through it. For some there is the added disadvantage of needing to communicate through an interpreter. The challenges to social workers, interpreters and other service providers in making their services accessible, acceptable and intelligible to families from a different culture will be discussed in Chapter 6.

This section has raised a number of concerns about how minority ethnic families may experience discrimination and disadvantage in child protection and court systems. However, it would be wrong not to highlight some of the many examples of excellent practice with minority ethnic families that have been noted in the various studies already mentioned. To stay with one of the most recent studies based on court applications, Brophy *et al.* (2003a) demonstrated that some social workers, guardians *ad litem* and other professionals involved in the child protection and family justice systems went to great lengths to try to meet the cultural and religious needs of some of the families. For example, at times advice was sought from specialist minority ethnic teams or workers; relatives from Asia were contacted regarding the needs of a particular child and assessed as potential carers; independent specialist workers were brought in to help. High quality, culturally sensitive, practice goes on, but appears to occur inconsistently throughout the different local authorities and courts.

Chapter 5

Children Looked After Away from Home or Placed for Adoption

Britain is a very racist country, I have to say. Racism is a very hard thing to cope with. If you are not white it's harder and I think that while a child is in care they should be taught about racism. (Care leaver quoted by Ince 1998, p.80)

I really feel part of this family – they didn't chuck me out – they didn't say 'Oh she's an outsider, she's not part of our family'. They treat me like I was born into the family... They treat me with respect and love. It's been different being adopted, because most kids don't have what I have – two families. (Asian teenager adopted by Asian single parent quoted in Thoburn, Norford and Rashid 2000, p.195)

An overview of the research

When compared with children in need of family support and child protection services, there is considerably more research on children cared for away from home, both conducted in the UK and overseas. Our literature search has included non-UK sources, but we have concentrated here on UK research. Because of the different characteristics of 'in care' populations around the world, research conducted in other countries has to be interpreted with caution: the results can be misleading. For example, most European studies of the adoption of ethnic minority children concern children adopted from overseas. Unlike the majority of UK children adopted by parents not previously known to them, most of those adopted from overseas have been abandoned or are adopted at the request of their parents. Some of the main US adoption studies that report on ethnicity combine international and in-country placements for adoption, and some on the placement of older children use a definition of 'foster care' which includes children in what, in the UK, is referred to as 'residential care'. (The US term equating with the UK 'foster care' is 'foster family care'.) However, outcome studies undertaken outside the UK that provide clarity about the children being placed and placement experience and the social work and therapy provided were included in our review of research and some are cited in this synthesis. Studies that describe the satisfaction of young people, birth parents and/or carers with the services provided and with the experience of out of home placement also 'travel' fairly well across national boundaries. We have included some UK studies published some time ago to provide context since they can tell us about changes over time. However, when they are available we have given more weight to more recent studies.

The main focus is on children looked after by local authorities or placed for adoption, but some of the findings are relevant to children in private foster care and children 'in need' who are living with relatives or in boarding schools but not formally 'looked after'. Much of the writing on ethnic minority children who are looked after provides accounts of practice or is about how practice might be improved. (See, for example, Ahmed, Cheetham and Small 1986; Banks 1995; Barn 1999a, 1999b, 2001; Barn et al. 1997; Berridge and Smith 1993; British Agencies for Adoption and Fostering 1998; Candappa 2004; Dutt and Phillips 2000; Dwivedi (ed) 2002; Kirton 2000; McRoy et al. 1982; O'Neale 2000; Prevatt Goldstein and Small 2000; Prevatt Goldstein and Spencer 2000; Richards and Ince 2000). Most of these writers address the issues around 'matching' and transracial placements and Rhodes (1992) focuses specifically on this.

Much research does not differentiate between children living away from home for short periods or long term; mixes up age groups and children with different sorts of need; combines children in residential and foster care; involves small numbers and does not differentiate between the different ethnic groups. Inevitably, long-term outcome or 'satisfaction' studies of children placed as infants describe practice before the Children Act 1989 and more recent adoption legislation and guidance were implemented, and when the ethnic composition of the in care population was very different from now (for example Kirton 2000; Kirton, Feast and Howe 2000; Thoburn, Norford and Rashid 2000; and the USA and Swedish longitudinal studies reported most recently by Brooks and Barth 1999, and Lindblad, Hjern and Vinnerljung 2003). There is no way around this problem, other than to point it out, since long-term outcomes can only be measured when the children reach adulthood.

Another point to be made at the start of this chapter is that comparisons between different samples must take on board whether what is being reported on is a 'flow' or 'starting to be looked after over a given period of time' sample, or a 'stock' or 'snapshot' sample of children who are looked after on a given date. The latter will contain more children who were older at placement, had been looked after for a longer period and came into care via the courts as a result of serious family problems and maltreatment. This is because those who are older or are more troubled when they start to be looked after are less likely to leave quickly, whether through adoption or return home.

Despite the large number of studies there are still very few relating specific interventions to welfare outcomes for the children, their birth relatives and the adoptive or foster families. There is more information from qualitative studies or those using mixed quantitative and qualitative methodologies about rates of satisfaction and attitudes of young people, their parents and carers to the social work and other services. However, most of these findings are drawn from small non-random samples. Some consumer accounts of being in care and leaving care are available, either written by care leavers themselves or reported by researchers.

Are the different groups of children of minority ethnic origin over- or under-represented amongst children looked after?

The *Looked After Children* annual reports (National Statistics and DH 2003b – now produced with DfES) provide statistical information on ethnicity alongside other basic data which can be compared with data from the 2001 Census. When looked after children are compared with the general population of under 18s in England (2001 Census and Labourforce Survey) children of minority ethnic origin are over-represented (18.5% of looked after children compared with 13% in the general population are of minority ethnic origin). However, as can be seen from Table 5.1, the pattern is different when the different ethnic groups are looked at separately. The largest grouping after the white children comprises the 3 per cent of 'other mixed background' – a very diverse census category that is over-represented amongst children looked after to a greater extent than any of the main ethnic groups. The three largest minority ethnic groups amongst looked after children are those of mixed African-Caribbean and white heritage; those of African descent and those of African-Caribbean descent. African-Caribbean children, those of white and African-Caribbean heritage and those in the 'other black heritage' census group are over-represented by more than two to one. Black African children are also almost twice as likely to be looked after as their numbers in the population would suggest. (It should be noted that around half of the 2100 unaccompanied asylum-seeking young people who are in the care system are of African descent.) Numbers looked after who have one white and one African parent, and those of white and South Asian heritage are small which makes comparisons less reliable. However, these groups are only slightly more likely to be looked after than are white children and not over-represented to the extent of the other groups of black or mixed heritage children.

Numbers looked after of Indian, Bangladeshi and Pakistani heritage are also very small and greatly under-represented. (In March 2002 only 200 Bangladeshi, 330 Indian and 500 Pakistani children were looked after.) As noted earlier, the 'snapshot' population includes many children who have been looked after for some years so it is worth looking at the 'flow' statistics – those who started to be looked after during 2001–2 to see if the same pattern is continuing. Table 5.1 shows that the comparison with the looked after statistics shows that the proportions are broadly similar except that slightly fewer children in the combined mixed heritage group are starting to be looked after (7%) than are in the 'snapshot' looked after population. However, for the census aggregated 'black' group (6.5% of those 'looked after' but 8% of those starting to be looked after) the likelihood of coming into care appears to be increasing. For the combined South Asian group the likelihood of being looked after is also slightly higher but these children are still very much under-represented amongst those starting to be looked after (3% compared with 6.4% in the child population). Those who do not fit into any of the other groups continue to be over-represented amongst those starting to be looked after.

The special issues for unaccompanied asylum-seeking children are explored in a special edition of *Child and Family Social Work* edited by Kohli (2003) in which Cemlyn and Briskman (2003) explore the international and legal contexts and Kohli (2003) and Kohli and Mather (2003) discuss the small amount of evidence on social work practice with those asylum-seeking young people who are accommodated. Jones (2001) bases her conclusion that there is incompatibility between UK child welfare and immigration legislation on a study of a group of young people affected by immigration controls. She found wide geographical variations in whether young people were accommodated (and thus benefited from the status of being formally 'looked after'), placed informally in lodgings or detained in detention centres or custody. This was particularly likely if there was dispute about the age of the young person. She found that young people under 18 were often detained for two to three months with inadequate advice before being referred to the local authority social services department as vulnerable young people who may be in need of Section 20 accommodation.

It is interesting to consider any changes over time by looking at earlier research. Bebbington and Miles used statistical techniques to estimate the likelihood of children with different characteristics coming into care and thus control for any differences between ethnic groups. They concluded that 'Afro-Caribbean and African children are a little more likely to come into care than white children, but the differences are not statistically significant. On the other hand, a child of mixed race is two and a half times as likely to enter care as a white child, all else being equal' (1989, p.356). It appears that the likelihood of being looked after has decreased to some extent for children of mixed heritage but increased for children of African-Caribbean and African heritage.

Table 5.1 Children looked after 31 March 2002, starting to be looked after 2001–2 and in the general population by ethnic group (England 2001 Census)

Ethnic group	% looked after 31 March 2002	% starting to be looked after 2001–2	% all children under 18 in the general population
White	81.5	79	86.5
Mixed heritage	7.37	7.3	3.2
Caribbean/white	2.84		1.2
African/white	0.48		0.3
Asian/white	0.9		0.9
Other mixed	3		0.7
South Asian	2.34	2.8	6.6
Indian	0.55		2.4
Pakistani	0.83		2.5
Bangladeshi	0.33		1.0
Other Asian	0.57		0.6
Black/ black British	6.53	8.1	3.0
Caribbean	2.5		1.2
African	2.68		1.4
Other black	1.4		0.4
Chinese	0.15		0.4
Other ethnic group	2.34	3.0	0.4

Source: Data adapted from National Statistics and Department of Health 2003b and National
  Statistics 2003, Table S101

The 1989 Rowe, Hundleby and Garnett research is still the largest study providing details on ethnicity for both the 'stock' and 'flow' of looked after
children. The authors found that, although ethnic minority children as a
combined group were over-represented, there were differences between
authorities in the extent to which over-representation occurred. Then as now,
Asian children were under-represented amongst children looked after. The
over-representation of African-Caribbean and African children was mainly
accounted for by their over-representation in the pre-school and five to ten age
groups where their admission rates were more than twice those for white
children. However, in the pre-school group, the majority of admissions were

very short term. In that study Asian children were less likely to come into care as pre-schoolers but more likely to be admitted in the five to thirteen age group. Importantly, the authors note that 'in areas with large black populations...mixed parentage children accounted for less than half of black admissions to care...but in [areas] where black people account for a small proportion of the population, the majority of black children admitted to care proved to be those of mixed parentage' (p.165).

In order to see if this may still be the case, we looked particularly at the Department of Health returns for West Midlands authorities, whose populations are more stable than is the case for many parts of London and where proportions of minority ethnic families vary considerably. The pattern of under-representation amongst looked after children we see for England as a whole is even more pronounced in respect of Asian children in Birmingham (33% of the child population but only 5% of the 'looked after' population). White children are over-represented (49% of the child population but 63% of the looked after population). The combined group of 'mixed ethnic origin' are, in Birmingham, only slightly more likely to be looked after than their numbers in the population would predict (6.3% of the population and 7.2% of those looked after). In Wolverhampton, the pattern in respect of white and Asian children is similar to the position in Birmingham, but interestingly, the combined group of black children are only slightly more likely to be looked after than their numbers in the population would predict (6.3% of the child population and 11% of those looked after). However, in neighbouring authorities with small ethnic minority populations the pattern is the same as for England as a whole. This lends support to the hypothesis of Rowe et al. (1989) that where ethnic minority groups are well represented in any community, either they are able to influence local policies or they provide greater support to families in their communities (or a combination of these and other factors) such that the need for children to come into care for long periods is diminished. It may of course also be that there are strong constraints preventing families seeking help through the care system such that children who would benefit from being looked after away from home do not receive the help they need.

The characteristics of ethnic minority children who are looked after

Following on from this discussion on the representation of the different ethnic groups, it should be noted that, in some areas, some change will have been brought about in the statistics by the presence amongst the 'looked after' populations of 2100 unaccompanied asylum-seeking children, 90% of whom live in the South East. Some (mainly from central Europe) come under the 'other white' grouping but the largest number (over 50%) are of African heritage. As we have seen in an earlier section, some qualitative studies have found that refugee and asylum-seeking families (in recent years often from African countries) may be particularly traumatised and living in severely stressful circumstances. This can have an impact on the ability of parents to meet their children's needs and on children's mental health and behaviour, resulting in a need for children to be accommodated or to come into care through the courts.

For all ethnic groups, the largest numbers of children looked after are over the age of ten, with more of the Indian children (57%) and the white children (58%) being over ten. African-Caribbean and African children are less likely to be looked after when under the age of one (3% and 2% respectively) than the average (4%) and in contrast to Bangladeshi children (10% of the albeit small number of Bangladeshi children looked after were under one year of age). When those starting to be looked after are considered, larger proportions in all ethnic groups are in the under-five age group, the difference between the two sets of statistics being largely explained by the younger children tending to leave care more quickly.

A slightly larger proportion of the black children than the white children in the Barn (1993) study came into care on a voluntary basis and as a result of their parents requesting help. Only Asian children were under-represented amongst those who started to be looked after at the request of a parent. Significantly more black children than white children came into care because of the mother's mental health problems. The recent statistical returns give data on reasons for becoming looked after broken down into the broad ethnic groups. (Though it should be noted that the 'reasons' groups allow some scope for interpretation by those completing the schedule as only one category can be chosen whilst in most cases there is more than one reason. For example, very few children are listed as starting to be looked after because of poverty, but this will have been a contributory factor to household stress for perhaps the majority.) The largest proportion in all groups start to be looked after mainly because of concerns about abuse or neglect. However, the proportion is highest for Asian children (47% of the small number of South Asian children starting to be looked after had this as the main reason); for those of mixed race parentage (48%) and for white children (45%) than for black children (30%) and those in the 'other' group. This suggests continuity with smaller scale qualitative studies that indicate that African-Caribbean children are more likely to be accommodated on a short-term basis after their parents have sought help and that Asian parents are less likely to request accommodation and may delay too long in seeking this form of help so that an emergency admission for protection reasons becomes necessary. The 'other' group may have less community support since they will all be in small minorities in any community, and may therefore be more 'visible' and thus referred for help at an earlier stage.

Brandon *et al.* (1999) found that roughly the same proportion of ethnic minority children (28%) and white children (25%) had their main placement away from parents during the 12 months following identification of actual or likely significant harm. Ethnic minority children were slightly more likely to be removed from home via an Emergency Protection Order or taken into police protection, but less likely to remain away from home on a Care Order. The studies of Hunt *et al.* (1999), Hunt and MacLeod (1999) and Harwin *et al.* (2003) found that children of minority ethnic origin were slightly more likely than white children to be placed back at home with parents but still on a care order.

When comparing the reasons for admission, the patterns for white children and those in the mixed ethnicity group are broadly similar. This is not unexpected since the more detailed research studies indicate that many are living with their white single mother at the point of entry into care. For these two groups 'abuse and neglect', 'family dysfunction' and 'family in acute stress' are the largest categories (15% and 13% respectively for 'dysfunction' and 13% for both groups under 'acute stress'). For Asian and black children the proportions in the 'family dysfunction' group are similar to those for white families, but there is a marked difference in respect of the 'acute stress' category (4% for Asian children and 7% for black children). The most marked difference between ethnic groups is in respect of the 'absent parenting' category (defined as 'children whose need for services arises mainly from having no parents available to look after them'). Whilst this was the main reason for only 6 per cent of the white children and 8 per cent of those of mixed heritage starting to be looked after, it was the main reason in the cases of 22 per cent of the Asian children, 30 per cent of the black children and 42 per cent of those in the 'other' group. This category will include the small number who start to be looked after prior to placement for adoption but may also be the category used for some 'home alone' and for unaccompanied refugee children. The larger proportion of single parents amongst African-Caribbean families may also be a partial explanation since there is often not another parent around if the main parent becomes incapacitated. This may indicate some continuity from earlier studies that found that African-Caribbean children in some authorities were more likely to be provided with short-term accommodation as part of a family support service.

Similar proportions started to be looked after because of the disability of a parent (around 9%). Given the higher rate of severe disability amongst Asian children reported in Chapter 3, at first sight it appears surprising that disability of the child was the main reason in respect of only 4 per cent of the Asian children – though this is higher than for the other groups (3% of the white children and 1% each for the other broad groups). However, this may be misleading as children who start to be looked after as part of a series of short-term episodes (the majority in respect of children with disabilities) are omitted from this analysis. From a review of the limited amount of available research, Flynn (2002a, 2002b) concluded that, over a ten-year period, the take-up of short breaks for their disabled children by black families had barely improved, and that a disproportionate number of families was using institutional rather than family-based care when compared with white families.

The categories relevant to characteristics of the children starting to be looked after are unsatisfactory, and the requirement to give only a main reason may conceal the extent of difficulty amongst the children that contributed to their starting to be looked after. For example, there is an overlap between the categories on 'disability of the child' (which could include 'challenging behaviour resulting from a mental health problem) and 'socially unacceptable behaviour'. Around 8 per cent of the white children and of the black children are recorded in the national statistics as starting to be looked after mainly because of the 'socially unacceptable behaviour' of the child (compared with 5% for the mixed heritage children and 3% of the Asian children and those in the 'other' group).

Meltzer and colleagues (2003) followed up their prevalence study of children with a mental disorder in the general population (around 10% of children aged between 10 and 15) with a study of children looked after (45% of the 1039 children surveyed had 'any disorder'). The threshold for inclusion in the 'any disorder' group was a disorder that 'causes distress to the child and has a considerable impact on the child's daily life'. None of the differences between children in the different ethnic groups (combined into the broad groupings of white, black, and other – including 8 South Asians, 2 Chinese and 57 in an 'other' group that included mixed heritage children) is statistically significant and the authors caution care in interpretation of the descriptive prevalence table because of small numbers. Using the data descriptively, more of the white looked-after children in the sample had 'any disorder' (46% compared with 40% of the black children and 36% in the 'other' group). Broadly the same proportion of white and black children had conduct disorders (38%) but fewer of the black children than the white or 'other' children had emotional disorders (6%, 12% and 11% respectively). More of those in the 'other' group (5%) than the white or black children (4% and 1.5%) had 'less common disorder', the most common being 'pervasive developmental disorder'.

Child placement as family support or short-term intervention

Between 75 per cent and 80 per cent of children starting to be looked after will have 'left care' within two years. A small proportion will have been adopted, and some will have gone on to independent living, but most will have returned to the care of their parents. This proportion remained fairly constant for about 15 years after the Rowe *et al.* (1989) analysis conducted in 1985–6. However, since the Children Act 1989, a larger proportion stay for between 12 and 24 months and then leave than was the case for the Rowe sample, when more left in the first 12 months (Dickens *et al.* 2003)

Rowe and colleagues (1989) found that young African-Caribbean children were the group most likely to be provided with short-term accommodation as part of a family support service and that they tended to leave after a short period as planned. However, children of mixed race parentage were more like white children and stayed longer in care than African-Caribbean, African or Asian children. The authors noted that there was a higher likelihood that pre-school children of mixed race parentage would be readmitted within a year than was the case for all other ethnic groups.

In one of the earlier studies, Barn (1993) found that black children came into care in a shorter period of time after seeking help or being referred by other agencies than was the case for white children. This may be related to the fact that black children were significantly more likely to come into care from single-mother households, and therefore with no other parent being available to care if the main carer became unavailable. Barn *et al.* (1997) found that much of the work concerning children leaving home was of a crisis nature, with more of the African-Caribbean and mixed-parentage children leaving home within two weeks of referral and staying longer in care than was the case for white or Asian children.

More recently, the research by Packman and Hall (1998) on voluntary care and accommodation after the implementation of the Children Act 1989, indicates that, in the majority of cases, parents find a short-term accommodation service to be helpful, even when, as is increasingly the case, it is provided in cases where there are child protection concerns. The numbers of children of minority ethnic origin in this study are small – one black child, one Asian child and 11 of mixed race parentage, together making up nine per cent of the sample. None of these was in the 'volunteered' group of mainly younger children accommodated at parental request, perhaps indicating, when read alongside the Barn *et al.* (1997) study, a change from the practice of using short-term accommodation as part of family support to help (particularly) African Caribbean families.

In the Packman and Hall (1998) study, half of the children of minority ethnic origin who were accommodated were in the 'at risk' group and half in the 'difficult teenagers' group. Although expressing caution because of the small numbers, the authors suggest that there may be pointers for practice in areas (like the two in the study) where there are only small numbers of minority ethnic families in the general population. They hypothesise that either agencies may be quicker to perceive risk when 'dealing with the unfamiliar' or families may only be drawn into contact with social services when problems have escalated. This is picked up in the overview of the Children Act studies (DH 2001, p.53) which comments that the use of accommodation as family support for ethnic minority families is 'in itself acceptable, even desirable within the framework of the Children Act. However, because accommodation was seen in some areas as the main gateway to compulsory action, these [ethnic minority children] may have then been inappropriately catapulted into care proceedings'. In another report in the series, Aldgate and Bradley (1999) found that ethnic minority children were under-represented amongst those being placed with foster families for a series of short-term breaks to help relieve stress on their parents. Flynn (2002a, 2002b) received 13 responses from a postal survey of 24 English short break schemes. Six schemes were visited and examples of good practice highlighted. As with studies of other support services for families, many parents of disabled children were found to be unaware of the service and how they might use it. From interviews with those who did, the researcher identified misconceptions and mismatches between workers, carers and parents about the role of social services and of the short-term breaks services. Parents were particularly concerned as to whether their child's culture, religion and language would be respected. As for all families in need of a short term break (see Aldgate and Bradley 1999 and Packman and Hall 1998) some parents feared that if they allowed social services to provide overnight care for their children they may never return home.

Nationally collected statistics on short term breaks analysed according to ethnicity and disability or family stress are not yet available. Butt (1994), Candappa (2004), O'Neale (2000) and Richards and Ince (2000), call attention to the fact that a poor standard of ethnic monitoring in most local authorities impedes ethnically sensitive service planning.

Dickens *et al.* (2003) reanalysed the statistics from 24 Eastern and West Midlands authorities and found that, when taken as an aggregated group, ethnic minority children were neither more nor less likely than white children to return home after a short period. However, when ethnic groups were considered separately, children of Caribbean and of Pakistani heritage and those in the 'any other black' group tended to stay longer.

Turning to the top end of the age spectrum, in a combined quantitative and qualitative study Lees (2002) examined the records of a cohort of young women starting to be looked after in one outer London borough in the 1990s and found that only 19 per cent were white. Young women of African and African-Caribbean heritage (including those of mixed heritage) were over-represented amongst those coming into care in this borough. Most came into care at their own request, and the numbers of African children were enlarged by asylum-seeking young people. The author concludes that explanations for over-representation are complex and interacting. They include the lack of extended family members, with single-parent families having fewer relatives to turn to for practical help and emotional support and some grandparents being in the home country; a higher level of material disadvantage; a higher tendency for black young women to be more autonomous and therefore more likely to run away from abusive situations at home. They note that the young women were 'often subjected to particularly strict forms of discipline and restrictions on their autonomy' (p.921).

Rowe *et al.* (1989, p.170) found that remands to care for young people of minority ethnic origin aged 14 to 15 were twice as likely as for white youngsters in this age group, but the pattern was reversed for young people aged 16+. They hypothesise that older black youngsters may have been more likely than their white counterparts to be remanded in custody and thus in prison service establishments. The proportion of African-Caribbean young people entering penal establishments through the care system was eight per cent – similar to that for white teenagers (6%) – but more than for Asian young people and those of mixed heritage. Caesar, Parchment and Berridge (1994) report on a specialist foster care scheme set up by Barnardos to provide long-term foster care to young people leaving youth treatment centres. The agency was successful in recruiting black and Asian foster carers in order to meet the needs of the young people leaving these secure units who were of minority ethnic origin.

Placement patterns of children looked after

Although there has been much emphasis in the UK on the placement of children from care for adoption (Performance and Innovation Unit 2000), the majority of children looked after for longer as well as for short periods are in foster care. Few children stay for any length of time in residential care (other than in secure units and very specialist provisions for children with severe disabilities or challenging behaviour). By the mid-1980s Rowe *et al.* (1989) found no differences in placement patterns between white and black children.

Foster care

The most recent large-scale study of children in foster care is that reported by Sinclair and Wilson (2003), Sinclair, Gibbs and Wilson (2004) and Sinclair Wilson and Gibbs (2004). According to data provided by their foster parents, 16 per cent of the 495 children in their care were of minority ethnic origin, the largest group (9%) being of mixed race parentage. The proportions in the other groups were: 2.2 per cent Asian, 1.9 per cent African, 1.7 per cent Caribbean and 0.2 per cent 'other'. Nine out of ten of the foster carers of these 495 children described themselves as white and of English, Irish, Scottish or Welsh origin. The authors comment that the small number of ethnic minority carers in some areas points to difficulties for these local authorities in making appropriate placements. In contrast, the fact that over 70 per cent of the carers in one area were from ethnic minority backgrounds demonstrates success in recruiting ethnic minority carers within established communities.

Summarising the research evidence Sellick and Thoburn (2002, p.18) and Sellick, Thoburn and Philpot (2004) comment that practice initiatives from the

1980s onwards to recruit and approve black foster carers 'have clearly been effective in areas where there are substantial numbers of ethnic minority families in a particular community. Methods for supporting them and retaining their services have, however, been less well scrutinised' (Sellick and Thoburn 2002, p.18). Waterhouse and Brocklesby (1999) surveyed placement choices for children in temporary foster care in five local authorities. Almost half the children were of minority ethnic origin (mainly African-Caribbean or unaccompanied asylum seekers from African countries). Just over half of the foster carers were white. Social workers and foster carers placed the importance of matching ethnicity and culture at the top of their list of important factors to be considered. The researchers considered that three-quarters of the placements were an appropriate match in terms of the child's ethnic and cultural needs. There were only four placements in which the placement definitely did not match the child's ethnic origin (two of these involving white children).

Barn *et al.* (1997, p.75) found that 'the vast majority of African-Caribbean and Asian children were being placed in substitute families which reflected their own ethnic and cultural backgrounds' – but that the placement of other groups, including those of mixed race parentage gave cause for concern since 40 per cent were placed with families where the single parent or both parents were white.

> The baby [mixed parentage] was put with a white family and the older child (African-Caribbean) with a black family... They're telling me they had no other foster mums. I think they put her there because she is mixed race and they thought she would be better off with a white family. But they placed my other daughter with an African-Caribbean family. That was wrong. Why separate my girls? (black mother quoted by Barn *et al.* 1997, p.70).

There were 12 young people of minority ethnic origin (9 of them of mixed heritage) in the Farmer *et al.* (2004) study of 68 adolescents newly placed in foster care. Eighty-three per cent of the 68 were placed with carers of the same ethnic origin. However, whilst only one white child was placed transracially – with a single carer of mixed parentage, 10 of the 12 children of minority ethnic origin were placed with parents of a different ethnic origin, mainly white. However, six were placed with families where, for example, a white single parent had birth children of mixed heritage, or a child of mixed heritage joined a family with two African-Caribbean parents. The lack of choice in placements for teenagers was brought out in the finding that 9 per cent of the social workers considered the placement either fairly or very unsuitable and only 51 per cent thought it very suitable.

In some metropolitan areas, especially London, there are more African-Caribbean and mixed white/African-Caribbean carers than there are African-Caribbean children. For example, information was provided during the workshops that in one inner London borough, 62 per cent of the short-term foster carers are black (mainly African-Caribbean) and only 26 per cent are white British. Three-quarters of the short-term placements in this borough in 2002–3 were transracial, mainly involving white children or those of mixed race parentage or of African descent placed with Caribbean foster families. White teenagers were especially likely to be placed transracially (see Flynn, 2000, on transracial placements of white children). In contrast, Sellick and Connolly (2001) found that 82 per cent of foster carers recruited by the independent fostering agencies described themselves as white, but that 25 per cent of the last ten children placed by the participating agencies were of minority ethnic origin. The issue is complex since in areas where the proportion of minority ethnic families in the community is low, the children coming into care who have special cultural needs are more likely to be of mixed heritage and to have parents who are also of mixed race parentage (listed in the statistics as 'other (non-mixed)' or 'other').

From qualitative and descriptive studies, including interviews with parents and children, it appears that, for short-term care, proximity to the home and family and therefore to friends and schools where the child's culture is well represented are considered to be as important as, if not more so than, ethnicity. This must go along with the qualities and values of the foster carers, including well-developed and flexible parenting skills, culturally sensitive attitudes, the ability to empathise with the parents and the children and the ability to encourage and facilitate comfortable and safe contact with family members and friends. However, in view of the fact that increasing numbers of short-term placements are confirmed as 'permanent' the question of the match between ethnicity, class, language, culture and religion is of considerable importance, even for 'short-term' placement. Looking to the future, it is likely that, especially in parts of London and other areas where white families are in a minority, more minority ethnic parents will take on the role of long-term carers/adopters of children of a different cultural background from their own who were already placed with them on a temporary basis and have 'put down roots'.

Kinship placements

The 'looked after children' statistics (National Statistics and DH 2003b) show that there has been a big expansion since the 1989 Children Act in the practice of placing children looked after with friends and relatives (often referred to as kinship care), to the extent that more children are now placed with relatives than in residential care. Much of the research on kinship placements is North American (see the review by Broad 2001). Caution is needed when applying findings from these studies to the UK context since there are many differences around poverty and restricted access to welfare benefits as experienced by ethnic minority families. In the USA, kinship placements often result in adoption and the payment of an adoption allowance whereas in the UK and other European countries the legal severance of ties with birth parents is rarely considered appropriate. In the UK there is more variability as to how the placements are financially supported, especially once the young person ceases to be looked after (Richards 2001). Small-scale studies and research reviews in the UK have concluded that ethnic minority children were more likely than white children to be placed with relatives. In the Brandon *et al.* (1999) study, 5 of the 14 black or Asian children placed away from home, but only 2 of the 23 white children, were placed with relatives. Barn *et al.* (1997) found with their 'snapshot' sample, including long-stayers, that placement with relatives and friends was considered more often for African-Caribbean, Asian and Chinese children than for white children. Broad, Hayes and Rushforth (2001) researched 50 children looked after in Wandsworth who were in kinship placements. About half the sample (all over 11) were young people of African-Caribbean or Guyanese ethnic origin – a larger proportion than for the whole group of children looked after. The reasons for being looked after included child protection issues, a previous placement breakdown, and behavioural difficulties. Richards (2001) interviewed a 'volunteer' sample of grandparents who were mainly looking after their grandchildren outside the local authority 'looked-after' system. She found that, whilst a large proportion of the white grandparents and those of African-Caribbean heritage were looking after their grandchildren as part of a (mainly informal) 'child welfare service' to a child 'in need', all the South Asian and Chinese grandparents interviewed were providing the service as an expected part of family membership.

In their study of care plans, Harwin *et al.* (2003) found that, although 86 per cent of the sample were white, as many ethnic minority children as white children (seven in each group) were placed with kinship carers – though here there is an unusual definition of 'kinship placement' since it includes fathers who had not been part of the household when the child left home. The authors note that kinship care was more likely to be used in local authorities with large ethnic minority communities and a tradition of putting resources into family support services.

Residential care

> When I was in the residential home a black woman helped me out, you know, talked to me and that. (Ince 1998, p.79)

> Well I Don't know About me but I just wanna Leave care as soon as possible, cause like I live in a children's home with four people Like there's 3 girls and there's one Boy that Lives in a children's home, it's a Bloody nightmare ahh! Someone save me please Before anything else happens to me if ya get me… (16-year-old African-Caribbean young woman responding to a Who Cares? survey, Timms and Thoburn 2003, p.16).

Earlier studies of the placement of minority ethnic children have noted that they have been placed disproportionately in children's homes. Although the numbers of places available in residential care at any one time have decreased, residential care is still a placement through which an important minority of (especially older) children pass, usually staying for comparatively short periods of time. There is an increase in the use of residential care for parents and children together, often as part of the assessment before deciding whether a young child can safely remain with the parents. We have no data on the extent to which these placements are used by ethnic minority parents and children but would suggest that this is an area worthy of further study.

The small numbers who spend periods of years in group care settings will be in secure units, small residential units for children with complex learning or physical difficulties and often also challenging behaviour and schools for children with emotional and behavioural difficulties (EBD). Small children's homes are often not dissimilar from large foster homes. Little recent information is available about those who spend substantial periods of their childhood in residential care, and even less about the numbers of these children who are of minority ethnic origin. However, unaccompanied asylum seekers are currently spending much of their adolescence in children's homes and hostels (25% in March 2002 compared with 11% of white children, National Statistics and DH 2003b).

A study that concentrates on children of minority ethnic backgrounds is that of Robinson (2000). Taking a child development perspective she compared the self-esteem and racial identity attitudes of 40 African-Caribbean young people living in children's homes with a matched sample of 40 young people not in care. She found that the two groups had relatively high levels of self-esteem and of internalisation of their identity as black young people. Self-esteem was most likely to be high for those who strongly identified themselves as belonging to the black community.

Three recent studies of residential care which contain information on ethnicity are those of Berridge and Brodie (1998), Berridge et al. (2003) and Sinclair and Gibbs (1998). The Sinclair and Gibbs study collects together the information on children of minority ethnic origin in an appendix as well as integrating it in the text. This mixed methods study included a statistical analysis of data on 223 young people who had lived in 48 children's homes in five authorities at some point during the 12 months of the study, 75 of whom were of minority ethnic origin. The largest group (35 young people) were of mixed African-Caribbean/white parentage; 19 were African-Caribbean; 13, Asian; 11 were of mixed Asian/white ethnicity and 3 were of 'other' ethnic origin. Ethnic minority staff as well as young people were over-represented, especially amongst staff who had been there for shorter lengths of time. They tended to be younger than their white colleagues. Two homes had high proportions of black and Asian staff members (64% in one home) but 22 homes had no ethnic minority staff. There was no obvious 'match' between ethnicity of the young people and the proportion of staff of minority ethnic origin, except that only 17 per cent of the children in the home where over half the staff members were black or Asian were of minority ethnic origin.

Berridge and colleagues (2003) are undertaking the second phase of a study comparing 257 adolescents in children's homes, foster care and residential EBD schools. A quarter of the young people in the sample (including ten unaccompanied asylum seekers, nine of whom lived in children's homes) were of minority ethnic origin. Few of the black or Asian teenagers attended residential special schools.

Placements in long-term / permanent foster families

There are far more research studies on children in long-term or permanent placements than in short-term placements. Though most of these, especially in recent years, are on adoption, some include children in 'permanent' foster placements alongside children placed for adoption (for example Charles, Rashid and Thoburn 1992; Fratter *et al.* 1991; Quinton *et al.* 1998; Rushton *et al.* 2001; Rushton, Dance and Quinton 2000; Rushton, Treseder and Quinton 1995). Most 'snapshot' studies of foster care (for example Barn 1993; Sinclair, Gibbs and Wilson 2004; Sinclair, Wilson and Gibbs 2004) include a proportion of short-stay as well as long-stay children which may explain some differences in findings.

Although many of the early studies of foster care were of long-term fostering, since the mid 1980s when adoption became the placement of first choice for children who could not go home, research on long-term fostering has declined. Because it was unusual to define a foster care placement as 'long-term' it proved too difficult to find sufficiently large numbers of such placements for robust evaluation. However, Rowe *et al.* (1989, p.112) write: 'There is no historical benchmark against which the decline in long-term fostering can be measured but we thought that those placements might have declined to a mere trickle. It was not so. We found that long-term fostering is certainly still alive, even if it might not be considered to be very healthy.' This 'decline in long-term fostering' in the 1970s and 1980s is of interest for our purposes because it coincided with a period when strenuous efforts were made to recruit black foster parents, many of whom became long-term foster parents (see Ahmed, Cheetham and Small 1986 and Thoburn, Norford and Rashid 2000 for reviews of these developments). Few of the studies specifically focusing on long-term foster care include large enough numbers of ethnic minority children for purposes of quantitative analysis but insights from interviews with these children and their foster parents can assist in understanding their experiences and these have contributed to our overall conclusions (Beek and

Schofield 2004; Berridge and Cleaver 1987; Schofield *et al.* 2000; Schofield 2002; Sinclair, Wilson and Gibbs 2004).

Children placed as long-term foster children are more likely to be included in 'permanence' studies alongside those placed for adoption (Charles *et al.* 1992; Rushton *et al.* 2000; Thoburn, Noeford and Rashid 2000). Just under a third of the 297 ethnic minority children in the Thoburn, Norford and Rashid study were placed as permanent foster children. They were placed in the early 1980s and followed up some 15 years later. Half of them were of mixed-race parentage and the majority were placed with white families. A purposive interview sample included around half who were placed in 'matched' families. An important finding was that children both of whose parents were of the same minority ethnic background were more likely to be placed as permanent foster children rather than for adoption than was the case for children with two white parents or those of mixed-race parentage. This is to some extent explained by the fact that the children of mixed heritage tended to be younger at the time of placement, and younger children were more likely to be placed for adoption than were older children. However, the children with two black or Asian parents were more likely to be placed with black or Asian new parents, and these parents were more likely to foster than to adopt. Although for some it was a question of needing the fostering allowance or valuing continuing social work support, for most, there were principles involved, such as not wishing to sever a child totally from the birth parents and siblings. These foster children tended to see more of their birth parents and were more likely to be in a placement with their siblings. When motivation was discussed, the foster parents were more likely than the adopters to mention wanting to give a home to a child in care who was of their own ethnic background. They were also more likely to empathise with the birth parents as well as with the children and to list amongst their reasons for deciding to foster rather than to adopt that they did not wish to further harm the birth parents who had had many difficulties in their lives. This aspect of the study is explored more fully by Rashid (2000).

Lowe and Murch (2002) explore the reasons why plans were made for either adoption or long-term fostering for 220 children, aged under 12 in 1999, who had been looked after for at least 12 months. They found that children of mixed race parentage were greatly over-represented amongst the children being placed for adoption. The original plan for the child was long-term foster care in 40 per cent of cases, adoption in 29 per cent of cases and 'other' (including return home) in 31 per cent of cases. Twelve months later, the plan had changed to long-term fostering in 47 per cent of cases, adoption in 23 per cent of cases and 'other' in 29 per cent of cases. Ethnicity of the child is one of the variables included in the analysis of whether adoption or long-term fostering is the plan of choice. Of the 22 children whose parents were of minority ethnic origin, 65 per cent were the subject of a plan for long-term fostering compared with 53 per cent of the white children. As with other studies, children of mixed ethnicity were more likely than those with two black or Asian parents to be placed for adoption rather than with long-term foster families.

Adoption

There is no shortage of reviews and overviews of adoption research, most of which have something to say about the placement of minority ethnic children. Much of the emphasis (overseas and in the UK) is on placements of black children in white families. Parker (DH 1999b) includes an overview of the research on ethnicity and adoption in his review of Department of Health funded adoption research completed in the 1990s. Simmonds (2001) provides an analysis and discussion on 505 people making enquiries about becoming adoptive parents during the 1998 'adoption week', 25 per cent of whom provided information that they were of were of minority ethnic origin. Thoburn (2002b) has summarised recent research in a *Quality Protects Briefing* and Rushton (2004) has provided an overview of adoption research in a *Knowledge Digest* prepared for the Social Care Institute for Excellence (SCIE). Statistics routinely collected from local authorities and published annually have started to provide data on children placed for adoption, but these do not yet provide detailed information on the ethnicity of the children and birth or adoptive parents (National Statistics and DfES 2003). The most detailed statistical information on adoption and ethnicity is to be found in Ivaldi's (2000) reanalysis of national and local statistics and Lowe, Murch *et al.*'s (1999) survey of adopters approved and children placed by 85 local authority and 30 voluntary adoption agencies in 1993–4. Thoburn provided a cross-national comparison of adoption for the prime minister's review (Performance and Innovations Unit 2000; Thoburn 2002a). Selwyn and Sturgess (2001); Triseliotis, Shireman and Hundelby (1997) and Warman and Roberts (2003) have also provided research overviews on adoption in an international context and Selman (2000) summarises the research on inter-country adoption which is mostly also transracial.

Coming back to children in out-of-home care in the UK, data are beginning to be available from the newly set-up Adoption Register for England and Wales (2003) on children for whom an adoptive home is sought because one has not been quickly available within the child's local area. Twenty-two per cent of the 3200 children whose details were or had been on the register during a six-month period were of minority ethnic origin – a slight over-representation when compared to the 18 per cent of ethnic minority children looked after. However, children in a combined group comprising 'mixed and other' are greatly over-represented (17% of those on the register but 9% of children looked after). At 2 per cent, those in the 'Asian or Asian British' group were on the register in the same proportion as their numbers looked after. However, those in the 'Black or Black British' group were greatly under-represented amongst those for whom an adoptive family was sought beyond their local agency (3% compared with 6% of the looked after population). This may be understood in terms of the smaller number of black children who start to be looked after when under one – the age group that comprises the largest group placed for adoption. Ninety per cent of the 3000 prospective adopters were white, 6 per cent were in the 'mixed or other' group and 3 per cent were in the 'Asian or Asian British' group. There were more Asian prospective adopters than Asian children on the register but more black children than black adopters. The report makes clear that most children referred to the register have a range of special needs and that there is a mismatch between the needs of the children and the prospective adopters. Forty per cent of this 'hard to place' group on the register were aged six or over but only 28 per cent of the adopters on the register were approved to take a child of six or over.

A similar pattern is found with children referred to BAAFLink and Be My Parent (British Agencies for Adoption and Fostering 2000). Twenty-six per cent of all children referred to this service in 1998–9 were of minority ethnic origin. Twelve per cent of those referred (almost 50% of those referred who were of minority ethnic origin) had one white and one African-Caribbean parent. The large proportion of the referrals of children under five who were of minority ethnic origin is probably explained by authorities in areas with a largely white population needing to use national agencies to look more widely for a suitably matched family. There is support for this in the survey by Ivaldi (2000), who found that children of minority ethnic origin were more likely than white children to be placed by a different local authority or a voluntary adoption agency than by their local care authority. Ivaldi's data from 116 local authorities, although less recent, provides a more comprehensive picture in that it includes all children and not just the harder-to-place. Ten per cent of the 1330 children placed for adoption were of minority ethnic origin. The large proportion of children of mixed parentage placed for adoption, when compared with those with two parents of the same ethnic origin, merits further study. This should be read alongside the research cited in the earlier section on foster care indicating that more black and Asian children than mixed parentage children are placed in permanent foster care. The combined group of black and Asian children started to be looked after at a younger age (average four months) than those of mixed race parentage (mean age of nine months) and the white children (mean age of one year two months). They were also more likely to have started to be looked after under voluntary arrangements (54% of them), than the mixed parentage and white children (21% and 20%).

Since the majority of children now being placed join their new families as infants and toddlers, it is interesting to compare the data from the first stage of a more detailed longitudinal study by Neil (2000) which focused on 168 children placed for adoption in 1996–7 when under the age of four. Nineteen per cent of these children were of minority ethnic origin. Mixed heritage children were over-represented in this group of children but not to the same extent as in the Ivaldi study. The diversity within this small group illustrates the complexity of the task both of placement workers in taking account of ethnicity and culture and of researchers. All the children with parents of the same ethnicity and those with one white and one black or Asian parent were placed in a family of a similar ethnic origin. The small proportion placed with white families had either three white grandparents or had two parents of different minority ethnic origin. Neil found that the children of minority ethnic origin were placed more quickly than the white children but this was explained by the white children being, on average, older and more difficult to place. Relinquished white infants joined their new families on average at a slightly younger age (mean age 4 months, than those with two black or Asian parents, mean age 6 months) and those of mixed parentage (mean age 10 months). For those adopted from care following care orders, the mean ages were hardly different (22 months for white children, 18 months for those of mixed parentage and 13 months for those with two parents of minority ethnic origin).

Ethnic minority children were more likely than white children to be relinquished by their parents. There appeared to be two main reasons for this. Some of the Asian young women felt they had no choice since single parenthood was not supported or sanctioned within their communities and some were afraid of being physically assaulted if the pregnancy became known. Although the numbers are small, if this pattern is repeated across the country, it could indicate that Asian women who become pregnant outside marriage do not have the same choices as other young women either to keep their children or place them for adoption. Their children also may suffer from this total severance model of adoption because even indirect post-adoption contact was rarely planned for.

The Lowe *et al.* (1999) survey of 1557 children placed when over the age of five included 15 per cent who were of minority ethnic origin (9% of mixed race parentage; 3% African-Caribbean; 2% Asian and 1% from another minority ethnic group). Only a small proportion was placed transracially, including some white children placed in families where at least one adopter was of minority ethnic origin. In the Ivaldi (2000) survey also, the majority of children were in ethnically 'matched' placements and more of the children with two black or Asian parents came into care through voluntary agreements than was the case for those of mixed parentage, or white children.

It is important to note that the children in the studies reported above were actually adopted. There is evidence in some states in the USA (see, for example, Barth 1997; Kemp and Bodonyi 2000) of a failure to find adoptive families (whether same race or of a different race) for African-American children, including some who enter care and are freed for adoption when very young. We have no robust evidence to indicate that this happens to young ethnic minority children coming into care in the UK but it seems unlikely. However, we have less information on whether older children of minority heritage are disproportionately represented amongst the children for whom plans change from adoption to foster care because no adoptive family is found. There is some evidence from the Be My Parent and other linking services that this may be the case but data are not collected at a national level on children 'freed for adoption' who 'age out' of care without being adopted.

In concluding this section on numbers of children adopted from care in the different ethnic groups it is important to stress how small are the numbers, even in what appear to be large cohorts. When the different groups of children are combined for purposes of quantitative analysis (as with the Ivaldi and the Neil studies) differences between ethnic groups may 'cancel each other out' leaving important information relevant to one group unreported.

Turning to placement patterns prior to placement for adoption, a finding from the Ivaldi (2000) study is that white children and those of mixed parentage were more likely to have had repeat admissions to care than was the case with those with two black or Asian parents. Thoburn, Norford and Rashid (2000) summarised studies which specifically focused on ethnic minority children placed several years ago, especially the longitudinal research on the work of the British Adoption Project which set out to counteract the institutionally racist view, widely held at the time, that black children were 'unadoptable' (Gill and Jackson 1983; Raynor 1970). This review set the context for their longitudinal survey of the placements of 297 minority ethnic children, 71 per cent of which were made with the intention that the child would be adopted. Much has changed since the children in these studies were placed, both in terms of the demographic characteristics of the general population and of the characteristics of the 'in care' population. For example, more were older boys placed from residential care than would be the case with more recent cohorts. Only 30 per cent were placed when under the age of five, 26 per cent were aged between five and eight at placement and 39 per cent were aged nine or over. The biggest change over time is that far more were placed with white families (71%) than is the case with more recently placed cohorts. The study will be referred to more fully when outcomes are considered. However, it highlights some factors that may still be relevant, particularly about children of mixed-race parentage.

In common with others looking at populations of children in care at that time, the study found that the largest group of these children had an African-Caribbean father and a white mother. However, when placed with mixed partnership families, it was most likely that the father was white and the mother of African-Caribbean, African or Asian heritage. The authors draw attention to the problematic nature of the terms 'same-race', 'transracial' and 'matching'. Whilst 83 per cent of the children placed with African-Caribbean families had two black parents, some of these were of African descent. Whilst 53 per cent of the children placed with ethnically mixed partnerships were of mixed race parentage, 47 per cent had two black or Asian parents. It was far more likely that the children placed with white families would be of mixed race parentage (66%) than was the case for children both of whose parents were of minority ethnic origin (34%). Older children were most likely to be placed with two black or Asian parents, and ethnically mixed partnership families were most likely to have the youngest children placed with them. When other characteristics associated with 'hard to parent' children such as behavioural and emotional disturbance and a history of maltreatment are considered, white and black parents were equally likely to take into their homes children known at the time of placement to have problems, whilst the mixed partnership families had fewer such children placed with them. When the ethnic minority children were compared with the white children in the original cohort of 1165 children (Fratter et al. 1991), those with two black or Asian parents were more likely than white children or those of mixed race parentage to have continuing contact with a birth parent and to be placed with a sibling. This was most likely to be the case for children who were placed with two (or a single) African-Caribbean parent/s, irrespective of whether this was a placement for adoption or as a permanent foster child.

The detailed interviews with a purposive sub-sample of adopters and foster parents in this study, and others that include small numbers of minority ethnic children, provide detailed information on the attitudes of parents and children. (See for example Quinton et al. 1998; Rushton et al. 2001; and Owen's 1999 study of 30 children adopted by single parents.) Studies in Europe and the USA also give insights into the issues and provide data on outcomes, but these mainly concern children adopted from overseas. (See Triseliotis et al. 1997 for an overview of the American studies and Armstrong and Slaytor's 2001 edited volume of the accounts of young adults who grew up in adoptive families who were visibly different from themselves.)

What do we know about interim and long-term outcomes for children and families?

> Things are different now. Ive applied for College next year. I have 2 jobs. I have support. I see a Counsellor to help me to get over my past. I have an effectionate caring, and Supporting boyfriend of 17. and This time next year ill have my own counsel flat. Im So Glad for all the support of all the carers who are out there. (Young woman of mixed heritage quoted in Timms and Thoburn 2003, p.101)

Most studies that are large enough to take account of the way in which the differences in the child and his or her circumstances influence success rates use whether the placement lasted as needed or broke down as the only 'outcome measure'. Some, for example the Rutter et al. (1998) research on children adopted from Romania, use a range of measures of well-being, as do most of the smaller-scale interview studies More recently, data are routinely collected on the educational achievement of young people leaving care (Bhabra, Ghate and Brazier 2002; DfES 2003) but the national statistics are not as yet undertaken with ethnicity as a variable. In countries such as Sweden, where data are routinely collected for the whole population, it is possible to use health and education records and criminal convictions to track the long-term outcomes for cohorts of children. Examples are the longitudinal study by Bohmann and Sigvardsson (1990) of children placed for foster care and adoption compared with a general population of children brought up by their parents, and the more recent study by Lindblad, Hjern and Vinnerljung (2003) comparing adults who came to Sweden through inter-country adoption.

Outcomes of short-and medium-term foster placements

Although now dated, the study by Rowe *et al.* (1989) is the only large-scale source of data on outcomes for minority ethnic children placed for short-term care in the full range of placements. Even with larger populations than is often the case, the researchers urge caution when interpreting their findings on outcome for the different ethnic groups. Because a higher proportion of the ethnic minority children (especially young children of African-Caribbean descent) were placed for short periods, and placements with the aim of 'temporary care' was the most successful, more of these children had successful placement endings than white children. The researchers therefore looked at a group of children whose placements ended when they were aged 11 years or over. Forty-five per cent of ethnic minority children had successful placement endings compared with 42 per cent of white children, with Asian children and those of mixed parentage having slightly more successful placement endings than African-Caribbean and African children. When only foster care placements are included, there were no differences overall between placements that had lasted as needed for the different ethnic groups. However, there was a slight tendency for the placements of Asian children and those of mixed race parentage to last 'too long'. More of the placements of Asian children in residential care had a successful ending than was the case for the other groups.

The Rowe *et al.* (1989) study did not collect information on the ethnic background of the carers. The overall breakdown rates for children in long-term, intermediate and short-term placements in the Berridge and Cleaver (1987) (smaller numbers) study were no different for ethnic minority children than for white children, even though two-thirds of their foster carers were white.

The conclusions of Rowe *et al.* on short-term foster care are that, for children under 10 around 88 per cent of placements for temporary care for all ethnic groups achieved their aims, and the proportions were only slightly lower for those aged 11 years and over. The only difference between ethnic groups was that African-Caribbean/African adolescents were more likely than the other groups to have unsuccessful placement endings if the aim was 'treatment' or 'assessment'.

Recent studies following up children who have returned home from care or accommodation do however indicate that insufficient planning and support goes into ensuring that the move back to birth parents or relatives is successful. Since 'placement at home with parents' is a route often taken by ethnic minority children, the finding from recent studies that this is the least successful placement type for children on care orders should be the subject of further research (Harwin *et al.* 2003; Hunt *et al.* 1999; Sinclair, Wilson and Gibbs 2004).

Outcomes of long-term/permanent foster family care and adoption

> It is so difficult to gain knowledge of and a familiarity with a heritage I was not raised with. Somehow I can read all the books in the world on Chinese history and culture but can never be familiar with it. (Armstrong and Slaytor 2001, p.103)

> Seeing my natural father and my adoptive mother sitting next to each other chatting at my wedding… It was fantastic. (Kirton *et al.* 2000, p.15)

Several UK studies provide information on longer-term outcomes for permanently placed children, including some of minority ethnic origin, though sample size and representativeness differ greatly as does time between placement and follow-up (Berridge and Cleaver 1997; Fratter *et al.* 1991; Gill and Jackson 1983; Howe 1997a, 1997b; Howe, Feast and Coster 2000; Kirton *et al.* 2000; Quinton *et al.* 1998; Rowe *et al.* 1989; Rowe, Hundleby and Keane 1984; Rushton *et al.* 1995; Rushton *et al.* 2000; Sinclair, Wilson and Gibbs 2004; Thoburn 1990). Rushton and Minnis 1997 and Triseliotis *et al.*1997 review the USA as well as the UK studies and specifically consider the question of transracial adoption.

Rowe *et al.* (1989, p.17) found that 27 per cent of the foster placements made with the aim of 'care and upbringing' (50% of them in respect of teenagers) had broken down between one and two years later, and that 'placements of black and mixed parentage children broke down slightly less often than those of white children'. For all ethnic groups, breakdown was related to age at placement. In line with other studies of the placement of teenagers, Farmer, Moyers and Lipscombe (2004) reported a high rate of placement breakdown (40% in the first year) for the 68 adolescents in their research. Because only 12 were of minority ethnic origin, numbers are too small for analysis of outcomes by ethnic group.

Numbers of same and transracial placements in the Berridge and Cleaver (1987) study of placement breakdown in long-term foster families were insufficient for statistical analysis, but the authors 'would not conclude that the association between the racial characteristics of foster parents and children was paramount [in explaining placement breakdown] although there was some tendency for mixed race children placed with white, long-term foster parents to experience more breakdowns than one might expect by chance' (p.67).

The Sinclair et al. study (Sinclair, Gibbs and Wilson 2004; Sinclair and Wilson 2003; Sinclair, Wilson and Gibbs 2004) provides detailed information on a sample of 528 foster children. They provide outcome data on those that could be traced three years later. For the 464 in respect of whom this information was available from the foster carers, the expectation at stage one of the study was that 34 per cent would remain in this placement until the age of 18 or beyond. Three years on, 28 per cent of the sample were with the same foster family (including 3% adopted by that family); 15 per cent were with other foster families; 4 per cent were in residential care and 18 per cent were living independently. Seventeen per cent had returned to live with birth parents and 12 per cent had been adopted by families other than those they were with at stage one. There were no apparent differences in outcome between the white children and those of minority ethnic origin.

Care has to be taken to look at the nature of the sample when comparing adoption outcome studies. Those which include children adopted by foster parents or, as in the case of many USA studies, by relatives, report fewer placements breaking down than those where all the placements are with substitute parents not previously known to them. Because of the large sample size, the Fratter et al. (1991) cohort study of 1165 'stranger' placements for older children and those with special needs has the most reliable information on breakdown rates (measured between two and five years after placement). That study found that when other variables were held constant there was no difference in the rate of placement breakdown for children both of whose birth parents were of minority ethnic origin and white children, but that there was a higher risk of placements of children of mixed ethnicity disrupting. Charles et al. (1992) re-examined the records on these children between six and ten years after placement. At least 24 per cent of the placements had disrupted (not all the records could be traced for the full ten years). When age at placement was held constant, there was no difference in placement disruption rates between those placed as foster children and those placed for adoption.

Although we have concentrated on the placement of UK children from care, there are important lessons to be learned from inter-country adoption studies. Rutter and colleagues (1998, 1999) are following up a cohort of 165 Romanian children placed with UK adopters, mainly after the children experienced adverse conditions in institutions. These children will be followed up until adulthood and their well-being compared with a cohort of English children placed for adoption as infants. When assessed by the researchers at the age of six the children had caught up on physical and cognitive development but, especially for those placed over the age of two, there were concerns about the social development and behavioural problems of an important minority of the children. Because inter-country adoption has a longer history and is more widespread in other European countries and the USA than the UK there is more information on adult adoptees. Lindblad *et al.* (2003) found that most of the 5942 inter-country adopted adults (mainly of Korean or Indian heritage and almost all adopted by white families) were leading satisfactory adult lives. However, on a range of measures they were doing less well than the general population in the same age group and their non-adopted Swedish siblings and about the same as children from the same ethnic groups who had migrated to Sweden with their families. Adoptees were more likely than the other groups to have psychiatric problems (including substance abuse) and to be long-term recipients of welfare benefits.

An area we have barely touched on in this review and where more work is needed is that of the fostering of children through private arrangements. There are no nationally collected statistics but it is thought that most of those in long-stay arrangements are black African children placed with white foster parents. For some, the lack of legal security appears unproblematic because of the good relationships (often now involving two generations) between the families. But for others the lack of adequate monitoring and support for the foster carers and the vulnerability of the children to unplanned removal and to poor parenting can be seriously harmful. Philpot (2001) has reviewed the knowledge base on these families and the Social Care Institute for Excellence is commissioning further research to help to fill this important gap in research knowledge.

Outcomes of kinship placements

We are not aware of any UK studies specifically on the stability and disruption rates of kinship placements for children of minority ethnic origin. However, since ethnic minority children are more likely than white children to be placed with kin, we make the assumption that outcome studies that do not specify ethnicity will have relevance. Across the age groups, on average, kinship placements are reported by the majority of researchers to be more successful than 'stranger' placements. The main research studies are American, and these include large proportions of children of African-American, Hispanic and mixed race parentage. Caution is urged in applying this research to the UK context since there are issues specific to the US discussed earlier. Caution is also needed when looking at UK research since most of the outcome studies took place before the Children Act led to an increase in these placements. The Sinclair, Wilson and Gibbs research (2004) does not report the same positive findings about kinship placements that were reported by Rowe *et al.* (1984; 1989) and Berridge and Cleaver (1987). However, using satisfaction as an outcome measure, the black children and their carers interviewed for the Broad *et al.* studies (2001) were in the main strongly in favour of being placed with kin.

In some respects there are similarities between outcomes for birth parents and outcomes for kinship carers. Some kinship placements end by the child being placed for adoption outside the birth family, in which case research on post-placement contact and other aspects of the continuing role of the kinship carers in the life of the child is relevant (see, for example, Neil 2000, 2003).

Outcomes of residential placements

The largest study of placements in residential care that includes an analysis of placements of ethnic minority children is that of Rowe *et al.* (1989). That study found no difference in the patterns of placement for ethnic minority children and white children, except for a slight trend towards Asian teenagers having more successful placement endings in residential care than the other groups. Across the ethnic groups, Rowe *et al.* found that there was no difference in the proportion of 'successful' endings of placements in residential and in foster care.

Only 18 of the 223 young people interviewed in the Sinclair and Gibbs study (1998, 1999a, 1999b) were of minority ethnic origin, so the researchers advise caution. The conclusion drawn from these interviews was that 'the black and ethnic minority young people did not feel particularly victimised but did find the homes an uneasy and uncomfortable place in which to be' (1998, p.267). Their comments on how they were treated by the staff were similar to those of the white young people, but they were significantly more likely to say they had a problem with the food and 'with police checking on people with whom they might stay'. Unlike those responding to two *Who Cares* surveys (Fletcher 1993; Timms and Thoburn 2003) these researchers found no direct evidence of racism between residents or on the part of staff, but note that this may be a feature of the research design and the fact that all the interviewers were white, though pilot work was undertaken by a black interviewer. The broad conclusion from surveys of young people's views is that there is no clear preference for one form of care rather than another, some having good reasons to do with their own histories for preferring foster care and some residential care. Some small-scale studies focusing specifically on black young women (Lees 2002; Robinson 2000) found generally positive results for the young people and high rates of satisfaction, especially when staff were of the same ethnic background. However, Sinclair *et al.* reach a more negative conclusion about the quality of life of the young people in all ethnic groups in the 48 children's homes taking part in their research. They particularly note the high rate of bullying, sexual harassment, and involvement in delinquency by young people who had not offended before going into residential care, although they also note differences between the homes.

Outcomes for birth parents, including when children in care are placed with parents

Very few studies have looked at the outcomes for the birth parents of children placed away from home. Those that have, generally use birth parent satisfaction as an outcome measure. Richards and Ince (2000) report on what they value and what they find unhelpful. Except for this, and the studies cited earlier of Asian disabled children that provide some information on parents' satisfaction with respite services, we have found no studies that specifically explore what ethnic minority families are looking for from placement services and whether they find them helpful. We therefore have to turn to general studies, some of which include data from interviews with ethnic minority parents (Charlton *et al.* 1998; Freeman and Hunt 1998; Packman and Hall 1998; Packman, Randall and Jacques 1986; Schofield *et al.* 2000; Smith and Logan 2004; Thoburn, Murdoch and O'Brien 1986). There is no reason to suppose that the findings on parental satisfaction do not apply across the ethnic groups. There are clues in the detailed qualitative studies about how the needs and wishes of parents of different ethnic and cultural backgrounds may differ. They are most likely to express concerns about the detail of substitute parenting, especially concerning how children are helped to respond to racist behaviour, and about how religious and cultural observances are encouraged. The way in which parental control is exercised by the carers is also seen as important by birth parents.

In summary, birth parents generally find short-term care helpful, whether it is provided as a series of short-term placements, at a point of crisis or in response to a particularly stressful period in their lives. This is especially so if it is provided in response to their request for this type of help, but even when it results from emergency protection measures, if the family is helped both whilst the child is away and when he or she returns home, the parents tend to rate the service positively. Some parents greatly value a placement service for teenage children whose challenging behaviour is placing the young person, and sometimes siblings, at risk because of inappropriate sexual behaviour or violent outbursts. This is a service that some adopters also seek and value when it succeeds in enhancing rather than cutting the links between themselves and their troubled adopted child (Thoburn, Norford and Rashid 2000).

On the other hand, it is very rare for birth parents to consider that they have been provided with a good enough service if their children are placed in long-term care or for adoption against their wishes, although this occasionally happens when they continue to receive social work support and especially if they are helped to maintain meaningful links (Fratter 1996; Logan 1999; Neil 2003). This is important since many of the ethnic minority parents are themselves under 18 and therefore children themselves, or are vulnerable because of mental health problems or learning disabilities or having themselves had a troubled background, including being in care. It is also important since, especially if the child is placed in a family of a different ethnicity and culture, they hold essential information about the child's heritage, religion and culture. The Thoburn, Norford and Rashid (2000) study did not include interviews with birth parents but, at second hand through the foster or adoptive parents and the young people, the researchers learned that some birth parents had become reconciled to the placement. Some social workers and some substitute parents have been praised by birth parents because of their continuing support after their child went into care.

Satisfaction as an outcome measure

> I wouldn't change anything about my family. But at the end of the day I wouldn't advise any black person to go to a white family. Because you miss out on all the culture and everything. But I do appreciate what they did for me. There is nothing I would change about what they did for me. (Thoburn, Norford and Rashid 2000, p.143)

A 'softer' but no less important measure of outcome is the satisfaction of those involved in adoption or foster care. The satisfaction of the carers with the placement experience, and with the social work and support service is also relevant. Many of the research studies and surveys already referred to provide information on the views of young people, an important source being studies involving interviews with young people who have left care. Some of these studies, including that of Ince (1998) on young people of mixed parentage who grew up in care, Thoburn, Norford and Rashid (2000) and the Richards and Ince (2000) report of focus group discussions with young people looked after, their birth parents and carers, are specific to young people of minority ethnic origin. Others include some interviews with black and Asian young people as with the Garnett (1992) and Biehal et al. (1995) leaving care studies. A range of research methods is also used to assess well-being and satisfaction rates amongst adult adoptees and those who have grown up in long-term foster families (Howe, Feast with Coster 2000; Schofield 2002). Studies reporting interim outcomes closer to the time of placement are richer sources of data about satisfaction with social work and other services around the time of placement, since memories are more easily recalled (Beek and Schofield 2004; Lowe et al. 1999; Neil 2002b; Quinton et al. 1998; Schofield et al. 2000; Thomas et al. 1999). Even when only small numbers of black and Asian children and/or their carers are included, what they have to say can convey important messages, especially when combined with those from other studies.

Because numbers of ethnic minority children in any one study are small, researchers rarely analyse the data in terms of ethnicity. However, taken together they provide an eloquent commentary on some of the special issues around being looked after as a young person of a different culture from the majority. What follows is a summary from all the research already cited that seeks information on the satisfaction of young people either through their own voices or those of their parents and carers. They share many of the feelings and aspirations of all young people in care. Most are saddened by having to leave home but understand the reasons for it. Some are greatly relieved that they were taken away from an unsafe, frightening or distressing environment (Timms and Thoburn 2003). They want consistent, skilled, but above all affectionate and caring, parenting that provides them with a sense of belonging, boosts their sense of self-worth and competence and strengthens their pride in their appearance and personalities. They want help to make sense of their histories and want to be accepted as part of the foster or adoptive family even though most want to retain their links with their first families. They also want their carers to be good at the social aspects of parenting, helping them to make positive social relationships and supporting them in achieving their potential at school, college or in employment. In addition, black and Asian young people, and others who are visibly different, want the reality of racism and discrimination because of appearance or disability to be understood by their carers and they want help in devising strategies to deal with it. They recognise that parents and carers of a different cultural background don't find this easy, though they value the fact that they try their best. Some want to be given approval to find their own sources of support to deal with racism alongside any help their carers and social workers try to give them. Living in a community where many others share the same appearance and culture is a great help.

Continuity and consistency from a social worker who cares about them, puts him or herself out to be available when needed and involves them in planning for their future as well as the detail of their daily lives is important. Given all these essentials, they value having a social worker of a similar ethnic background and culture. In this respect, class, language and religion are important as well as ethnic group and shared physical characteristics.

If they cannot return home, they want to be loved and welcomed as part of an alternative family, even if they find it difficult to give love back. They want their past to be respected as integral to the person they are, and to find ways of understanding and coming to terms with what has happened to them rather than to have it locked away as forbidden territory, too terrible to talk about. Most want to be placed with siblings and to go on seeing birth parents, siblings they are separated from, and other people who have been important to them in the past, including previous carers.

> I would really like to be a T.V. journalist on ITN. I would love to be rich and donate £2,000,000 to social services to help other children in care. I think that it is important for every young person to get what they deserve. I would love to get in contact with my Dad and find out about my history and my Mum. There are a lot of secrets in my family and no one is willing to share

them with me. I want to know why my Mum is manic-depressive, I want to know why Nan and Grandad split up. I want to know why none of my uncles apart from two came to see me when I was younger. I want to prove to everyone who had stereotypical views about me to be put to shame and shown that foster children can get really far if they just believe in themselves. (Young woman of mixed heritage, Timms and Thoburn 2003, p.99)

Studies from around the world convey similar messages, and there is congruence between the messages from those adopted away from their country of birth and those placed 'in-country' but away from their culture and familiar territory (see, for example, Armstrong and Slaytor 2001 and Grotevant and McRoy 1998).

The satisfaction of the carers is also important since feeling they are doing a good job, and that the agency values them sufficiently to put in the necessary support, can help maintain a placement when the going gets rough, as it usually does at some stage. Satisfaction is related to motivation for taking up a career as a residential social worker or foster carer or welcoming a child into their family on a long-term basis. Put simply, those who achieve what they set out to achieve are more likely to find the experience satisfying and to keep doing it. The research indicates that successful carers blend self-directed motives with altruism. Foster carers and adopters of minority ethnic origin have the same combination of reasons for taking on a caring role. Additionally, many speak of their shock in learning that many children from their own culture and religion are 'in care'.

For them, an important aspect of altruism is a determination to provide a home for a child of a similar background whose life has been less fortunate than their own. Some who have themselves had a difficult childhood and been distressed by racist abuse want to help the next generation to overcome these obstacles as they themselves have done.

> They were in a children's home in a mainly white area. He was very damaged. He had lost his identity. He would talk about 'Bournville Selection'. I said 'Hold on a minute. You are either black or you are white, and you are black.' 'I'm not', he said, 'I'm a light darkie'. I got really worried because I didn't realise that there were black children who had got sold down the line like that. (African-Caribbean long-term foster mother quoted in Thoburn, Norford and Rashid 2000, p.126)

For many, this empathy encompasses the birth parents. More ethnic minority than white parents talk about a spiritual or faith dimension to their wish to help. Whilst this does not lead them to condone the way in which parents have maltreated, neglected or otherwise failed their children, it is their empathy for parents of a similar culture who have struggled with adversity that leads them to extend their wish to help the children to also helping the parents (Arnold and James 1989; Rashid 2000).

They asked me about adopting Clive and I said 'no'. Clive's daddy loved him in his own way and he had that link with his dad. And I don't think it would have been fair to rob him [the birth father] of someone that he had loved in his own way. (Thoburn, Norford and Rashid 2000, p.91)

The general consensus from a range of studies is that somewhere between 75 per cent and 80 per cent of adopters or long-term foster parents rate their experience of parenting in this special way as generally positive. Whilst fewer than 10 per cent are totally dissatisfied, another 10 per cent or so express some disappointment or have mixed feelings. Surprisingly, unlike breakdown rates, this does not seem to be linked to the age of the child at placement, bearing out the above comments about aims and motivation. Because they can see progress, some foster or adoptive parents of older children with very challenging behaviour feel satisfied even if the child never grew to love or trust them. On the other hand, some adopters of infants or toddlers whose motivation was to have a family or to enlarge their family have told researchers of their sense of disappointment that the child never really felt part of the family. These apply irrespective of the ethnic background of the children or the carers or parents, but for black families, the sense of achievement also results from bringing up young people who have a strong sense of pride in their appearance and culture, especially if the child came to them with a negative perception of his or her ethnic group and cultural heritage.

What do we know about what makes a difference?

To conclude this chapter we consider whether some characteristics of the children, their parents and carers, or the social work or placement processes are associated with more successful outcomes. Although there are some studies that consider longer-term or interim outcomes, few are sufficiently robust to unpick the impact of different characteristics of the child, the new family and the placement and helping process. Even fewer have attempted to do this specifically with respect to ethnic minority children. We summarise here the conclusions of the quantitative and qualitative research from the UK and overseas already referred to and only cite the main quantitative studies or those that have data on minority ethnic children.

Characteristics of the children

The variables that affect outcome are broadly the same for all ethnic groups. Most of the difference between more and less successful placements is explained by the characteristics of the children and their pre-placement experiences. Those placed when younger who remain with the same carers for as long as needed or until adulthood generally do better than those placed when older

(Barth and Berry 1988; Fratter *et al.* 1991; Lindblad *et al.* 2003; Rutter *et al.* 1997, 1999; Thoburn, Norford and Rashid 2000). Children who have suffered early privation or been maltreated or neglected, and those who had emotional or behavioural problems at the time of placement, tend to have less good outcomes than those who have not (Fratter *et al.* 1991; Hodges and Tizard 1989; Lindblad *et al.* 2003; Quinton *et al.* 1998; Rushton *et al.* 1995; Rutter *et al.* 1997, 1999; Thoburn, Norford and Rashid 2000). For older children and teenagers, violent or sexually inappropriate behaviour is particularly associated with poor outcomes (Farmer and Pollock 1998) Other ('softer') variables identified as associated with positive outcomes by some researchers are the willingness of the child to 'cut their losses' on the first family and join a new family (Fitzgerald 1990; Thoburn, Norford and Rashid 2000); or coming into care with all their siblings and not being 'singled out for rejection' (Rushton and Dance 2003). From interview studies it is clear that wanting to find a place in a new family is different from being willing to lose all links with the first family. Several studies give examples of children who were only willing to join a new family if they could go on having contact with members of their birth family (Thomas *et al.* 1999; Thoburn, Norford and Rashid 2000).

Turning to the characteristics of the foster carers or adopters, the small number of outcome studies that have looked at ethnicity of the carers as a variable have found no difference in rates of placement breakdown for those children placed with families of a similar ethnicity and culture and those placed transracially. (For the moment, this means placed with white families, as numbers placed transracially with ethnic minority families are too small to have been the subject of outcome research.) As with the short-term foster care studies, and studies from America (see Brooks and Barth 1999; Rushton and Minnis 1997; Triseliotis *et al.* 1997), when other variables such as age at placement are held constant, Thoburn, Norford and Rashid (2000) found no statistically significant difference between placement breakdown rates for UK children placed with white families and those with families of similar heritage to the child. However, when gender was introduced into the statistical model, Moffatt and Thoburn (2001) found that boys of minority ethnic origin placed with white families were less likely to experience placement breakdown than those placed with 'matched' families, but girls were less likely to have a placement that broke down when placed with families of similar ethnic heritage. A similar trend was noted by Sinclair, Wilson and Gibbs (2004) in their study of foster care outcomes. This finding may be sample specific but the authors note that most studies of adoption report gender differences on a range of outcome measures (see Howe's 1997b summary of research on outcomes for adopted children and Lindblad *et al.* 2003). There is a note of caution in the Lindblad *et al.* finding that a larger proportion of the young adults adopted (mainly transracially) from overseas by Swedish families had mental health problems than was the case for their peers. Whilst some of this difference will be explained by early adversity, the researchers comment that the experience of discrimination, especially in the sphere of employment, and of racial abuse were added areas of stress for the transracially adopted young people.

The qualitative research, using a wider range of outcome measures, adds complexity to this generally positive conclusion that parents with the appropriate attitudes, motivation and skills can successfully parent a child of a different ethnic background and culture to their own. Kirton *et al.* (2000) found a difference in their retrospective study between transracially adopted people and white adults adopted by white parents in terms of how they described their growing up experience. From their responses, the researchers classified 45 per cent of ethnic minority children as 'alienated' and only 21 per cent as 'integrated', the corresponding figures for white adopted people being 29 per cent and 48 per cent. From interviews, reasons identified were: being treated differently by members of the adoptive extended family and by neighbours.

Thoburn, Norford and Rashid (2000) found differences on some 'softer' measures of well-being between children placed transracially and those placed with families of the same race in respect of identity, strategies to combat racism, and pride in their appearance and heritage. They conclude, along with authors of smaller scale interview-based studies, that some white families can successfully parent children who are visibly different and have a different heritage from themselves, and can nurture in them a sense of pride in their race and heritage.

> I am very conscious and very interested in black culture. I am still learning today. My mum knows that. I'm more into my blackness than my white side – a lot of that is down to my mum... And I respect her for that. I don't find it a problem. I find being black a positive thing. I think I feel more black than white at the moment because of the friends I have got now and the area I am living in now. (Thoburn, Norford and Rashid 2000, p.141)

However, they have extra obstacles to surmount when compared to parents who are of the same ethnic origin.

> A big part of wanting to find [birth parents] was some kind of sanity and some sort of equilibrium about my sense of race. (Kirton *et al.* 2000, p.13)

> ...there are things I can't talk to her about because she doesn't have that understanding of it. I suppose what I'm saying, it's not just about having the colour, it's living it and you can live with it as my mum has done but it's different to living it. It's about living black. (Kirton *et al.* 2000, p.17)

The US literature, much of it based on inter-country adoption, provides more, and more detailed, studies on the question of 'racial' pride and identification.

Qualitative and mixed methods studies conclude that transracially placed children tend to do better if they can be placed near to home so that they do not have to lose their friends and change schools and places of worship and can more easily retain contact with their families. When new parents and the young people are interviewed, the majority speak well of the growing up experience and of strategies they have worked out to combat racism and develop a strong sense of pride in their appearance, culture and religion. However, most conclude with the majority of researchers who have explored this issue that family placement presents enough challenges as it is without adding the extra challenge of different ethnicity and culture.

> Love is great but it's not everything. It really isn't everything – because I had all the love I could possibly ask for but I'm not alright. (Kirton *et al.* 2000, p.17)

Ince (1998) gives voice to young care leavers who tell of their sense of alienation, and of racist attitudes or insensitivity on the part of white carers. For some, being placed with a white family led to the breakdown of their placement and to social, relationship and/or mental health problems for them as adults.

> When I was in Devon there were a lot of white people and me. How can they understand, when the white kids said 'Look a nigger'. They couldn't understand. They did nothing. (19-year-mixed heritage man in prison quoted by Ince 1998, p.76)

In other respects, the characteristics of carers associated with more successful outcomes are, unfortunately for practitioners and researchers, not easily measurable. The good news is that a very wide range of parents can be successful adopters. What seems to be important is that self-directed motives such as wanting to become a parent should be combined with an element of altruism. This shows up in the ability of the adoptive parents to empathise, not only with the child but also with his or her biography, and to develop an understanding of the problems in the birth family which led to the need for placement. As noted above there is some evidence that ethnic minority carers or adopters are more likely to have these characteristics, stemming as they do for many of them from a deep understanding of racism, disadvantage and discrimination.

Although sample size for many of the qualitative studies is too small for placement breakdown and other outcomes such as improved well-being to be analysed by ethnicity of children or carers, the detailed accounts provide messages about the parenting styles that appear to be associated with more or less successful placements. (See for example Beek and Schofield 2004; Howe 1997b; Lowe *et al.* 1999; Neil 2002b; Quinton *et al.* 1998; Rushton *et al.* 2001; Schofield 2002; Schofield *et al.* 2000; Sinclair *et al.* 2004; Thoburn, Norford and Rashid 2000). Berridge and Brodie (1998) and Sinclair and Gibbs (1999b) comment on associations between the cultures and working practices of children's homes and better outcomes for children. Sinclair and Gibbs concluded that better outcomes were associated with the head of home having a clear sense of autonomy and purpose and there being agreement amongst the staff about how the home should be run.

The third set of variables associated with different outcomes concerns the social work and legal processes before, during and after placement. This can be divided into decision making and 'helping' including support, education for parenting and therapy. The key decisions are whether and when to accommodate the child; whether the child can go safely home; what sort of placement to make and for how long; what the legal status should be; and matching the child with a particular residential establishment, foster carer or adoptive or long-term foster family.

Another key decision is about the sort of contact with birth family members that will be helpful. Both studies of the views of young people and those that provide data on long term outcomes conclude that most children benefit from being placed with siblings (Fratter *et al.* 1991; Rushton *et al.* 2001; Thoburn, Norford and Rashid 2000). Surveys and interview studies indicate that most children want contact with some, but not necessarily all, close relatives (Thomas *et al.* 1999; Timms and Thoburn 2003) but that it is very common for looked after or adopted young people not to see as much of their birth parents, close relatives and siblings placed elsewhere as they would like. Whilst most longitudinal studies conclude that post-placement birth family contact has either a neutral or a positive impact on placement stability (Fratter *et al.* 1991; Grotevant and McRoy 1998) recent studies have shown that, for children placed when past infancy, contact when badly managed can lead to avoidable distress and even contribute to disruption (Beek and Schofield 2004; Cleaver 2000; Sinclair, Wilson and Gibbs 2004; see also the debate on research findings on contact in Quinton *et al.* 1997; Quinton and Selwyn 1998; Ryburn 1997).

The help needed to maximise the chances of contact having a positive impact includes support to the birth parents, especially if there are new siblings at home (Beek and Schofield 2004; Neil 2003; Thomas *et al.* 1999). Contact with a parent (usually a father) they lost touch with before leaving home can be especially important for children of mixed race parentage so that they are in touch with both parts of their heritage. The efforts of social workers or new parents to help them to seek out 'lost parents', at the time most appropriate to them and not necessarily waiting till they are 18, is spoken of with warmth by young people interviewed as adults (Howe *et al.* 2000; Kirton *et al.* 2000; Masson, Harrison and Pavlovic 1997). As they get older, children want a greater say in the whether, how, when and with whom of contact. More recent studies are providing the sort of detailed information that can help social workers and carers reduce the stresses and maximise the benefits of birth family contact. The finding that children with two ethnic minority parents are more likely to have continuing post-placement contact is therefore encouraging. The impact of losing out on birth family contact on children of dual heritage, and on adoptees placed as infants without even indirect 'letter box' contact, are areas for further study.

Because the same themes run through all aspects of child welfare services, the characteristics of the social work practice and therapy that are most likely to be associated with better outcomes will be discussed in the next chapter. There is much detailed information in the placement studies already discussed, as well as the many practice texts that build on the research, about how the essential elements of effective practice can be taken into work with children, carers and birth parents when a child is looked after. They indicate that appropriate and appropriately timed therapy, and the advice of clinical and educational psychologists, can make a difference when adoptive and foster families are under stress. The importance of a dependable casework service provided by a worker they can trust, who is available when needed and helps them to put together packages of support for themselves and their children, is a theme that runs through many of the studies.

However, the conclusion to be drawn from a wide range of studies on successful and unsuccessful placements is that the most important aspect of the work of the family placement team lies in their family finding work. This involves recruiting, selecting and training enough of the right sort of carers from all ethnic backgrounds. It will then be possible at the crucial matching stage to find a family that meets all the child's identified needs, including the need to be brought up within the culture and religion of their birth. This greater choice will contribute to managing the tension between moving as quickly as possible to avoid the damaging impact of uncertainty and possible multiple placements, but not rushing into the wrong placement and exposing the child to the harm of either another placement breakdown or insensitive and unskilled substitute parenting.

In summary, the weight of evidence points to the conclusion that, in the generality of cases, neither the ethnicity of the child nor of the birth parents or new parents has an independent impact on outcomes. Although children from some ethnic groups are more likely than others to be in out of home placement, once placed, outcomes for children from the different minority ethnic groups are, on average, not different from those for white children who are in other respects similar. This is despite the additional problems they encounter that we have identified in earlier chapters, including racist abuse and harassment, discrimination at school, in the health services, in seeking employment and in the criminal justice system. This should not obscure what research has to tell us about the important minority who are significantly harmed by the initial failure to protect them from damaging early experiences before coming into care and then are failed by the care system. There is powerful evidence that in some cases there is a failure to provide the placements and services that will repair the damage. Inappropriate placements and practice compound earlier harm and leave some young people confused about their histories, culture and identity, with low self-esteem and, for some, long term mental health problems.

This brings us full circle. To understand more about why some children from minority ethnic groups do less well when placed out of the home we have to understand more about the environment and vulnerabilities of families in the different minority ethnic groups that led them to be in need of family support and protection services in the first place. Because parental mental health problems, substance misuse and domestic violence now occur so frequently in the biographies of children in short- and long-term care, studies that focus on ethnic minority families' experiences of these difficulties could prove helpful in understanding how best to help their children in and out of placement.

Chapter 6

Messages from Research on the Social Care Services to Parents and Children of Minority Ethnic Origin

[Family centre worker helped] a tremendous amount because she under-
stands where I'm coming from…the fact that she's black gives me a little bit
more of a secure feeling that she is going to put our interests at the forefront
and listen to what I have to say. (Butt and Box 1998, p.89)

Much of the research focusing on child welfare services to minority ethnic
families referred to in earlier sections provides descriptions of practice and
draws conclusions about how it might be improved. However, there is very
little research that considers in detail the effectiveness for ethnic minority
children and parents of different social work and social care approaches nor on
their views on the quality, acceptability and helpfulness of the workers or the
methods and approaches used. This chapter synthesises parental views from a
number of studies, as well as highlighting some key issues emerging from the
research for professionals and service planners.

Five fairly recent research or evaluation reports have looked more broadly
at social work and social care services for children and families of minority
ethnic origin. The research by Barn et al. (1997), referred to in earlier chapters,
included interviews with social workers and managers. They concluded that
most staff were aware of the complexities of working with families from a different ethnic group from that in which they themselves had grown up. The
second was undertaken by O'Neale (2000) and Social Services Inspectorate
(SSI) colleagues. This report drew on evidence from inspection reports on
services to ethnic minority children and families in eight local authorities in
England in 1998–9. It provides information on services for families whose
children were looked after as well as those who were considered to be in need
of formal protective services. The study concluded that seven out of the eight
authorities had little clarity on policies relevant to race equality. In these

authorities, the response to who was driving the agenda for race equality was 'no one' or 'don't know'. Staff from minority ethnic groups were appropriately represented in residential and field-work posts, especially in inner-city authorities, but there was a significant under-representation in managerial positions. Six out of eight authorities had poor consultative mechanisms with minority ethnic groups, and few departments had strategies for enabling ethnic minority groups to become service providers. Some departments saw training on issues around race, culture and religion as no longer necessary, whilst others had structured mandatory courses for all workers.

Richards and Ince (2000) found that all the authorities included in their survey had translated the relevant leaflets and guidance about services but failed to distribute them effectively. Qureshi *et al.* (2000) interviewed managers and social workers about their perceptions of services for South Asian communities in Luton. Despite the high percentage of South Asian people in the area, most managers felt that services and policies catered primarily for white residents. Concern was also expressed over the under-representation of minority ethnic social workers in the workforce. Candappa (2004) provides a detailed process analysis of four demonstration projects (associated with the Quality Protects programme) to improve services for children and families in different ethnic communities.

The nature and quality of the social work and other services provided

Many thousands of words have been written about the essential elements of effective social work practice. Much of this research focuses on a particular method, and concludes that certain methods are more effective for some parents or children in some circumstances. However, the studies referred to in earlier sections emphasise that the complexity of the difficulties facing many ethnic minority families will require the provision of a co-ordinated network of services and a range of social work and therapy approaches and methods. For example, Sellick *et al.* (2004), when discussing the social work and other services provided to adoptive and foster families, point out that there are many different interventions by professionals between the placement of a young child and a more or less successful outcome for him or her as a young adult. It is impossible to say what contribution to success was made by a particular method of recruiting the adopters, or the provision of therapy to the child at the age of 15 because of behavioural problems. There is some evidence that some methods or techniques can lead to behavioural change in the short term. For example, there are promising reports that parent training groups, or home visiting services, can help parents to feel more confident in handling difficult behaviour of their children (Barlow *et al.* 2003; Frost *et al.* 2000). However, the outcome studies rarely refer specifically to how members of different ethnic groups respond to these initiatives.

The overarching conclusion from social work research is that, irrespective of the broad approach or specific methods used, it is the relationship between the family members and the worker, and the personal and professional qualities of the worker, that make the major contribution to outcome. The particular characteristics associated in many studies with a positive outcome are accurate empathy, warmth and genuineness. These are demonstrated when the worker is reliable, a good listener, honest, gives accurate and full information about services available and agency processes (particularly important when the formal child protection process is involved or a child is looked after), and puts him or herself out to be available at times of stress. As an example, many adoptive families mention how important it is to be given the phone number of their link worker so that they can contact him or her out of office hours (and how rarely they use it). Families also value a worker who is knowledgeable about the specific concerns that brought them into contact, whether this results from a disability, problem behaviours or the need for help in claiming benefits. When particular skills or techniques are used, they appreciate those skills, but only in the context of an empathic and reliable relationship. There is much evidence from the qualitative studies reported here that these characteristics are what all ethnic groups are looking for in their workers.

However, there are additional challenges for agencies and workers when providing services to members of minority communities to ensure that their services are perceived as relevant and therefore used by those who need them. Black and Asian workers interviewed for O'Neale (2000) emphasised sensitivity; open-mindedness; demonstrating respect; acknowledging that you don't always have a clear understanding or an answer; seeking advice from independent workers from the same community or faith group who speak the first language of the family; not appearing arrogant or superior and being open and honest. Cultural sensitivity, including an awareness of the impact of racism and racial abuse and of ways of challenging it at the institutional and individual level, was seen by those interviewed as an essential prerequisite for working with minority ethnic groups. The term 'cultural competence' is often used in the US literature (Vonk 2001) especially in the context of white workers and carers to describe the necessary values and skills for those working with or caring for children and parents of a different heritage from their own. Richards and Ince (2000) give examples of how this can be achieved and particularly stress the importance of training.

Family members and their satisfaction with services

Survey data from the parent-completed questionnaires in the O'Neale (2000) research indicated that parents more often than not rated the service positively in terms of ease of contacting staff, being kept informed and finding the service helpful. Around 70 per cent of the service users returning completed question-naires 'generally agreed' or 'strongly agreed' with a set of positive statements about the service they received. This is a slightly lower rate than that for general populations of parents allocated to a social worker's caseload in two other studies (Thoburn, Wilding and Watson 2000 and Tunstill and Aldgate 2000). The highest rating (83% of responses were positive) was on being fairly treated and treated with respect by social services staff. The lowest ratings (in the low 60s) were on receiving all the services that were needed and receiving them at the time they were needed. This supports conclusions from other studies that ethnic minority parents, in common with all service users, are more likely to be *un*satisfied than *dis*satisfied. Thoburn, Wilding and Watson (2000) sought examples from parents and in the records of good or poor practice. Forty-six per cent were considered to have had a generally good service whilst 39 per cent received a poor or inappropriate service. There was a trend, which did not reach statistical significance, for more of the white than the ethnic minority families to be rated as receiving a generally good service (68% compared with 48%). This was explained by more of the white families receiving a longer-term service because of their long-term problems. There was a tendency for the cases of the minority ethnic families to be closed once immediate problems had been 'patched up'. Those who were allocated to a social worker's longer-term caseload were as likely as the white families to get a good service and to find it helpful. However, since they were less likely to receive this sort of service, many were 'unsatisfied' because important needs remained unmet. The researchers also found that more of the services to ethnic minority families appeared inap-propriate to their needs.

Several of the researchers cited in earlier sections have reported that families responded positively to practical support including day-care, transport to school, and grants for clothes as well as to the provision of emotional support and a planned social casework service. Parents interviewed valued a longer-term service provided by a worker they could trust that combined the provision of a person-centred service with practical help. This message came most strongly from parents whose child had a disability, but was echoed by parents involved in the formal child protection system and by adoptive parents.

> With my social worker I could bounce ideas off – both negative and positive. I did not have to know it all. I did not have to get it right. I could say to her, 'I feel awful', but I wasn't getting anywhere and she wouldn't take this as the end of anything. (Black single-parent adopter talking about white social worker quoted by Thoburn, Norford and Rashid 2000, p.164).

It comes as a very powerful message from children looked after that they bitterly resent frequent changes of social worker. The person carrying this key worker role will sometimes be a family support worker (as indicated by Gray

2002a,b) or a volunteer or advocate, who can act as a 'bridge' to the professional helping network. When parents who attended family centres were asked by researchers in the Butt and Box (1998) study what was particularly good about their family centre, the responses related to the welcoming atmosphere, the ethos of the centre that promoted service user participation and the specific services that the centre offered, for example an Asian Women's Group.

O'Neale (2000) concluded that ethnically sensitive and culturally competent services generally rested on the good assessments of individual workers. Where workers were knowledgeable and tenacious they were able to achieve more positive results for families. However the lack of specific support systems for ethnic minority children and their families made it difficult for workers to access the most appropriate packages of care. The report concluded that in areas where a particular ethnic group was under-represented, the service quality to that particular group tended to be less adequate. (See also Derbyshire 1994.) This conclusion is supported by the statistics that point to the over-representation amongst looked after populations when a particular ethnic group is represented in very small numbers in that community. However, accounts are beginning to appear which focus on practice with people of minority ethnic origin living in more rural areas or in urban areas where there is a low proportion of minority ethnic families in the community (Devon County Council 20003; Radford 2004; Scourfield *et al.* 2002).

O'Neale (2000) found that assessments were often partial. In terms of the Assessment Framework (DH 2000) the three domains (children's needs, parenting capacity, and environment) were often considered by social workers, but rarely put together holistically, to look at the needs of minority ethnic families. Many of the case files scrutinised provided little indication that issues of race and culture had been taken into account in the social work assessment. The study also found that some children had complained of racial and verbal abuse, yet in only 3 per cent of cases had racial harassment been identified as an issue in the assessment recorded on file.

Generally, the findings from the study indicated that ethnic minority family members did not feel included in the planning of services and that consultation was often poor. Similarly, ethnic monitoring was problematic in that managers and other staff members lacked understanding of the reasons for monitoring the ethnic group of service users and staff members. The reasons given for poor quality monitoring were varied, but one explanation given was that some staff felt awkward about asking questions concerning ethnicity. Also problematic was how some staff categorised a family's ethnicity: for example, children of mixed heritage were often defined as 'other' or 'unclassified'.

Like O'Neale, Barn *et al.* (1997) found that lack of resources was a significant factor that had a direct impact on the specific needs and concerns of black children and their families. They found that in the face of financial cutbacks, specific resources directed towards black families were the first to disappear.

Owen and Farmer (1996) found from their study of 'heavier end' cases that, when specialised support or therapy services were required for minority ethnic families, there were usually delays in assessment and the provision of treatment. There was also a shortage of Asian and African-Caribbean residential workers and foster carers. In common with other researchers, these authors comment on the shortage of Asian psychologists and psychiatrists. Another feature of cases involving minority ethnic children concerned the uncertainty experienced by families and agencies. For example, only 7 per cent of investigations were deemed inconclusive in the main sample, compared to 50 per cent in the sample involving minority ethnic families. As a consequence, the researchers noted that there were ambiguities in the assessment of risk, and the interventions tended to be vague. This may help to explain the Hunt and Macleod (1999) finding that cases involving ethnic minority children tended to move more quickly into the court arena. In the workshop discussing these findings it was suggested that one explanation might be that time limits allowed for assessments were too short for the complex issues in the cases of many minority ethnic children to be fully considered.

Cultural issues and matching the social worker to the family

> My daughter did have a black social worker from the local authority. She was very nice and I was able to talk to her about race and cultural issues. This worker did not come specifically to talk to her about black issues. It was just that she was young, black and trendy and Martine was able to relate to her. (White adopter of African-Caribbean young woman quoted in Thoburn, Norford and Rashid 2000, p.168)

Prevatt Goldstein (2002, p.771) found that the black social care workers she interviewed 'overwhelmingly wanted to contribute to equal opportunities for black service users'. However she also points to the 'Catch 22' situation when a policy of allocating social workers to clients on the basis of 'race' 'essentializes black and white service users and black and white workers by focusing on racialized experiences and needs only' (p.772). O'Neale (2000) reported that some parents found difficulty accessing services because of a lack of understanding of the role of social services departments and Richards and Ince (2000) found similarly in respect of grandparents caring for their grandchildren. Those responding to the O'Neale survey gave a mixed response when asked how satisfied they had been with the services provided. Dissatisfaction tended to arise because detailed concerns that could have been quickly resolved were not picked up and their importance to the families understood. Two concerns identified were the unavailability of halal meat for children who were living independently, and the failure of social services to recognise the religious needs of minority ethnic children who were looked after.

A number of key themes emerged from the Gray (2002a,b) study, pointing to possible explanations for the high level of satisfaction found in that study. One of these was that most of the workers involved in these home-based family support services were from the same community and were usually women. The researcher reported that the advantage for these workers was that they often had an inside knowledge of some of the difficulties experienced by the families. Gray concludes that cultural sensitivity, a shared language, and listening skills are the foundations of a multi-racial service in a multi-racial urban area. The potential for workers over-identifying with the families was countered through regular supervision and debriefing sessions with managers. The ethnicity of the family support workers also helped to inform child protection interventions that were appropriately sensitive to the cultural practices and religious beliefs of the families, and engendered a feeling of shared community involvement. Gray notes that families in the area receiving social work services were more wary of accepting this help since social workers usually became involved because there was an allegation of child maltreatment. They concluded that too many professionals were involved for too long a period of time without adequate explanation of their roles. However, an important role for family support workers was to interpret the issues for the families to the other professionals alongside providing an explanation to families of the formal child protection processes. As a result, most family support workers were still viewed in a positive light by families subject to child protection enquiries.

Thoburn, Wilding and Watson (2000) found that a high proportion of social workers and team managers were South Asian or African-Caribbean and several were actively involved in community groups. They hypothesise that a greater willingness of black and Asian workers and managers to seek to understand the reasons underlying certain patterns of parenting (especially around issues of child supervision and autonomy) may have been part of the explanation for the higher likelihood that ethnic minority referrals would be provided with services via the family support rather than the child protection route. Having more black and Asian social workers and reception staff may also be relevant to the willingness of families to refer and re-refer themselves for services. Many parents interviewed by researchers have spoken of their appreciation of having a social worker who understood the cultural issues that might be important to them. The black adopters and foster parents interviewed by Thoburn, Norford and Rashid (2000) were particularly thoughtful about this issue.

> Talking to her, I felt free to say just how I felt about it. But if I was dealing with a white worker, I would probably be wondering 'Now how do I put this so it doesn't seem as if I'm trying to make trouble, but they do understand what I'm

saying'. It's not essential [to have a black worker] but it's necessary that it should be available. I think that's the right way of putting it. (p.167)

In the Thoburn, Wilding and Watson (2000) study, the agencies' information leaflets were all provided in appropriate languages, a relevant factor since in one authority over half of the parents interviewed did not have English as a first language. Owen and Farmer (1996) also noted a more community development based approach to addressing child protection concerns in some cases.

The high proportion of black and Asian social workers in some teams taking part in research studies is in contrast to the position reported by Qureshi et al. (2000). They found that most of the referrals were due to child protection matters with few families seeking help voluntarily, another contrast with some of the other studies. The social workers interviewed, all of whom had worked with South Asian families in the previous 12 months, told researchers that they lacked confidence in working with families from different cultures. They wanted to undertake culturally sensitive work but felt impeded by a lack of knowledge and skills. The minority of South Asian people in this study who had had direct contact with social workers considered that social service departments were failing them. Focus group participants who had visited social services offices reported that it was very frustrating trying to see a social worker, particularly if their first language was not English. Those who had been in contact with social workers reported that they had made an effort to respond appropriately to language and cultural differences. However, reception staff were viewed less positively and were more likely to display discouraging or negative attitudes.

Also addressing this question of the role of black staff, O'Neale reported that in some authorities a 'colour-blind' approach was adopted where workers recruited from minority communities were required to carry out the same duties as other staff. In other authorities, black workers were seen to have special skills, for example concerning language, which could be used to benefit service users. However, other researchers have concluded that the question is more complex and that families should be involved in a discussion about whether they would want their worker to be from the same ethnic group. African-Caribbean and Asian social workers interviewed for the Thoburn et al. (1995) study, who worked in an area where a majority of the families were of South Asian heritage, played a major part in ensuring that the whole team was sensitive to cultural issues. The Asian workers did not wish to work only with Asian families but took on a consultancy role with their white and African-Caribbean colleagues. In this study on family involvement in child protection work, 78 per cent of parents were involved in the child protection process if the main social worker was black or Asian, compared to 41 per cent if the social worker was white. Prevatt Goldstein (2002, p.772) reminds readers of her study that service users can lose out because of 'attempts to reverse the racist undervaluing of the competence of black workers by assuming all black workers automatically have the skills and empathy to work with any black service user'. This young man of African-Caribbean heritage, whose social worker was of a similar ethnic background, gave this response when asked if he had any advice for social workers:

> Being a social worker is a treacherous job. You either have it or you don't. There's no tips I can give. Social workers need to be able to read between the lines and observe young people, because they may not tell them everything. You can't teach this sort of thing. Social workers either have it or they don't. My social worker didn't. Or if she did, she couldn't care a damn. (Thoburn, Norford and Rashid 2000, p.164).

Barn *et al.* (1997) noted that black workers and managers often differed from white workers in their perceptions of the same problem. However, there was not a unified view. Some were concerned that Eurocentric child protection procedures meant that ethnicity was not adequately taken into account, resulting in discriminatory services for black families, but others considered that white workers were too ready to condone abusive behaviour as culturally approved.

Brandon *et al.* (1999) noted different approaches to services for different ethnic groups, and cited a project in one local authority where support workers from the same ethnic groups were allocated to families. However, these parents tended to be less positive than those interviewed in the Gray (2002a, b) study. This was because a key role given to these workers was to report incidents of abuse or neglect and this was experienced by some families as being 'spied upon'. Accounts of workers' actions as part of child protection work, including perceived breaches of confidentiality, would often be passed on within the community, causing potential for division and resentment, and deterring others from seeking help. The local support workers were sometimes seen as 'coming between' the parent and the social worker.

> My social worker is very good but I cannot talk to her myself. It always has to be through the family worker and I am not sure what they say or whether the social worker knows what I am asking for. (Brandon *et al.* 1999, p.114)

The researchers concluded that what workers need when providing services to families of a different ethnic or faith group from their own is '…not so much the need for a set of guidelines about race or ethnicity for workers to follow, but a leap of imagination and extra sensitivity to be made in order to empathise with families' (Brandon *et al.* 1999, p.155).

In looking at the area of domestic violence, Mullender *et al.* (2002) concluded that service responses were often inadequate and inappropriate. Asian women in particular were often not aware of the support available to them, or they distrusted it. Professionals in the field were found to have little understanding of mental health issues and less appreciation of the complex interactions between culture, gender and self-harm. Many managers within the statutory services highlighted the practice of 'ethnic matching' and relied on the expertise of ethnic minority clinical and social work staff as the key to providing culturally appropriate services. The authors argue, however, that the need for appropriate and accessible support goes beyond shared language and culture. These researchers report conflicting opinions as to whether vulnerable young Asian women would positively choose to receive their care from someone else from the same community background or not, owing to the fear of potential breaches of confidentiality. Even when social workers were 'matched', empathy and understanding could not be taken for granted. In some instances, women were found to be criticised more by members of their own communities. Owen and Farmer (1996) concluded from their discussions with parents and the use of standardised scales to measure interim outcomes that the best outcomes for the black and minority ethnic children were when the worker and main caretaking parent were matched across gender, race and culture. Out of the four cases where such matching occurred, three were progressing well; but in the six remaining cases there was only one which was satisfactory.

In their study of 'heavier end' cases that went to court, Brophy *et al.* (2003a, 2003b) found that fewer than half of the sample of consultants (mainly psychiatrists) had received training in assessing children and parents from minority ethnic backgrounds. Some psychiatrists had undertaken to inform themselves about working within different cultures, whilst others were uneasy about assessing children and or parents from minority ethnic groups. Yet others felt their knowledge and skills were transferable across cultural boundaries. The researchers noted that paediatric reports were least likely to pay attention to issues of diversity and that this information was better in child and family centre assessments and reports from child and adolescent psychiatrists. Several studies give examples of cases where minority ethnic parents were unaware that a particular parenting practice would be of concern to professionals. (These were most often 'home alone' or 'excessive chastisement' cases and often concerned families recently arrived in the UK.) Qureshi *et al.* (2000) cite social worker and health visitor concern about young children sharing their parents' bed, though the parents considered this to be good parenting practice. Communication problems around a lack of familiarity with welfare and protection services were sometimes compounded by language difficulties. Brophy *et al.* (2003a, b) cite a case involving a Nigerian teenager considered by professionals to be beyond the control of her mother. In her statements to court, the mother detailed her fears about her immigration status and how she felt undermined by the social worker. From the records scrutinised by the researchers it appeared that her request for a black social worker had been refused, leaving her with a sense that her opinions were worthless and ignored. This could also be a problem for British-born African-Caribbean parents, but there were more examples in the research studies of the request for a black social worker made by African-Caribbean parents having been acted on.

Finally, leading on to the section on interpreters, several researchers reported concerns from social workers and parents about the problems that can arise over miscommunications and misunderstandings when worker and client have been brought up in very different cultures. Brandon *et al.* (1999) noted in one case that '…it was extremely difficult for the social worker to explain why social services were involved, and it took time and patience to establish with both parents the basis for intervention. Had this been possible earlier, recourse to the courts might have been avoided, or better understood' (p.112). One African refugee couple in the study spoke about the importance of telling newcomers about the law in respect of the supervision children require at different ages, acceptable methods of discipline and allocation of responsibilities to children. These researchers noted that in some cases matching of social worker to the family on the basis of ethnic origin could be unhelpful, as when an African-Caribbean social worker was allocated to an African asylum-seeking family when a French-speaking worker with some knowledge of African cultures would have been better able to understand the very complex dynamics of the traumatised parents and children. In this case an (appropriate and timely) request for a very troubled child to be accommodated was not picked up and the child was subsequently seriously physically assaulted and placed in long-term care.

Research on the use of interpreters

O'Neale (2000) found that in some areas visited by the SSI teams the reception areas were not equipped to be able to engage families whose first language was not English. In contrast, there were area teams where staff at all levels were proficient in more than one of the languages in common use in the communities they served. In terms of translation and interpretation generally, all the authorities had systems in place for the use of interpreters which operated in different ways, and with varying degrees of success. From their interviews with parents they concluded that language was often a barrier for ethnic minority families. For example, service users in two local authorities believed that their inability to speak English was a barrier to the receipt of services: 'if you can't speak English they won't deal with you properly – it's degrading', was the comment by one service user (p.15).

Richards and Ince (2000) found that only 42 per cent of the departments responding to their survey who regularly used interpreters provided them with specific training about child welfare work; only 69 per cent 'vetted' the interpreters and only 29 per cent involved family members in the choice of interpreter.

> I speak very little English but I could see that my interpreter was struggling to understand and even made some of it up (p.27)

Qureshi *et al.* (2000) also reported concerns amongst members of the Asian community participating in focus groups about the role of interpreting services. Some considered that such services were less likely to be available for certain minority groups. There was also some confusion about the interpreter's role, with some participants not clear whether this was confined to interpreting or whether they were also advocates. Confidentiality was also raised as an issue.

Brophy *et al.* (2003a) highlighted many areas within reports and court processes relevant to language and interpretation services. There was evidence that the failure of agencies to recognise and address the cultural and language issues resulted in some cases deteriorating to the extent that care proceedings became necessary when earlier family support services could have prevented the need for them.

Humphreys *et al.* (1999) reported that 12 out of 20 South Asian families required an interpreter. Although there was a 100 per cent attendance of interpreters when needed at child protection conferences, this became more sporadic the more informal the meeting. It appeared that the interpreting service put less value on work outside formal conference meetings. The lack of an interpreter when one was needed led to the non-English-speaking partner being unable to take part and some professionals assumed that this was because of a lack of commitment to, or co-operation with, the protection process. In some cases, too little time was allowed for meetings at which interpreters were needed, resulting either in interpreters having to leave before the end of the conference or the proceedings being rushed to keep within the allotted time. Because home visits by social workers did not routinely include interpreters, at times the English-speaking husband or a child was pushed into, or allowed to take on, the role of 'gatekeeper' to information both to and from the mother. It also presented problems for South Asian women (especially if sexual behaviour was being considered) that most of the interpreters were men (19 out of 21 in this study). The researchers noted that few social workers or conference chairs had training in the use of interpreters, a structural issue which the researchers felt discriminated against many Asian families. This generally poor service in respect of interpreters, alongside other service inadequacies, contributed to their conclusion (Humphreys *et al.* 1999, p.289) that 'while white children may often be experiencing a second class service, the service extended to Asian children can only be rated as third class when, for a range of reasons, attention is not given to meeting their identity needs'.

In this and other studies where meetings involving interpreters have been observed by researchers who speak the language of the interpreter and client there were occasions when either mistranslations occurred or, more commonly, an interpreter failed to translate something important said by a parent. Brandon *et al.* (1999) found that the provision of interpreters was patchy and that issues of confidentiality and cultural acceptability were often not addressed. Some parents stressed that it was essential that care was taken to ensure that the interpreter was from outside the family's network. At times, interpreters were observed to take on the role of advocates or advisers. The observers also found that the meaning and context of child protection procedures were not always conveyed to the family and that the interpreter sometimes spoke on behalf of a parent, or told a parent that something they had said would not be translated because it may count against them. Families have also reported being told by interpreters that, since they were in the wrong, having abused their child, they should remain silent. The researchers concluded that 'when all the members of the conference are dependent on one interpreter, error and misunderstanding may occur' (p.114).

Owen and Farmer (1996) also reported concerns raised by social workers and parents they interviewed around the use of interpreters. Lack of availability of interpreters was noted, particularly to make a home visit with a social worker when there was an emergency child protection investigation. Professionals reported that they could never be sure that complex meanings (especially in the area of sexual abuse and about child protection processes) were being accurately and sensitively conveyed. It was also noted that parents under threat often sought an alliance with the people who could communicate with them easily, which may mean that they need an advocate or friend as well as an interpreter.

In summing up their conclusions on interpreters Brophy *et al.* (2003b, pp.138–139) comment: 'there were numerous documented instances of failures to use interpreters at crucial points in interviews with parents both prior to, and after the instigation of court proceedings. For example when children were removed from parents under emergency measures, where there was likely to be a conflict of interests between parents, mothers were not interviewed separately. There were also reported instances of interpreters arriving late and not matched for language or dialect, and indications of the use of family members rather than professionals.' The researchers conclude that these and related findings '…raise some serious questions about access to justice for parents whose first language is not English'.

Chapter 7

Next Steps in Researching Child Welfare Services for Minority Ethnic Children, Parents and Carers

This book is already a summary and synthesis of research so no attempt will be made in this final chapter at further summary. What we shall do is to draw out from the overview of what we know, what we half know and where we know nothing, some pointers for future research agendas at the national and local levels. This concluding chapter is also informed by comments from the two national seminars for practitioners and policy makers at which our emerging conclusions were aired, as well as the emails that came in afterwards. Much of the discussion has centred around the rather ugly shorthand terms 'aggregation' and 'disaggregation' when identifying appropriate samples to answer the research questions being explored. Our conclusion is that the decisions about whether to research, and to analyse data, in terms of whole populations of people of minority ethnic origin or of smaller groups who share many aspects of culture and patterns of family life, have been too often taken for reasons unconnected with the aims of the particular research study. Some researchers have tended to combine disparate groups in order to have large enough numbers for robust quantitative analysis and have compared 'white' with 'black', ignoring the many different ethnic and cultural groups within these two. The result, as we have seen, is that diversity has been lost and practitioners and planners have been able to take little of value from these studies to help them to plan services. Other researchers and commissioners of research have tended, for reasons explored in Beverley Prevatt Goldstein's introductory chapter, to keep to the 'black' and 'white' groupings. For a study of the impact of racism and discrimination this has been an appropriate research strategy. Being 'white' in a society where white people have for centuries set the rules and held the power makes for a different experience from being 'black' and immediately recognisable as different from the majority population and therefore easy targets for discrimination and racism. One of the gaps we have identified is that there is very little research that specifically aims to explore the extent, nature and impact of discrimination, racism, and racist abuse and harassment in the child welfare services. There are accounts and some powerful statements recorded by researchers from those who have been on the receiving end of racism and discrimination, but this is usually as one aspect of qualitative studies whose main focus is something other than an exploration of racism. In this sense, child welfare research lags behind research in the fields of employment, health, education, housing and criminal justice.

But an overarching question posed by our research, which is beginning to be answered by a new generation of researchers, is which groups should be combined in research samples in order to provide information that will be helpful to those devising policies and providing services. This applies whether the subject under investigation is the impact of racism or discrimination, or a more detailed child welfare issue such as how to provide a more appropriate and acceptable parenting support, short-term break or adoption service. To seek an answer to some questions it may be appropriate for a local authority to commission research on asylum seekers in their area to include white Europeans and black and Asian asylum seekers. It may be appropriate, in a study of interpreting services, to include all those, across ethnic groups, who have to rely on interpreters. Or, to answer a particular question, it may be appropriate to select a research sample comprising small groups with very distinct needs, such as West African young asylum seekers, or teenagers 'trafficked' from Eastern Europe to be abused through prostitution.

In short, just as there is no 'gold standard' in terms of research methods, with the choice between a quantitative, qualitative or mixed-methods approach based on the specific aims of the study, so also must the decision about the ethnic composition of research samples depend on the questions the research sets out to answer. The reasons for selecting general populations or focusing on particular groups need to be more clearly spelled out by the researchers than has been the case in many of the studies we have included in this review. Similarly, researchers and research funders need to take decisions as to whether a particular research aim will be best achieved by a national, regional or local study. Our overall conclusion is that, although there is an important place for research on the national and even international level, more children and families will gain more from well-conducted local studies that focus on how to meet the particular needs of those living in particular areas. But alongside this must go a national programme of collation and co-ordination of these studies. In the way that the Joseph Rowntree foundation has co-ordinated a research programme on ethnic minority families living with disability, there is a need for a national body to take on the role of 'clearing house' for the small-scale local research studies on ethnicity and child welfare. This could perhaps be through the extension and more formal recognition of the information and library service already provided by the Race Equality Unit. We have been made aware that these studies exist, and have even played a very modest 'clearing house' function by putting local researchers in touch with each other in the later stages of the project. The opportunities now available for putting these studies on the web provides a mechanism for in-house and 'independent' researchers, community and service user groups to share methodologies and compare and pool findings.

Within this framework of general conclusions, we pick out some of the areas for future research, using the chapter headings of family support, the formal child protection services and child placement. We end with suggestions about research that focuses on the continuities and discontinuities as particular groups of minority ethnic children and parents 'journey' through the child welfare services from family support through care to reunification, adoption or independent living. This is not intended to be an exhaustive list. Some readers will agree with what we have picked out and others will have come to other conclusions.

Family support

It is in the area of family support services to parents, children and carers of minority ethnic origin that most benefit will be gained from research commissioned and carried out at local level, in partnership with local communities. These may be defined by 'geography' – all those living in a particularly run-down area and exposed to high levels of crime or racist abuse; by ethnic group; by religious faith; or they may be 'communities of interest' such as parents of children with life-threatening or life-limiting illnesses.

A research agenda, at national and local level, could start with what we have learned about the differential use made of family support services by the different ethnic groups. The 'under-represented' and the 'over-represented' groups need different research agendas. The barriers stopping families who need child welfare services seeking them out should be examined, as well the deficits in services that lead to their either being unsatisfied (offered no service or no service that they find helpful in meeting their needs) or dissatisfied with the services provided. The impact of racism and discrimination should be explored, both as contributors to family stress and the widespread depression that researchers have identified amongst parents needing family support services. An essential prerequisite for such research is a sensitive but comprehensive system for agencies to be sure that they have an accurate picture of the diversity of the settled and more transient populations in their areas. Without accurate and detailed record-keeping (with proper safeguards on confidentiality and systems for ensuring that service users know what is being recorded) agencies cannot know whether there is a 'match' or otherwise between those using family support services, those providing the services, and the ethnic and faith group composition of the area.

In terms of specific ethnic and needs groups, there is research that can be built on that focuses on the needs and attitudes to service use of South Asian families. There is the potential to learn from the research already completed to design national and local studies on the support needs of these and of other under-represented groups. For example, like South Asian children, Chinese, Vietnamese and other East Asian families are greatly under-represented amongst those who use family support services. The approach of researchers and practitioners working with local groups to identify barriers to seeking help, and to continuing to make use of it, provides ideas for new studies to build on. How to encourage self-referral and avoid the additional problems caused by waiting until coercion through the formal child protection or courts systems becomes necessary could be one focus of these studies. Along with this goes a study of effective methods of communication about the services available, and the circumstances in which family members might find them helpful. There is a synergy here between research and practice in that partnership-based models of research, and the opportunity for community and service user groups to initiate and play a fuller part in research, should lead to services being more appropriate and therefore more effective.

Looking at areas of need, research on children and parents with disabilities and on the impact of domestic violence and substance abuse is beginning to appear. The growing body of research on ethnicity and adult mental health services needs to be taken into the area of the impact of parental mental ill-health on children, and how this, and the services needed, might differ with different ethnic groups. Similarly, we came across very little research on how parents in different ethnic groups who have learning disabilities parent their children and the sort of help they need. There is some research into these issues from the perspective of 'young carers' but this may (or may not) be the best way of providing services to these families. There is some information that some parents retreat from a service approach (and possibly a research approach) that labels their children as 'young carers'. Turning to the children, there is room for more research on disturbed, disturbing and challenging behaviour, sometimes identified by parents when the child is very young and brought to the attention of the child welfare services. The qualitative research provides accounts from parents of all ethnic groups of their unsuccessful attempts to get help, only to find themselves blamed at a later stage as their children are labelled as 'antiso-cial', 'disruptive', 'uneducable' or 'criminal'. Though greatly over-represented in care, young black boys are even more likely to be over-represented amongst those experiencing a custodial sentence.

Given the continuing over-representation of African-Caribbean children, and those with one white parent and one African-Caribbean parent, amongst those who spend long periods in out-of-home care, it was striking that we iden-tified very little family support research focusing specifically on these groups. The other group, and the hardest to research, is the very diverse group of children of mixed heritage whose parents are of different minority ethnic origin and are often isolated from family members and others of the same culture and heritage (Wilson (1987), Prevatt Goldstein (1999) and Tizard and Phoenix (2002) point to issues needing further study). The issue with these two groups is not so much to encourage self-referral, since it appears that those who need help are likely to seek it out or to be referred by teachers or health visitors. Although encouraging self-referral is important, the challenge appears to be to make sure that appropriate services are available when families do seek help. Research that tracks those who were refused a service or received only a very short-term service might be helpful to practitioners and policy-makers.

There are indications that two services that African-Caribbean parents and children have found helpful are now less available than they were. The first of these is the provision of open access neighbourhood family centres. Sure Start developments, Children's Centres and 'extended schools' may, or may not, provide equally acceptable and effective services. There is evidence that short periods of accommodation for young children or teenagers at times of stress (particularly valued by single parents) are less available than they were, and it is not clear that they have been replaced by equally helpful and valued home-based family support services. A national study focusing on African-Caribbean families who requested an accommodation or short-term break service because of family stress or relationship problems might lead to some important revelations on how to cut down on the over-representation of African-Caribbean children in long-term care. A similar study of white single parents of mixed heritage children could provide some important information. The move towards closer working between schools and social services should bring opportunities for research on those excluded from school and on ways of preventing racist bullying, as well as helping parents and children for whom this adds to the stresses that make them more vulnerable.

There is little research on the way in which African families view and make use of family support services and there is a need for both local and national studies, taking on board the many important differences within the broad grouping of 'African'. Africans Unite Against Child Abuse (AFRUCA) 2002 are leading the way in the field of child abuse research.

Within vulnerable groups across the ethnic groups, there is scope for focusing on children of minority ethnicity abused through prostitution, possibly linked with research on young runaways.

The child protection services

There is now some research comparing the different ways in which families from different ethnic groups get drawn into the formal child protection and court systems, but very little on specific child and family welfare outcomes. The major focus now should be on working with community and faith groups to design research that focuses specifically on particular communities and cultures, exploring the issues around supervision, household and family responsibilities, discipline and control as they are understood in different cultural and faith groups. New research on family support should include explorations of how families from different ethnic groups and cultures slip into situations when the formal child protection processes have to be used. Because of the smaller numbers, these studies are likely to be nationally commissioned. Cohorts should be identified, for example, of Indian or Chinese children at a particular threshold, such as the child's name being placed on the register or the making of a Care Order. The researchers could then, through interviews with family members and workers, look back in order to understand whether opportunities had been missed to provide help at an earlier stage. Such studies would allow for an exploration of the family patterns that lead to serious abuse as well as the way in which the formal child protection processes are understood and how they might be made more culturally sensitive.

Highly focused studies are needed into abusive practices that affect a very specific group, such as genital mutilation or the racial abuse of mixed heritage children being brought up in white families. The lower incidence of sexual abuse referrals amongst minority ethnic families could usefully be explored through research focusing on attitudes towards sexuality in different cultural and faith groups, or through small-scale qualitative studies exploring those cases that are referred, looking backwards and following them up prospectively. Many questions arise from the studies we have summarised that could be explored. Are the time limits for initial assessments too tight for culturally sensitive work to be completed to ensure that families in very complex situations (such as refugee families) are not drawn unnecessarily into the formal child protection and courts arena? Can the child protection conferences and court hearings involving family members be adapted so that they are more sensitive to the needs of particular ethnic or faith groups? In what circumstances and with which ethnic and faith communities is the family group conference approach acceptable to parents and children and likely to provide effective protection? How can community and faith groups become more involved in the planning of ethnically sensitive and culturally competent child protection services?

Children looked after or placed for adoption

There is far more research on children (including some studies of children of minority ethnic origin) looked after for long periods than for short periods, yet far more children are looked after for periods of weeks or months than for years. In view of the evidence that pre-Children Act 1989 'voluntary care' was a service that was both used and found useful by African-Caribbean and lone white parents caring for dual heritage children, there would be merit in looking at how they are faring under the new 'family support' and 'accommodation' provisions. Very few ethnic minority children and parents have been included in studies of accommodation and short-term break schemes for families under stress, although studies of respite care schemes for disabled children of minority ethnic origin have been undertaken. The decreased availability of short-term accommodation, without its replacement by suitable and acceptable intensive support schemes, may help to explain why more African-Caribbean and mixed heritage children are coming into care for reasons other than maltreatment, and staying for long periods. This applies to children of all ages, but the reasons are likely to be different for the different age groups, so separate studies are indicated. Looking specifically at teenagers, there is evidence that some have found 'voluntary care' or 'accommodation' a safe and positive way out of a conflictual and possibly abusive family, and that it has helped them to move into independence without having to lose all contact with the more supportive members of the family. If this route is not available, more will join the growing numbers of young runaways and those vulnerable to abuse through prostitution or drawn into criminal behaviour. On the other hand, research is needed on whether families who are unfamiliar with the workings of the British child welfare system (especially those who are new to the country, speak little or no English or are isolated from family and community supports) are especially vulnerable to Section 20 'voluntary' accommodation being used as a back-door route to court action.

There are two groups of minority ethnic children whose longer-term 'care careers' should be the subject of further research focusing on particular ethnic groups. Those who need to be cared for away from home because of maltreatment or serious neglect may come into care at any age. Those for whom there is no place in their birth or extended family are likely to be infants, older children whose difficult behaviour makes them 'unmanageable' or teenagers in serious conflict with a family member – often a stepfather or parent's new partner. Starting with the youngest children, research is needed on the small number of young single parents, mainly of South Asian origin, who feel they have no choice but to place their babies for adoption and to sever even indirect links. The other group of parents who feel obliged to place their babies for adoption or whose children come into long-term care as toddlers are those who come into the census 'other' or 'other mixed' categories. Understanding why their children are over-represented to such an extent amongst those coming into care and placed for adoption is especially important, since they are the ones who will wait longer for a permanent placement and will rarely be placed with a family who fully reflects their complex heritage. The extent to which residential family assessment units are used for minority ethnic parents in order to assess whether they are able to care safely for their children is another area for study. Does the gender mix, for example, allow them to cater for the special needs of Muslim families?

Turning to research on the different placement options, specific studies are needed for each ethnic group and each placement type, including return home to parents and placement with relatives, both of which appear to be used more frequently for minority ethnic children. In particular, the adequacy of financial, practical and the right sort of emotional support available at the right time for the parents or relatives should be studied further.

There are already some studies on which to build. There are conflicting messages about residential care for young people of minority ethnic origin. The way in which children are protected from all forms of ill-treatment by other residents as well as by staff, including racism and racist bullying, merits further study. It would also be helpful to practitioners if more detailed studies could be provided of those residential environments which are positively rated by young people of different ethnic backgrounds and in different circumstances. There are, for instance, some very positive findings about the value of group care for African-Caribbean teenagers and asylum seekers from all ethnic groups. Much research has already explored the issues around the placement of black children with white parents. There is a small number of studies that have examined the issues for black and Asian adoptive and foster parents and mixed heritage families. Since most placements now are with families of a broadly similar cultural and ethnic background to the child, it is important for research to focus on the ways in which these parents manage the challenging tasks of proving a short- or long-term home for children whose early experiences have left them with scars and traumatic memories of loss and abuse. There is some research on the ways in which family placement workers recruit, train and support ethnic minority families, but little to say whether some methods are more successful than others. Some researchers have explored the ways in which children are helped to have a positive racial identity, and how continuing contact with birth relatives is facilitated, but more is needed. For South Asian adopters, many of whom will have brought up a child from infancy in a closed adoption, research is needed on how they approach the task of helping an adult 'child' who wishes to search for birth family members, some of whom may not know of her existence. There will of course be a growing number of children transracially adopted from overseas. There is a great deal of research from other countries and some longitudinal UK studies, but research will be needed on how these parents can best be helped to provide for the identity needs of their children as they move through adolescence and into adulthood.

A holistic approach to researching child welfare services for minority ethnic children and families

As well as focused research on specific ethnic groups at particular stages of a child's development and in contact with specific child welfare services, it is important for research studies to look at the 'journey' through the child welfare system of groups of children and their parents. It is our conclusion that researchers should move on from 'comparative' studies of different ethnic groups and use the findings already available to design studies to provide answers to the questions identified by these earlier studies. Two examples are given here. A prospective longitudinal study of eight- to ten-year-old African-Caribbean boys excluded from school and referred for a family support or child protection service because of difficult family relationships will be able to explore the reasons for different outcomes. A proportion will remain with their families and, with good family support services provided on a one-off basis or episodically when needed, return to school and go on to college or into employment. Others will settle down in the first foster home in which they are placed, retain links with their parents and siblings, do well at school and also go on to college or employment. But a proportion will eventually go missing from a children's home or be sentenced to youth custody at 16, having come into care when beyond the control of their parents and having experienced the breakdown of several foster care placements. The research will explore whether there were differences in the early history of these children that appeared to be associated with different outcomes; or whether it was the availability, accept-ability, timeliness and quality of particular services or a relationship with a par-ticular teacher, social worker or short- or long-term foster mother that appeared to make a difference. Another study (of necessity a national study because of small numbers) might identify a cohort of Pakistani teenagers who become pregnant outside marriage and approach an adoption agency for advice and the possibility of the baby being placed for adoption. Some will decide that they will keep the baby, with or without parental or community support, and be enabled, with good family support and education services to finish their educa-tion and have a fulfilling family life. Others will decide to place the baby for adoption, retain indirect links with the agency and the adopters, and meet up with their adult 'children' to explain why adoption was necessary. In other cases, either the mother or the adopted child will grieve for the life they might have had together. Or the mother may become isolated from her family, struggle to care for the child for a year or so, suffer the combined effects of racism, poverty and loneliness with which she receives little or no help and feel she has no option but to ask for the child to be adopted. The research will look for explanations for these different pathways, and point to ways in which the child welfare services helped, or missed opportunities to help, the parents and their children, and result in coherent plans for practice developments.

Whilst some studies will focus on clearly defined groups of children and parents, other are needed that focus on broader aspects of the service that are relevant at any stage of the child welfare process. An obvious example would be interpreting services. A series of linked studies on different aspects of interpret-ing services could be commissioned, some looking at the special issues concerning child protection conferences or courts, others at how interpreters can work closely with neighbourhood family centres and at the special issues concerning confidentiality when interpretation is provided by members of the local community. A programme of research on these lines could inform national standards and training requirements for interpreters providing a service to child welfare agencies and the family courts. There is much discussion in the research studies we have reviewed on the 'matching' of social worker or family support worker and family in terms of ethnicity, language, gender or religion. Whilst this is feasible in some areas and with some ethnic and religious groups, in many areas this is not always possible. This may be because of the sheer diversity of the population or the fact that in some areas one ethnic group (usually, though not always, white British) forms a very large majority alongside very small numbers from a range of ethnic, cultural and faith groups. There are examples in the research of teams of social workers, family support staff or child placement workers who have, according to parents interviewed for the studies, succeeded in providing an ethnically sensitive service where all team members are culturally competent to work with diversity. An ethnographic approach to research, with a strong element of parent and older child involvement and peer interviewing in the research process, could focus on social services or family centre teams. Such studies are needed both in areas of ethnic diversity and in areas where there are only small numbers of minority ethnic families to understand further how cultural competence is established in different geographical areas.

This leads on to a final point on methodology and selection of research teams. We have been struck by the divide in the research studies between those undertaken by empirical child welfare researchers and those (mainly focusing on general populations) undertaken by cultural theorists, social anthropologists, sociologists and social psychologists. Some of these are referred to in Chapters 1 and 2 but barely touched on in the rest of the review. The next generation of studies will best be carried out by research teams that bring together the knowledge, insights and skills of a combination of research traditions. They will also greatly benefit (as have a small minority of the studies we have described) from the involvement, as research planners as well as research subjects, of practitioners, community groups and parents and young people who have been on the receiving end of child welfare services.

Part II

Summaries of the Main
Research Studies

Summaries of the
Main Research Studies

Five potentially relevant groups of publications and research reports were identified. Summaries are provided of research on child welfare services that is either specific to minority ethnic families, or identifies and analyses data on minority ethnic children and families within a wider sample. Since the focus is on UK child welfare services, descriptive and process research on populations in other countries is only included if there is no UK research on the area under consideration, or it reports on a large-scale outcome study the findings of which can contribute to an understanding of the UK context. Research for which the fieldwork was undertaken before the implementation of the Children Act 1989 is only included if it provides the opportunity of exploring changes over time. Shorter entries are provided on 1.) research on general populations of minority ethnic families but not specifically exploring child welfare services and 2.) research on child welfare that is relevant to minority ethnic populations but does not specifically analyse the data in terms of ethnicity or where no/very few minority ethnic families are included in the sample. The reference list includes books and articles referred to in the text that do not come into the above broad categories. We do not claim that this is a comprehensive list of all relevant literature, but the reader should find the cited texts offer a way into the extensive background literature that provides context to our particular focus on child welfare services to minority ethnic children and their families.

Axford, N., Little, M. and Morpeth L. (in preparation) *Children Supported and Unsupported in the Community*. Totnes: Dartington Social Research Unit.

Aims, methods and sample characteristics

This research (in progress) aims to provide evidence on the nature of need among children living in deprived communities; on the extent to which they and their families use children's services; and on how these interventions, together with coping strategies, affect children's development. One of the two communities studied is ethnically diverse. Data were collected between 1998 and 2001. Three methods were used to describe ethnicity: self-report, census categories and responses to questions about different aspects of culture and ethnicity, including languages spoken and religious observance. If the census categories are used it is possible to report on at least some of the groups separately. In the London community only 16 per cent of the 464 children in the sample were described as 'White

British', 24 per cent were 'Black African', 11 per cent 'White Other', 23 per cent 'Other' and the remainder were evenly distributed across the rest of the census categories. Just under a quarter of the children were born outside the UK and 39 per cent were Muslim. The method comprised three components: screening the community, collecting data from families and collecting data from agencies.

Main findings/ Conclusions

A cluster analysis of the children in both areas produced ten 'needs' groups. Children from minority ethnic groups were found in all groups, and were no more likely than other children to be in particular groups. Only 19 per cent had no or few unmet needs. The data suggest that 37 per cent of children would be 'in need' by the Children Act 1989 definition. Children for whom English was not their first language were disproportionately likely to be in need. The proportion of children in need but not in contact with social services was roughly 1.6 times the proportion of children in need who were actually receiving social work assistance. Although there is a relationship between severity of need and service receipt, significant numbers of children in need do not get help, while others with less pressing needs do receive assistance.

The data have yet to be analysed with specific reference to children from ethnic minority groups. However, some of the broader messages apply to these children.

Barker, C. (1999) Protecting Children from Racism and Racial Abuse: A Research Review. London: NSPCC.

The report reviews the research on how children identify themselves with an ethnic group and conceptualise differences between themselves and other children. It also summarises findings from research on the extent of racial abuse, racial bullying, racial harassment and violent racism and their impact on the health, economic situation and educational achievement of family members. It goes on to consider the reasons why adults and children racially harass or abuse others.

Barlow, J., Shaw, R. and Stewart-Brown, S. (2003) Parenting Programmes and Minority Ethnic Parents. York: Joseph Rowntree Foundation.

The authors review the research that has set out to evaluate the effectiveness of parenting programmes in meeting the needs of minority ethnic parents and children. Quantitative and qualitative research studies are included. The authors found very few studies of the effectiveness (whether measured by parental satisfaction or improvements in functioning of child and/or parents) that included data on minority ethnic families. The authors group parenting programmes into 'behavioural programmes' (based on social learning theory and seeking to help parents to make changes in their children's behaviour) and 'relationship' programmes (including a diverse range of approaches broadly based on the development of insight and making sense of relationships within families). They note that most programmes ignore racial and ethnic diversity but that some 'culturally sensitive' programmes have been developed. Some of these are well-established programmes available widely to general populations that have been translated into the language of those likely to attend (referred to as 'translated' programmes). Others use programmes designed around white families but adapt them to take account of cultural and religious beliefs and family patterns (adapted programmes). The third group are designed specifically around the parenting patterns and belief systems of a specific ethnic group or a combined group of minority ethnic families from different cultures (culturally specific). The authors report that there are examples of all three in the UK. None has yet been evaluated in terms of welfare outcomes though accounts of parental satisfaction are beginning to appear, as with Hylton's (1997) account of the group-based Moyenda project. The report reviews the USA research but concludes that there are many problems with research methodology which require caution when interpreting results of these studies. The biggest problem is that initially a high proportion of those invited to attend a group do not do so, and there is then a high drop-out rate. In the USA and UK there is a higher likelihood that minority ethnic families will decide against attending and be more likely to drop out of programmes. Those who decide to attend and then attend regularly have different characteristics from those who never arrive or drop out, detracting from the reliability of random allocation research designs. The report concludes that 'the evidence to support the effectiveness of culturally specific parenting programmes is not strong' but attributes this to the inadequacy of the research rather than the inadequacy of the programmes. They also find evidence in their detailed studies of the research in the USA that providing a choice of programmes is important, which implies that a range of programmes with different approaches to parenting support should be available.

Barn, R. (1993) *Black Children in the Public Care System*. London: Batsford.

Aims, methods and sample characteristics

The research aimed to identify the circumstances surrounding the admission of children into care and to explore whether black children were disproportionately represented in the care system in one London authority. The cohort included all children who were in care in one London Authority's four area offices in 1987. The sample comprised all the 294 children in care, over half of whom were black (around 50% African-Caribbean; 10% West African; 35% of mixed heritage and small numbers of South Asian or Turkish Cypriot descent). Seventy-four per cent of the children were from single parent families (83% black and 64% white). Eighty children who had entered care within the six months prior to the survey were studied in depth, giving a portrait of practice just before the implementation of the Children Act 1989.

Main findings/Conclusions

Black families were more likely than white families to be referred for reasons such as family relationships, financial and material difficulties and the mother's mental health problems. White families were more likely than black families to be referred because of concerns about neglect or abuse. Black children were more likely than white children to enter care quickly. When compared to the general population in the area studied, black children were over-represented in the care system especially with respect to children under five.

Barn, R., Sinclair, R. and Ferdinand, D. (1997) *Acting on Principle: An Examination of Race and Ethnicity in Social Services Provision for Children and Families.* London: British Agencies for Adoption and Fostering.

Aims, methods and sample characteristics

The study considers how social services departments responded to the Children Act 1989 requirement for local authorities to seek to place with families who could meet their racial, cultural and religious needs. In doing so it also looked more broadly at social work practice in child and family social work teams. Records were scrutinised of 196 cases that were currently allocated to social workers in parts of three local authorities. Just over half were of minority ethnic background (18% African-Caribbean; 14% Asian and 16% mixed parentage). Around two thirds of the cases involved children looked after and a third were receiving a family support service. Files were analysed and interviews completed with 73 family members, carers and social workers in respect of a sub-sample of cases, or workers in respect of a sub-sample of cases; departmental policy documents were read and 11 interviews took place with senior managers. Those interviewed included 18 children, 19 birth parents and 5 foster parents, drawn from all the ethnic groups represented in the sample. Of the 36 field and residential workers, 16 were African-Caribbean, 13 white and 7 Asian. The interview data are analysed according to key themes and the case summaries and quotes are used to illustrate the quantitative data.

Main findings/ Conclusions

- Fifty-seven per cent of the children lived in or came into care from single-parent families; 39 per cent from nuclear two-parent families and a small minority were part of an extended family household. African-Caribbean children were the biggest group who came from a single-parent household (61% were African-Caribbean) followed by 51 per cent of mixed parentage children; 43 per cent of white children and 25 per cent of Asian children.

- Of the 30 mixed-parentage children about whom data were available, 27 had a white mother. Eleven of the fathers were African-Caribbean, five were Asian, five were white, three were African and three were of mixed parentage.

- Ninety-two per cent of the children were born in the UK and the first language of over three-quarters was English. Religion was recorded in only 102 cases but was recorded for all the Asian children (43% Sikh; 32% Muslim; 25% Hindu).

- Referrals were made by family members (20%), the police, schools and health services. White parents (including the white mothers of mixed-parentage children) were more likely to refer themselves for help than were black or Asian parents. Fifty per cent of the referrals of African-Caribbean children and 71 per cent of the referrals of Asian children were made by the statutory agencies.

- Almost a quarter of the children in the whole sample were on the child protection register but three-quarters of the 28 Asian children were, or had been, on the child protection register. The combined group of black and Asian families was more likely than white families to be on the register for reasons of physical abuse or neglect (though neglect was least likely in respect of Asian children) and less likely than white children to be registered because of concerns about sexual abuse.

- There were no written policies about the placement needs of minority ethnic children and interviews produced evidence of differences of interpretation of unwritten policies.

Numbers in the different ethnic groups are too small and age ranges too wide for a reliable estimate of over- or under-representation, and for discussions about the different routes into care and placement patterns for the different ethnic groups. Rich qualitative data are provided from managers, practitioners, children, parents and carers, especially about the nature, adequacy and cultural sensitivity or insensitivity of the social work service. The researchers conclude that 'there have been significant improvements in recent years in social services provision for black children and families' (p.93). They note that a serious attempt had been made by each authority to adopt 'equal opportunity policies in respect of employment and service delivery although there was less evidence of implementation of anti-discriminatory policies and procedures' (p.92). Detailed recommendations are made for further improvements to policy and practice at national and local levels.

Becher, H. and Husain, F. (2003) *Supporting Minority Ethnic Families: South Asian Hindus and Muslims in Britain: Developments in Family Support.* London: National Family and Parenting Institute.

This literature review and synthesis makes an important contribution to the knowledge base on the provision of family support services to British South Asian families. It especially highlights religion as an important component of group and ethnic identity. It starts with a synopsis of writing in this area, summarising earlier research on South Asian families and detailing the extent of disadvantage across the areas of poverty, employment/unemployment, education, physical and mental health and exposure to crime, including racially motivated crime. It describes key areas of family life amongst the different British South Asian communities. The authors then provide an overview of the approaches to family support as reported in the research, policy and practice literature and summarise the main studies. They provide a synthesis of the findings about what seems to work and the policy and practice barriers to the provision of appropriate support and improved services. 'Best practice' initiatives and projects from the UK and overseas are described.

Berridge, D., Beecham, J., Brodie, I. et al. (2003) 'Services for troubled adolescents: Exploring user variation' Child and Family Social Work 8, 4, 269–280

One of the Department of Health funded 'costs and effectiveness' programme studies, it compares the young residents in children's homes, foster homes and EBD (Emotional and Behavioral Difficulties) schools and the similarities and differences in the services provided and their costs. A quarter of the 257 adolescents in the study were of minority ethnic origin (including ten unaccompanied asylum seekers, nine of whom lived in children's homes. Few of the girls or the South Asian teenagers attended the EBD schools, in which white children were over-represented.

Bhabra, S., and Ghate, D. with Brazier, L. (2002) Consultation Analysis: Raising the Educational Attainment of Children in Care. Final Report to the Social Exclusion Unit. London: Policy Research Bureau.

Summarises 201 written responses to a consultation exercise on approaches to raising the educational achievement of children in care. Only a small number of respondents commented on any special issues for the education of ethnic minority children who are looked after, in itself an important finding. The report provides useful background on strategies being pursued under the Quality Protects initiative to improve the educational achievement of looked after young people.

Bhardwaj, A. (2001) 'Growing Up Young, Asian and Female in Britain: A Report on Self-harm and Suicide.' Feminist Review 68, 52–67.

Aims, methods and sample characteristics

The report starts from statistics that indicate that Asian women between the ages of 15 and 35 are two to three times more vulnerable to committing suicide and self-harming than their non-Asian (white, African and Caribbean) counterparts. The qualitative research, carried out in 1997 at Newham Asian Women's Project, aimed to explore the reasons why young Asian women self-harmed and to evaluate the response of service providers; to account for the poor mental health experiences of Asian women; and to evaluate their perceptions of mental health support services. There were in-depth interviews with Asian women who had a history of attempted suicide and guided focus group discussions with young Asian women. There were also structured interviews with a sample of service planners and providers from health, social services and the voluntary sector. For some, the self-harm acted as a coping mechanism for the unbearable distress that they faced in their lives. Others described how it helped them to survive from day to day, acting as a form of power and control over their lives. For some it was a response to a pervasive sense of self-loathing and others used it as a response to feelings towards others that they felt unable to articulate.

Main findings/ Conclusions

The researcher concluded that self-harm amongst Asian women was related to competing expectations of them in their daily life, e.g. parental, family and community-related. The research concluded that 'violence and physical abuse towards young women continued to be a community-sanctioned method of curbing their independence' (p.59). The service response was found to be inadequate and often inappropriate and such services as there were were poorly publicised amongst those who needed them. Professionals in the field were found to have little understanding of mental health issues and less appreciation of the complex interactions between culture, gender and self-harm. The women interviewed gave conflicting opinions about whether it was desirable to have a worker from the same ethnic group.

Biehal, N., Clayden, J., Stein, M. and Wade, J. (1992) *Prepared for Living?* London: National Children's Bureau.

Biehal, N., Wade, J., Clayden, J. and Stein, M. (1995) *Moving On. Young People and Leaving Care Schemes.* London: HMSO.

Aims, methods and sample characteristics

Quantitative and qualitative data from social workers and young people were used to analyse and evaluate transitions from care and leaving care schemes in three English Local Authorities between 1991 and 1993. The quantitative survey included 183 participants, 17 of whom (14%) were black, Asian or of mixed heritage. Nine of the 74 young people interviewed were from minority ethnic groups. The sample young people were followed up twice, the final interview being 18–25 months after they left their care placement.

Main findings/ Conclusions

The young people from minority ethnic groups in this study were 2.5 times more likely than the white young people to have entered care before the age of five and twice as likely to be looked after for ten years or more. Despite doing slightly better in terms of educational achievement, the employment situation, though poor for most of the young people, was worse for young people from minority ethnic groups. Qualitative research amongst these young people pointed to the conclusion that identities were not fixed, but rather changed over time. The researchers question the concept of 'black identity' as the young people interviewed talked of an identity based on ethnicity as only one of many complex and fluid identities they experienced in the context of their work and family lives. However, in contrast, social workers were often found to view 'black identity' as largely a fixed biological attribute and could be viewed as pathologising young people's problems. The researchers therefore highlighted the need to question social work attitudes and responses to issues around ethnic and cultural identity.

Bignall, T. and Butt, J. (2000) *Report: Between Ambition and Achievement: Young Black People's Views and Experiences of Independence and Independent Living.* London: Policy Press.

This community-based study reports on interviews with 44 young disabled people (aged between 16 and 30) of Asian, African or Caribbean origin to explore the attitudes and responses to their growing-up experience. The study took place in four local authorities and concluded that the majority had negative experiences of education. Many felt this was because professionals' expectations of them were low because of their race, culture and disability. All the young people were known to social services departments and had had contact with social workers at some time during their lives. However, at the time of the study, few were in contact with social care agencies and most relied on their family for care and support.

Brandon, M. and Lewis, A. (1996a) 'The Children Act Definition of Significant Harm – Interpretations in Practice.' *Health and Social Care in the Community 4*, 1, 11–20.

Brandon, M. and Lewis, A. (1996b)'Significant Harm and Children's Experiences of Domestic Violence.' *Child and Family Social Work 1*, 1, 33–42.

Brandon, M., Thoburn, J., Lewis, A. and Way, A. (1999) *Safeguarding Children with the Children Act 1989.* London: The Stationery Office.

Aims, methods and sample characteristics

This Department of Health funded post-Children Act study looked at the child protection work in parts of four local authorities. The sample was a total cohort of 105 children newly identified as suffering or likely to suffer significant harm. The authorities were mixed between urban, rural and inner-city areas. The cases were followed through for a 12-month period between 1993 and 1994. Fifty-nine per cent of the children were white and 46 per cent were of minority ethnic origin. Fourteen per cent were African-Caribbean, 2 per cent were African, 2 per cent Indian and 4 per cent Pakistani. Sixteen per cent were of mixed heritage, 5 per cent were of other European origin and there was one traveller family. Quantitative and qualitative methods were used. For the intensive sample of 51 families, parents, children and key professionals were interviewed twice, at an interval of 12 months. Standardised schedules and the DH *Looking After Children* dimensions were used to assess well-being of parents and children and changes over the year. Files were scrutinised and cases were then allocated with the use of 'researcher rating' protocols to more or less successful outcome groups. A further study of the children between 6 and 7 years later is in preparation.

Main findings/Conclusions

Reliable data on children in the different ethnic groups in the areas in which the study took place were not then available, but, taken as a combined group, the researchers estimated that the minority ethnic families were over-represented by around two to one when compared with white families. The well-being of more of the children of minority ethnic origin improved over the research period than was the case for the white children. However, there was less improvement in the well-being of the parents, irrespective of ethnic group. The detailed accounts of the reactions of the parents and children to the child protection process draw out some themes of particular relevance to minority ethnic families, including the use of interpreters and the selection of social workers to work with families.

Broad, B. (2001a) (ed) *Kinship Care: The Placement Choice for Children and Young People*. Lyme Regis: Russell House.

Broad, B. (2001b) 'Kinship care: supporting children in placements with extended family and friends.' *Adoption and Fostering* 25, 2, 33–42.

Broad, B., Hayes, R. and Rushforth, C. (2001) *Kith and Kin: Kinship Care for Vulnerable Young People*. London: Joseph Rowntree Foundation/National Children's Bureau.

This empirical study of 60 kinship care placements took place in Wandsworth in the early 1990s. Thirty-one per cent of the children were of Caribbean or Guyanese origins, a further 31 per cent were categorised as 'Non-Europeans' or 'other' and 27 per cent were 'English, Welsh or Scots'. In all but one case the ethnic origin of carer and child matched exactly. There was a much higher proportion of black children placed with relatives and friends (24% of the borough's 'looked after' black children) than was the case for white children. The authors concluded that the higher percentages of black children cared for in this way may say something about cultural preferences. They comment that the higher proportion of black children placed with relatives may be a 'good thing', in the sense of preventing more black children from being split off from their families in long-term care. On the other hand the higher proportion could be a 'bad thing' if black children and families are being inappropriately channelled down the kinship care route, with or without supports, and being denied other services of their choice. An alternative possibility is that the strengths of the black families are valued by social services but to a point of not offering further support because that is perceived as less necessary in a black extended family compared with a white family. The research evidence indicates that most extended families, both black and white, want ongoing social services support. The researchers conclude that the identification of potential carers from amongst family or friends is an especially important consideration in the placement of black and minority ethnic children. It is therefore important that social care staff are 'culturally competent' to work with these families.

Brophy, J. with Bates, P., Brown, L., Cohen, S., Radcliffe, P. and Wale, C.J. (1999) *Expert Evidence in Child Protection Litigation: Where Do We Go From Here?* London: The Stationery Office.

This is the first of four related studies exploring attitudes and approaches to the use of experts by guardians *ad litem* (now children's guardians) and experiences of child psychiatrists instructed as expert witnesses in care proceedings. A national stratified random sample of care cases was undertaken as part of a questionnaire survey with guardians. A return of 338 questionnaires (a 71% response rate) provided detailed information on 557 care cases concerning just under 1000 children. Information was also obtained on the training undertaken by guardians including any training in relation to equal opportunities issues. Interviews were conducted with 35 guardians and with 17 child and adolescent psychiatrists. When comparing the ethnic groups of children in the national survey of cases with data from the 1991 census, the study identified that 6 per cent of cases concerned black children (this compared with 2% of all children aged 0–5 in England and Wales); 2% of cases concerned children of South Asian origin (compared with 5% in the general population); 8% of cases concerned children of mixed parentage (compared with 1% of such children in the general population). The researchers comment that lack of ethnic monitoring by courts creates problems when trying to match minority ethnic children with appropriate guardians. Some child psychiatrists interviewed expressed a range of concerns about 'cross-cultural' assessments in care proceedings.

Brophy, J. (2000a) '"Race" and Ethnicity in Care Proceedings: Implications from a National Survey of Cases containing Expert Evidence.' *Adoption and Fostering* 24, 2, 70–72.

Brophy, J. (2000b) '"Race" and Ethnicity in Public Law Proceedings.' *Family Law* 30, 740–9.

Aims, methods and sample characteristics

These articles report a secondary analysis of the survey data based on section 31 applications (Brophy *et al.* 1999) which aimed to further explore the demographic, legal and evidential profile of care cases by ethnic group. Cases consisted of 54 Black children (disaggregated: 15 African, 35 African-Caribbean and 4 from 'other Black' groups); 36 children of South Asian origin (15 Indian, 13 Pakistani and 8 Bangladeshi) and 71 children of mixed parentage. An analysis is provided of the type, range and complexity of expert evidence filed in cases by ethnic group of the child, including the use made of any specialist cultural advisers as expert witnesses in proceedings. The data were analysed both by aggregated groups (Black and South Asian) and disaggregated (as above). The report highlights the need for caution, because of small sample size, with regard to findings for some disaggregated groups.

Main findings/ Conclusions

- The majority of the children in all ethnic groups were under six years of age.

- Cases concerning black children and children of mixed parentage were significantly more likely to be transferred to the higher courts. Cases concerning children of mixed parentage tended to be highly complex representing many challenges for courts, professionals and clinicians.

- Just under one-third of all cases contained some adult mental health evidence. The researchers highlighted their concern that very few minority ethnic parents filed *any* paediatric and child and family psychiatric evidence. Where black parents filed any expert evidence almost all of this was based only on psychiatric assessment of the parents or carers.

- Very few minority ethnic children were represented by a guardian who was 'matched' with the child according to ethnic group. At the time of the survey most guardians (57%) reported they had undertaken some training under the broad umbrella of equal opportunities training.

Brophy, J., Jhutti-Johal, J. and Owen, C. (2003a) *Significant Harm: Child Protection Litigation in a Multi-cultural Setting.* London: Department of Constitutional Affairs.

Brophy, J., Jhutti-Johal, J. and Owen, C. (2003b) 'Assessing and Documenting Child Ill-treatment in Ethnic Minority Households.' *Family Law 33,* 756–764.

Aims, methods and sample characteristics

This is a detailed empirical study, which explores further the questions raised in Brophy's earlier research and literature reviews. It aimed to provide information on whether the courts had access to information on ethnic, cultural, religious and linguistic diversity within families, and on the applicability of the 'significant harm' definition and threshold criteria to minority ethnic families. Quantitative and qualitative methods were used to explore a random sample of 100 cases, mostly completed between 1998 and 2000, concerning 183 children in one court circuit serving an area of considerable ethnic diversity. Documents were analysed according to the degree to which they identified and explored issues of cultural, religious and linguistic diversity in the context of allegations of harm and risk to children. Thirty-six hearings were observed. and interviews undertaken with 26 key court personnel (including judges, magistrates and legal advisers). The court file study consisted of 61 Black children involved in 34 cases (26 African, 15 African-Caribbean and 20 children from other Black groups); 42 children of South Asian origin involved in 25 cases (13 Indian, 15 Bangladeshi and 14 Pakistani); 32 children of mixed parentage (involved in 18 cases) and 46 White British children (involved in 23 cases). Information was collected and analysed for aggregated (Black, Asian and mixed parentage) and disaggregated groups. There were similar numbers of boys and girls. Forty-six per cent were under five years old at the date of application, with African-Caribbean and Indian children most likely to be under five compared to the white children in the sample.

Main findings/ Conclusions

- Cases involving children in the aggregated Black and South Asian group, and the mixed parentage group were more likely to be amongst the 41 transferred to the higher courts, the major reason for transfer being exceptional gravity and complexity. Cultural or religious reasons were included as part of the reason for case complexity and thus transfer in just over a third of the cases.

- At the start of proceedings, most children were already living away from their birth parents and this was most likely to be the case with South Asian children. South Asian children were also more likely than the other groups to be the subjects of Emergency Protection Orders.

- A reference in the reports to mental health issues and failure to accept professional help with these problems, was more frequent in respect of the South Asian group compared to the other minority ethnic groups; male violence was also higher in the South Asian group compared with other minority ethnic groups (but lower than in the White British group).

- There were numerous documented instances of failures of the agencies to use interpreters at crucial points in interviews with parents prior to, and after the instigation of court proceedings. This happened, for example, when children were removed from parents under emergency measures. In some cases where there was likely to be a conflict of interests between parents, mothers were not interviewed separately.

- Allegations of physical ill-treatment were highest in the white group (55%) followed by the South Asian group (41%) and lowest for the Black group (26%). Allegations of sexual abuse were highest amongst the mixed parentage group (27%), followed by the South Asian group (19%) (compared with 6% in the White group and 3% in the Black group). The researchers note that in all ethnic groups applications for care orders were based upon multiple allegations of child maltreatment amounting to 'significant harm' or likely significant harm and also multiple concerns about failures in parenting (i.e. they were not 'single issue' cases).

- Where cases included conflicts grounded in diverse norms and values, these were more likely to occur in cases concerning parents of South Asian and African origin. However such conflicts were seldom pivotal by the time the cases reached a pre-trial review and a contested final hearing was a rare event – in all groups.

- In the final stages of proceedings, the extent and quality of information about diversity issues increased, especially for cases heard in the higher courts, for which 83 per cent contained some analysis of issues relevant to culture and religion, often linked in with discussion of the local authority's care plan.

- For 18 per cent of the Black group and 6 per cent of the mixed-parentage group, statements identified that a parent, carer or child had been subjected to racial abuse or harassment.

- In terms of practice, there were examples of social services staff, guardians and other professionals going to great lengths to try to understand and meet the cultural needs of the family.

- The researchers found no evidence to indicate that the significant harm criteria require further review in order to meet the needs of minority ethnic children. They emphasise that, for some analytical and statistical purposes, the disaggregated numbers in some ethnic groups in their sample are small, but do point to the likelihood that there are different sorts of problems within and between different groups, and between male and female family members. They stress the importance of addressing and understanding the cultural and religious contexts when considering how families interact with and make sense of the welfare and court systems.

Butt, J. and Box, L. (1998) *Family Centres: A Study of the Use of Family Centres by Black Families.* London: Racial Equality Unit.

Aims, methods and sample characteristics

The research focused on the use of family centres by black families in the context of other aspects of family support work. The term 'black' was used to include people from Africa, the Caribbean and Asia. A questionnaire was completed by 84 family centre managers in 9 local authorities covering the whole of the UK except

Scotland. Thirty-eight of those working in the centres were selected because stage one responses indicated that they worked regularly with black parents and children. The researchers stress the importance of not making assumptions that the findings also apply to family centres that rarely work with black families. The fifteen focus groups included two groups specifically for children and one group for men. The survey provided data on the facilities provided by the family centres and included an analysis of their budget for the year 1995 to 1996.

Main findings/Conclusions

- The average number of services provided in centres was 9. Twenty-three family centres had services specifically for black children and parents, ranging from child protection risk assessments through to services around education for parents and children.

- About 65 per cent of centres were receiving either no money for growth or a cut in their budgets. Funds were allocated to services for black families in 15 out of 66 centres, with the amounts varying from £128 to £25,000. The small amounts of money tended to be used for celebrating religious and cultural festivals, whilst the larger amounts funded groups specifically for black service users.

- Black voluntary organisations and race equality councils were less likely than statutory agencies to be routinely informed about family centre activities. Only 6 centres routinely provided translations of publicity material whilst 28 centres reported that they did not translate any information or publicity into other languages.

- Managers of the 3 centres that had an over-representation of black parents and children considered that this was because the services were particularly designed around the needs and wishes of these communities. The problems with which black families most frequently sought, or were referred for help, included economic problems, problems related to crime, including racial harassment, and housing problems. Caribbean people were more likely to use the services than Asian or African parents and children.

- As well as the services that specifically catered for black families, childcare services, which included day-care and after-school clubs, were also popular amongst them. Services focused on child protection were least likely to have any service user involvement with regard to both management and delivery of services.

- Many respondents were positive about the services they had received from their family centre because they could: lessen isolation and loneliness; allow parents to have a break and time for themselves; provide practical help and advice and help improve relationships within families.

- Services for children mentioned positively were: the provision of safe spaces for play and the development of social skills, especially as for many parents their own accommodation was inadequate; support in times of crises, for example by helping children who had been abused, and fostering improvement in parent–child relationships and interaction.

- Service users particularly commented on the welcoming atmosphere and the ethos of those centres that promoted user participation; the services specifically for black and Asian families; and the qualities of the staff groups in family centres, who were held in high regard by many users.

The overall conclusion was that few family centres had made consistent attempts to meet the needs of black parents and children. When care was taken to consult members of minority ethnic communities in the area and to work in partnership with parents and children, the services provided were generally seen as appropriate and helpful, especially those services that recognised the impact of racism and environmental stresses experienced by parents and children.

Butt, J. and Mirza, K. (1996) *Social Care and Black Communities: A review of recent research studies*. London: HMSO.

A review, synthesis and critique of research and other data sources (mostly published between 1980 and 1996) relevant to people of African-Caribbean, African or Asian descent who receive a social work or social care service or would do so if an appropriate service were available. Combines in a single volume information on publications relevant to demography and the environments in which minority ethnic people live, services to children, elders and those with disabilities including mental health problems and their carers. The authors call for a greater involvement of black people in the design and carrying out of research, and greater clarity on the part of researchers about the particular groups and services that are the subjects of the research.

Candappa, M. (2004) *Improving Services to Black and Ethnic Minority Children and their Families: Four Demonstration Projects Under the Quality Protects Initiative*. Understanding Children's Social Care Series, No.6. London: Institute of Education, Department of Health.

An account and analysis of four demonstration projects co-ordinated as part of the Quality Protects programme, with a particular focus on processes for setting up, supporting and monitoring the projects. Each project aimed to develop best practice in services to a different group of minority ethnic children and their parents and focused on a different aspect of the child welfare service. In Bristol, the aim was to improve the placement choices and stability for children of dual heritage. The Manchester project focused on African-Caribbean care leavers. In Tower Hamlets, the initial aim of improving the educational attainment of

Bangladeshi looked after children was broadened to other minority ethnic groups when it became clear at an early stage that Bangladeshi children in the borough did as well as if not better than children from other ethnic groups at GCSE. The focus in Warwickshire was on listening to looked after children from the Sikh community ensuring that their views fed into policy, and on the role of councillors. However, since only five Sikh children were looked after, the remit was broadened to all ethnic groups. All the projects gave attention to ways of improving the quality of recording and data collection on the ethnic minority children and families.

Cawson, P., Wattam, C., Brooker, S. and Kelly, G. (2000) *Child Maltreatment in the United Kingdom: A Study of the Prevalence of Child Abuse and Neglect.* London: NSPCC.

Aims, methods and sample characteristics

Although a 'community' rather than a 'child welfare' study, this research is reported in some detail because it provides important background information on parenting practices in the UK at the start of the twenty-first century. As well as providing data on the incidence of abusive and neglectful behaviours, it informs the important debate about the circumstances in which discipline tips over into abuse. A computer-assisted data entry survey instrument was administered by researchers to a random sample of 2,869 young people aged 18–24, all born in the UK. There were 1235 young men and 1634 young women and the response rate was 69 per cent. Ninety-two per cent of respondents described their ethnicity as white; 5 per cent of the total sample described themselves as Asian (most identifying themselves as Indian or Pakistani); two per cent identified themselves as black (mostly African-Caribbean or 'black other'. Although this was broadly representative of national population figures, it did not give an adequate size of sample for detailed examination of the minority ethnic respondents, and an additional 'top up' sample was sought, bringing the number of young people of minority ethnic origin to 510. The analysis in terms of ethnicity has not yet been completed, and the results in the report refer primarily to the base sample.

Main findings/Conclusions

- For the sample as a whole, a large majority (77%) reported that they grew up in loving homes and a further 15 per cent slightly agreed that they 'had a warm and loving family background'. However, a sizeable minority (38%) grew up in families where there was 'a lot of stress'.

- In terms of discipline, methods such as reasoning, 'grounding' and withdrawal of pocket money or privileges were used by most parents, but 87 per cent of young people reported that they had experienced verbal treatment including being shouted and screamed at, sworn at, called names such as stupid or lazy, and threatened. Most had also experienced physical punishment. This was most commonly an occasional slap with an open hand on the bottom, arm or leg but 21 per cent had been slapped on the face, head or ears. A quarter of the sample (25%) reported more serious violence including being hit with implements, punched, kicked, burned or scalded, knocked down, and choked, with most of this occurring at the hands of parents, especially mothers. A detailed picture is also provided of the extent to which the young people were exposed to inappropriate sexual attentions from a family member or someone outside the family, were neglected or inadequately supervised or were psychologically maltreated.

- Of those who experienced bullying by adults, 15 per cent thought it was because of their 'race' and 4 per cent because of their religion. Bullying by other children was more common, most often taking the form of name calling and insults, but with a third experiencing physical assault. White respondents more often reported being bullied, but minority ethnic respondents more often reported that they had experienced discrimination. Of those who experienced bullying or discrimination by other children, 'race' was identified as the reason by 8 per cent of the whole sample, but by 68 per cent of minority ethnic respondents, compared to 3 per cent of white respondents.

- Preliminary examination of the results from the enhanced sample of minority ethnic young people (not yet published) give a picture of family life and relationships, and of maltreatment, which is broadly similar for all ethnic groups. However, where there are some specific differences between ethnic groups, these tend to be masked when all are included together as 'minority ethnic' respondents. Analysis compared results between Asian (Indian, Pakistani and Bangladeshi) and black (African-Caribbean, African and 'black other') respondents, 'other ethnicity' (including those of mixed heritage) and white respondents. Few of the differences between groups described below are large in terms of numbers – 5 to 10 per cent being the most common order of difference – but there are some consistent trends which, the researchers stress, need careful unpacking, since factors other than ethnicity could be having intervening effects. The main sample showed strong associations with socio-economic status and some aspects of child-rearing and of maltreatment, and this is a potential intervening variable. Another important issue is family structure, since many adverse childhood experiences were associated with having had changes of parenting and growing up primarily in single-parent families, and this was more common among black respondents and the 'other ethnicity' group than among Asian or white respondents. Consequently the results given here are provisional.

- Respondents from all minority ethnic groups more often said that physical violence had occurred between their parents: approximately a third of all groups compared to a quarter of white respondents. Levels of domestic violence were highest for black young people, of whom 13 per cent said it was 'constant' or 'frequent' compared to 4 per cent of white and 7 per cent of Asian respondents.

- The results do not fully support common stereotypes. For example patterns of physical punishment were very similar in most respects between black and white young people, with half of each reporting slaps with an open hand on the bottom, and 60 per cent slaps on the leg, hand or arm. Asian respondents were less likely to have these experiences (17% and 33%). However both black and Asian respondents were more likely to have been slapped on the face, head or ears (35% and 30% respectively) compared to white young people (20%).

- For all groups the mother was the most common instigator of this level of physical punishment, but less so for black young people (71% of those punished) than for white young people (80%).

- On the more serious forms of physical discipline, classified in the study as 'violent' treatment, black young people are three times as likely to report being hit with implements as are Asian or white young people, but it is still very much a minority pattern: 19 per cent reported being treated in this way, compared to 6 per cent of Asian and white respondents. Numbers of respondents punched, kicked, burned, choked or knocked down are low (approximately 5–10% of those receiving any violent treatment for all groups). Mothers are most often named as the person who did it, but in this instance most often by black young people (65% of those experiencing any of this treatment compared to 48% for Asian and white respondents.) Fathers were said to be responsible by approximately 40 per cent in all groups. Slightly more black young people in the whole sample said that this treatment happened 'regularly over the years' (9% of black respondents, 3% of Asian respondents and 6% of white respondents) and that it usually caused marks or soreness lasting till at least next day (13% of black respondents, 9% of Asian respondents and 6% of white respondents) but the differences are small, given the low base numbers involved.

- The authors conclude that none of these behaviours towards children, including hitting with implements, is culturally normative for the larger ethnic groups in the UK today. In the main sample, lower socio-economic group and lower levels of parental education were strongly associated with greater use of physical punishment and parental violence at all levels, and it is possible that differences in the minority ethnic sample can also be at least partially explained in these terms.

Chahal, K. and Julienne, L. (1999) 'We Can't All Be White!' Racist Victimisation in the UK. York: Joseph Rowntree Foundation. http://www.jrf.org.uk/findings/housing/697.asp

Using responses to in-depth interviews and focus groups, the researchers report the accounts of 74 people in ethnic minority communities in Belfast, Cardiff, Glasgow and London about their experiences of racism. The focus was on housing and neighbourhood safety and other related issues, but the accounts of those taking part are highly relevant to an understanding of how racism, racist abuse and discrimination impacts on the daily lives of parents and children. It provides insights about how the 'everyday' experience of racism and the serious racist abuse that sometimes occurs (and the fear of it occurring) force parents and children to change their behaviour and impact on their quality of life. The study documents the reluctance of families to report harassment and racist incidents and the generally inappropriate and inadequate response of agencies when community members do finally report the incidents.

Chamba, R., Ahmad, W., Hirst, M., Lawton, D. and Beresford, B. (1999) On the Edge: Minority Ethnic Families Caring for a Severely Disabled Child. Bristol: The Policy Press.

Aims, methods and sample characteristics

A postal survey (with questionnaires translated into Urdu, Punjabi, Gujerati, Bengali and Hindi) was completed in 1999 by 647 ethnic minority parents caring for a severely disabled child (a 66% response rate). Nearly a quarter of respondents were of African or African-Caribbean origin (combined for purposes of analysis); 38 per cent of respondents were Indian; 28 per cent were Pakistani and 12 per cent were Bangladeshi. The research followed a 1995 study which explored the experiences of 1000 white families caring for a severely disabled child and explored families' living conditions, levels of informal support, experience of services and unmet needs.

Main findings/Conclusions

- Families from minority ethnic groups caring for a disabled child were more disadvantaged than white families in similar situations.

- Poor interpreting support and limited availability of translated materials was a barrier to information services, particularly for Bangladeshi families.

- Indian and Black African/Caribbean families reported least support from their extended families (the main reason given by 50% was that no family members lived nearby), with levels of support lower than found amongst the white families in the earlier study. Mothers from all ethnic groups reported lower levels of support from their partners than had been reported by white mothers.

- Two-thirds of parents felt that they needed more breaks from caring for their disabled child but only a quarter had received short-term breaks. Indian and Black African/Caribbean parents were more likely to use short-term break services than other minority ethnic families.

- Parents across all ethnic groups generally agreed on the most serious problems they faced as service users: delays in service provision; having to 'fight' for services; lack of information and a sense that professionals do not understand what daily life with a disabled child is like.

Farmer, E. and Owen, M. (1995) *Child Protection Practice: Private Risks and Public Remedies.* London: HMSO.

Owen, M. and Farmer, E. (1996) 'Child Protection in a Multi-racial Context.' *Policy and Politics 24*, 3, 299–313.

Aims, methods and sample characteristics

These two linked studies were part of the Department of Health *Child Protection: Messages from Research* series of studies. The main research was carried out in two county authorities just prior to the implementation of the Children Act 1989.

To allow for an exploration of the views of minority ethnic parents who had been involved in child protection procedures, interviews were conducted with parents, social workers and team managers in a large metropolitan area.

Main findings/Conclusions

When the ten cases involving children of minority ethnic origin are compared to those in the main sample, they followed a broadly similar pattern. The inquiry and conference were generally experienced as stressful, but the difficulties for the ten (six of whom were of South Asian heritage) were compounded by language problems as well as by differences in the value-base and overall culture of the formal child protection system and that of the families. It was thus more likely that in these cases, when compared with those of white families, an investigation would end in uncertainty and the ensuing intervention was less well focused. As with white families, male abusers, whether of children or their partners, tended to opt out of involvement with social workers. The child's welfare was likely to be enhanced following the intervention when the needs of the caretaking parent/s were met, and this was related to a partnership-based model of practice. The researchers concluded that in both the main sample and the sub-group of minority ethnic families, some of the children and parents drawn into the formal child protection system would probably have been better served by the provision of a Section 17 family support service.

The authors concluded that there is benefit in the matching, wherever possible, of the ethnic background of the worker and the family members. However, matching should be based on an understanding of class and gender, located in a cultural context. The involvement of social services teams in networking and community development work was also pointed up as important in improving the relevance of child protection services to minority ethnic families.

Fazil, Q., Bywaters, P., Ali, Z., Wallace, L. and Singh, G. (2002) 'Disadvantage and Discrimination Compounded: The Experience of Pakistani and Bangladeshi Parents of Disabled Children in the UK.' *Disability and Society 17, 3, 237–253.*

Aims, methods and sample characteristics

A detailed descriptive and analytical study based on interviews with 15 Pakistani and 5 Bangladeshi families with one or more severely disabled children, aged between 5 and 19 years, living in Birmingham. The families were new cases referred in 1999–2000. Parents and adult carers were interviewed on their material circumstances, use of services, informal care arrangements and parents' social and psychological well being. The findings are set in the context of published research on disability. It is estimated that 400,000 disabled children are currently being brought up in the UK with over 100,000 being described as severely disabled (Department of Health 2000). In 1994 the SSI reported that only 5000 disabled children were living in communal establishments.

Main findings/Conclusions

- The study found that not only were most of the Pakistani and Bangladeshi families in the study socially and economically deprived but they also suffered high levels of anxiety and depression.

- The 39 family members interviewed reported little contact with professional service providers other than school and their GP. In general, 'families had difficulty in understanding the role of service providers, identifying who they were and where they came from. In some cases, families knew nothing more than the first name of a worker who came to the house' (p.244). Families in touch with social services reported that when they needed to contact social services they often got put through to a different worker each time.

- The language and ethnic background of the service provider was seen to be important to eight parents.

The authors suggest that many national surveys may have underestimated the extent of material disadvantage, and emphasise that health and social care professionals should not assume that Pakistani or Bangladeshi parents have access to high levels of extended family support. Whilst many parents with a disabled child reported difficulties in securing access to appropriate services, this was particularly acute for ethnic minority families. The researchers conclude that this indicates that these families may be having to contend with the additional dimension of institutional racism.

Flynn, R. (2002a) *Short Breaks: Providing Better Access and More Choice for Black Disabled Children and their Parents.* Bristol: The Policy Press.

Aims, methods and sample characteristics

This book, based on a Joseph Rowntree funded study, reviews the literature on access to short breaks for black disabled children and their parents. A postal survey of 24 short-term break schemes in England (13 responses), together with interviews with a small number of scheme managers, parents and carers, resulted in an exploration of the barriers to access and ways of overcoming them so that children and parents can benefit. Nine Scottish disabled children and young people of Pakistani and Chinese origins were interviewed about their lives and use of services as were two parents and three carers of South Asian or African-Caribbean origin involved in family-based short-break schemes in London and Nottingham.

Main findings/Conclusions

- The take-up of short breaks by black families had barely improved over a ten-year period. A high level of unmet need was noted, particularly among South Asian families.

- When compared with white families, black families were more likely to use institutional rather than family-based provision, but the reasons for this had not been explored.

- Home-based services such as sitting and befriending are very popular with black parents, particularly those of South Asian origin, as they are more able to control the quality of the service and ensure that it does not expose their children to culturally inappropriate parenting practices and values. Some parents also spoke of concerns that, if their children were provided with out-of-home care by the social services department they might not be allowed to return home.

- Information about services was often unavailable or ineffective and this was a major barrier to access for families. Schemes in areas with few families of minority ethnic origin were not proactive enough in making their services culturally competent. There was a tendency for social workers to take an initial response from parents 'at face value' rather than engaging with them to address their concerns and misconceptions and encourage them to apply to use the service. Consultation and direct communication with families was lacking.

The author concluded that a shortage of black social workers and short-break carers meant that in some areas services could not adequately represent the communities they serve. The need to keep accurate statistics of users and non-users of services is stressed. Schemes that succeeded in providing an available and acceptable short-term break service were those that were firmly located within their communities, with high visibility of scheme workers and carers amongst black families and organisations.

Gardner, R. (2003) *Supporting Families: Child Protection in the Community.* London: Wiley.

A detailed account of an evaluation of six NSPCC family centres set in the context of a discussion of family support services. The description of the six areas includes information on ethnicity. The researchers comment on the generally poor quality of ethnic monitoring. In one of the areas children of mixed parentage were over-represented on the child protection register. In another, in which 30 per cent of the general population were of minority ethnic origin, the proportion of those involved with child welfare services who were of minority ethnic origin increased with the seriousness of the intervention. They made up 42 per cent of the children in need, 46 per cent of children looked after and 50 per cent of children placed for adoption.

Ghate, D. and Hazel, N. (2002) *Parenting in Poor Environments: Stress, Support and Coping.* London: Jessica Kingsley Publishers.

This is a detailed report (part of the Department of Health *Supporting Families* research programme) of a nationally representative survey of 1754 families in poor environments, 198 of whom (11%) were of minority ethnic origin. Using questionnaires and interviews the researchers explore the differences between parents who are 'coping well' (46% of the sample) and 'coping less well' (2% coping badly and 52% sometimes coping and sometimes not). Taking the group of ethnic minority families as a whole, there were no differences between whether the parents would describe themselves as 'coping' or 'not coping' according to ethnicity but the authors point out that this may conceal differences between ethnic groups. There is a detailed analysis of the nature of formal and informal support available to families and the factors that influence the use of support.

Gibbons, J., Conroy, S. and Bell, C. (1995) *Operating the Child Protection System.* London: HMSO.

This research aimed to explore the wide variation in numbers of children placed on Child Protection Registers (CPR) in otherwise similar authorities. The survey was carried out in 1991 before the implementation of the Children Act 1989. A mixed methods research approach was used. In stage one, 90 completed postal questionnaires giving data on CPRs from 107 English authorities (a response rate of 84%) were analysed. The second part of the research involved a detailed study of six London Boroughs and two counties. In these, all referrals or re-referrals where the child was under 16, and there was a possibility of abuse or neglect, were notified to the research team, resulting in a sample of 2758 children. The researchers urge caution in interpreting the data on ethnicity because data on the ethnic origin of the children was often missing. Minority ethnic families as a combined group were less likely to be referred because of concerns about possible sexual abuse (20% compared with 31% of the referrals of white children). However, they were more likely than white families to be referred because of physical abuse (58% of minority ethnic families were referred for this reason compared with 42% of white families). Black African and South Asian parents were more often referred than those in the other ethnic groups for using a stick or other implement to inflict the physical punishment (40% of Asians and 43% of black Africans were referred for this reason compared with 30% and 16% respectively of African-Caribbean and white parents).

Gill, O. and Jackson, B. (1983) *Adoption and Race: Black, Asian and Mixed Race Children in White Families.* London: British Agencies for Adoption and Fostering.

This was the third follow-up report of placements for adoption of 51 black, Asian and mixed-parentage children made by the British Adoption Project (which was set up to challenge the prevailing view in the 1960s that adoptive families could not be found for black children). Half were placed when under six months old and all were placed when under two years old. Of the original 51 families, 44 were interviewed for this book when the children were adolescents. The children were also interviewed and much of the book comprises the comments of the parents and young people. Thirty-six of the children were placed with white families and eight were placed with parents at least one of whom was black or Asian, although most of these families lived in predominantly white neighbourhoods and only two of these could be described as culturally and ethnically well matched. These eight are discussed in a separate chapter and most of the book concerns the transracial placements. In all cases except one, the children were still in the family, and most parents and children spoke positively of their experiences of adoption. However, the authors comment that those placed with white families 'saw themselves as "white" in all but skin colour' (p.130). Because they had some concerns about whether the coping strategies of these children would serve them adequately as they moved into a world where their differences rather than their similarities with the majority community would be emphasised, the researchers emphasised the importance of the drive to recruit more minority ethnic adopters. Although practice and attitudes have changed since these children were placed, the study provides a benchmark to measure these changes.

Gray, B. (2002a) 'Emotional Labour and Befriending in Family Support and Child Protection in Tower Hamlets.' *Child and Family Social Work 7*, 13–22.

Gray, B. (2002b) 'Working with Families in Tower Hamlets: An Evaluation of the Family Welfare Association's Family Support Services.' *Health and Social Care in the Community 10*, 2, 112–122.

Aims, methods and sample characteristics

A broadly ethnographic approach was used to describe and evaluate the work of the Family Welfare Association's Tower Hamlets Family Support Services project. Project management records and 30 family case records were scrutinised and members of 22 families were interviewed and family interactions observed. Five family support workers were 'shadowed' on their visits to families and their work and attitudes discussed with them. Focus groups were held with family support workers and the project steering group. The ethnic minority population of the borough as a whole was 36 per cent at the time of the research, and in one project neighbourhood Bangladeshis formed the majority group, making up nearly 60 per cent of the population. Three projects were evaluated: home visits by family support workers to provide activities for parents and children and advice on parenting skills; home-based family support to parents with profound mental health problems; and the Quality Protects service taking referrals from across the borough for family assessment and child protection focused service. The main emphasis in the articles is on the first of these.

Main findings/Conclusions

- Many families reported that their children had been bullied at school and that there were racist undertones even when the bullying was not overtly racist. Somali children, as the newest arrivals in the community, were particularly vulnerable to bullying. Family support workers played a role in detecting bullying and facilitating communication with the schools to find ways of dealing with it.

- The family support workers (all women) were not qualified social workers but received in-service/vocational training. They were usually from the same community as the family being visited. This was valued by parents and there was evidence that it helped to cut through cultural and language barriers between the service providers and the family members. For recent arrivals they provided basic support and provided information and an introduction into the country.

- Family support workers worked closely with social workers in cases where there were concerns about domestic violence or possible child maltreatment. This did not appear to prevent the families from accepting their support. The family support workers were often able to explain the child protection systems and help the parents to participate. Professional supervision was seen as particularly important because of the close relationship that usually developed between the families and the workers.

- Families appreciated the intensity and duration of the services provided by the family support workers and the mental health project. The fact that the Quality Protects service was provided by a voluntary sector agency did not entirely mitigate the suspicion and anxiety family members felt at the high level of professional involvement in child protection cases.

The central conclusion is that trained and well supervised 'semi-professional' workers who share the culture and language of the families are well placed to provide longer-term practical help and emotional support. Through visiting the family at home at a fairly high frequency agreed with the parents, they can not only succeed in providing support but also facilitate participation of the parents and children in the more formal health and social work processes, including the formal child protection mental health and domestic violence systems. Equally important, they are able to influence interventions in the direction of being more sensitive to the cultural beliefs and views of the family members.

Harwin, J. and Forrester, D. (2002) *Parental Substance Misuse and Child Welfare: A Study of Social Work with Families in which Parents Misuse Drugs or Alcohol.* Interim report to Nuffield Foundation. London: Brunel University.

Only the phase one report of this study was available for inclusion in this publication. The research, undertaken in four London boroughs, poses the questions: what proportion of cases allocated for a 'child in need' or child protection service involve substance misuse? which substances are misused? what concerns are expressed about the children and how do they relate to the substance misuse? how do social workers assess and intervene in the cases? what are the outcomes for the children? The characteristics of the 183 'parental substance misuse' (PSM) sample are compared to the 348 non-substance misuse cases. Forty-six per cent of the cohort (246 children) were of minority ethnic origin and data obtained from records and from interviews with social workers were analysed in terms of ethnicity alongside other potentially explanatory variables. Thirty-nine per cent of the white British families were in the PSM sample, a larger proportion than for the other ethnic groups except that 48 per cent of the 73 children of mixed heritage were in the PSM group. In contrast, none of the 60 Black African children were in the PSM sub-sample. Black children of mixed parentage were over-represented amongst the care proceedings cases. Of the 14 mixed parentage children subject to care proceedings, 12 were in the PSM sample. Taking advantage of a total cohort of child and family cases in which there was a substantial proportion of minority ethnic families, the researchers provide information about these families. Some of the cases involved concerns with a cultural dimension, such as differences in relation to behavioural expectations for teenagers; the use of physical punishment and leaving children alone. But most cases involved a complex interplay between social, economic, cultural and individual factors and the researchers note that over-simplistic generalisations based on ethnicity and culture need to be avoided.

The researchers concluded that parental substance misuse is a very common concern in longer-term child and family social work. Yet the workers dealing with all types of substance misuse had received little or no training and were frequently dealing with complex cases without specialist input around substance misuse issues.

Harwin, J., Owen, M., Locke, R. and Forrester, D. (2003) *Making Care Orders Work: A Study of Care Plans and their Implementation.* London: The Stationery Office.

Aims, methods and sample characteristics

This DH funded, post-Children Act 1989 research aimed to investigate the influence of court care plans on case management and interim child outcomes. The study provides data on 100 children in 57 families who were subject to care orders in 1997 in 5 local authorities. Social service files were analysed, and social workers, some birth parents, current carers and 26 children over 7 were interviewed after 21 months. The study does not focus specifically on ethnic minority children but the variable of ethnicity is included in the analysis. Fourteen of the 100 children and young people (16%) were of minority ethnic origin. Ten of these were boys whereas in the white British sample girls outnumbered boys. Half of the ethnic minority children (as with the white children) were aged four years or under. Around a quarter in all ethnic groups started as emergency proceedings. Needs related to ethnicity or culture were mentioned in only 10 of the 100 care plans. Three of these plans were for white European children (e.g. Irish or Scottish). For half of the children of minority ethnic origin, the subject of their ethnicity was not mentioned in the care plans. The majority of the care plans in which race or culture was mentioned referred to the need to match the child's ethnicity in substitute placements (especially where adoption was planned). Half of the children of minority ethnic origin were to be placed with relatives. Of the other seven children, there were four (all of dual heritage) who had fostering plans and three very much younger children were to be placed for adoption. Remaining or returning to a parent was the plan for 22 white children but no children of minority ethnic origin. Interim outcomes were considered, using the DH *Looking After Children* dimensions as outcome measures. Of the eight children from ethnic minority groups who made good progress (four African-Caribbean and four of dual heritage) all were in fulfilled placements – six in kinship care and two placed for adoption. One child with mixed progress was also in a fulfilled kinship placement. Among the five children from ethnic minority groups who made poor or 'mixed' progress, three were also in placements that had been fully implemented.

Hatton, C., Akram, Y., Shah, R., Robertson, J. and Emerson, E. (2004) *Supporting South Asian Families with a Child with Severe Disabilities*. London: Jessica Kingsley Publishers.

Aims, methods and sample characteristics

This is part of the DH *Supporting Parents* group of studies. Taking as their starting point an estimate that the prevalence of severe learning disabilities amongst UK South Asian communities may be up to three times higher than amongst the general population, the researchers aimed to provide a comprehensive picture of the lives of UK South Asian families with a child with severe disabilities. Structured interviews (using schedules translated into four languages) were conducted with 136 parents, in 5 local authority areas. The sample included substantial numbers of Indian (17% of the sample), Pakistani (70%) and Bangladeshi (11%) families to allow comparisons to be made across these groups. Where possible, standardised measures used in previous research were used to enable comparisons with related studies. Semi-structured interviews were conducted at two time points with 26 parents. Qualitative and quantitative data were combined to build a comprehensive picture of the lives of South Asian families with a child with severe disabilities. Factors associated with positive and negative outcomes for families were explored.

Main findings/Conclusions

- Most main carers were mothers born outside the UK, but who had spent many years in the UK and cared for the family full-time. Substantial numbers of families had a lone parent (12%) or were caring for more than one person with disabilities (21%). Only a minority of main carers could speak, read or write English, with parents reporting a wide variety of spoken and written languages. Ninety-three per cent of main carers were Muslim.

- As with previous research, parents in this study reported a pattern of pervasive material disadvantage. Household income was inadequate, especially to meet the special needs of a disabled child. Unemployment was high, with patchy uptake of benefits. Housing was generally rated as unsuitable for the needs of the child, particularly in terms of lack of space and safety issues. There were higher rates of depression than in the general population and parents made explicit links between caring for their child with disabilities, particularly without support, and physical and mental health problems.

- Most parents described their children as fairly happy, sociable and affectionate, but over 80 per cent of parents also reported problems associated with eating, toileting and bedtime routines, and their child throwing things, yelling, screaming and throwing tantrums.

- Most children were diagnosed as having a disability by four years of age. Disclosure was mostly conducted by a medical professional in

English. Around half of parents reported understanding what was told to them at disclosure, with most receiving good support at the time from partners and the disclosing professional. Post-disclosure support was, however, lacking.

- Almost all children were in special schools, which were generally very highly rated by parents and were often the only reliable point of contact with services to gain information and support. However, very few schools were reported to provide for the language, cultural or religious needs of the children.

- Most parents reported having enough information about the child's disability, although fewer parents had enough information about *services* for the child or for themselves as parents. Parents using the English language were more likely to report having enough information. Parents also reported preferring to receive information in the appropriate language from a professional face-to-face.

- The most common source of informal support for parents was within the household. Few parents reported receiving support from extended families or religious organisations. This was partly owing to extended family members living too far away or being unable to provide support, although even when received this support was often rated as unhelpful.

- Less than half of parents reported collaborative relationships with professionals. Most parents reported difficulties in communicating with professionals and having to struggle to obtain needed support. Bangladeshi parents reported fewer problems with services, possibly owing to lower expectations of services, and Indian parents reported more problems with services.

- Few parents reported awareness and/or use of respite care services for their child. Respite care, when received, was usually in respite units managed by social services. These services were generally highly valued and responsive to the child's cultural needs, but the amount of respite available was insufficient.

- Although most parents reported needing an interpreter, less than half had been provided with one.

- A minority of parents (28%) reported having a keyworker, with social workers and health visitors often taking on a keyworker role. Where provided, keyworkers were almost always highly rated.

- Because the support needs of many parents were not met, the social lives and leisure activities of parents and children were severely restricted.

The researchers concluded that culturally sensitive support and services reinforce collaborative relationships between parents and professionals, thus reducing the unmet needs of families and helping to improve the physical and mental health of parents.

Howe, D, Feast, J. with Coster, D. (2000) Adoption, Search and Reunion: The Long Term Experience of Adopted Adults. London: Children's Society.

A retrospective quantitative and qualitative description and analysis of the experiences of 472 adopted adults placed by The Children's Society, mostly as infants. Of the 472, 394 were adopted people who had initiated a search for information and birth relatives (searchers) and the remaining 78 were non-searchers but had been approached by the adoption agency to let them know of a birth relative's wish for contact. The study is unusual as it focuses on the reasons why some adopted people seek information on, or contact with, a birth parent or relative and other adopted people do not. The 394 returned questionnaires represented a response rate of 87 per cent for searchers and 68 per cent for the 78 'non-searchers'. Thirty-two (8%) were of minority ethnic origin and all but two were placed with white families. Qualitative interviews were carried out with a large sub-sample of 74 adopted adults. Detailed information is provided about the experience of growing up adopted and meeting up with members of the birth family and the impact this had on the adoptive family. See Kirton *et al.* (2000) for more details on those of minority ethnic origin.

Humphreys, C., Atkar, S. and Baldwin, N. (1999) 'Discrimination in Child Protection Work: Recurring themes in work with Asian Families.' Child and Family Social Work 4, 283–291.

This article reports on two linked studies in two Midlands authorities in 1994–5. The first involved documentary analysis of the case files of a purposive sample of 20 families of South Asian origin (including children of mixed heritage) whose cases were considered at child protection conferences. These were followed by a semi-structured interview with a social worker. The second involved observation of child protection conferences, review conferences and core group and other meetings held in respect of 19 South Asian families. Data from files, observations and interviews were analysed thematically. Twelve of the 20 families required an interpreter and many problems in relation to interpreting were identified. Interpreters tended to be used only at formal conferences and not at other meetings and home visits. There was a lack of culturally sensitive and appropriate placements for children needing to be looked after. Physical and mental health issues for the parents were often ignored, yet one or both parents in 16 of the 20 families had an identified physical or mental health problem and in some families both were apparent. The researchers concluded that, when interpreting or placement services fell short of adequate, and when needs remained unmet because of the narrow focus on an incident of suspected abuse, with little attempt to understand the cultural context, the end result for both children and parents was both inadequate and oppressive.

Freeman, P. and Hunt, J. (1998) *Parental Perspectives on Care Proceedings.* London: The Stationery Office.

Hunt, J., Macleod, A. and Thomas, C. (1999) *The Last Resort: Child Protection, the Courts and the 1989 Children Act.* London: The Stationery Office.

Hunt, J. and Macleod, A. (1999) *The Best-Laid Plans: Outcomes in Judicial Decisions in Child Protection Proceedings.* London: The Stationery Office.

Aims, methods and sample characteristics

These three linked studies focus on children in three areas whose cases were considered by the family courts. Together, they aimed to analyse the decision-making processes; to investigate how professionals and family members viewed legislation in this area; and to evaluate the operation of the legislation. For the Hunt *et al.* study, data were collected on 104 child protection proceedings before the implementation of the Children Act 1989 and 83 post-Children Act cases. Forty-four per cent of the cases concerned a child of minority ethnic origin. The Freeman and Hunt publication reports on interviews with 35 adult members of 25 families, 44 per cent of whom were of minority ethnic origin. Hunt and Macleod were able to collect reliable data on 118 of these children, 52 of whom (40%) were of minority ethnic origin (14 'non-Caucasian, single heritage' and 38 of mixed heritage). Interviews were also carried out at this later stage with 19 adults from 17 families.

Main findings/Conclusions

- Some plans changed during the first year, but eventually 84 per cent of placement plans were achieved. It was more likely that adoption plans would be achieved than plans for kinship care, return to parents or long-term foster care.

- It was more likely that placement plans would be achieved for white UK children (75% achieved) than for 'single heritage' minority ethnic children (69%) or for children of mixed heritage (61%). Numbers in the different groups and different placement types were too small for reliable analysis but were provided for descriptive purposes.

- More of the white children were placed for adoption (29%) compared with only 2 of the 33 mixed heritage and one of the 13 single heritage ethnic minority children. The largest number of achieved care plans was for placement with parents and there was little difference in terms of ethnicity. This was the achieved plan for 39 per cent of the white UK children; 33 per cent of the children of dual heritage and 38 per cent of the single heritage ethnic minority children. However, the authors note that 'non-indigenous children [with care plans to return to or remain with parents] did seem rather more vulnerable to both breakdown and disruption' (p.36).

The three books in this series provide detailed case material and comments from parents and professionals, giving insights into how decisions are taken, the sorts of pressures families are under, the subsequent care careers of the children, and the impact of compulsory social services intervention and court processes on the parents and children.

Husain, F. and O'Brien, M. (1999) *Muslim Families in Europe: Social Existence and Social Care.* London: University of North London.

This European Union funded report provides information on the circumstances of Muslim families in England, Belgium and Denmark and on the statutory services available to support them if problems develop. Through interviews with social services staff and a small number of parents in the three countries the research team aimed to identify best practice initiatives in the non-profit and statutory sectors. A need was identified for improvement in interpretation services and the training and vetting of all interpreters. The need for training for social workers, managers and reception staff on issues affecting Muslim families was highlighted as was the importance of recruiting social workers from religious and ethnic minority communities.

Hylton, C. (1997) *Family Survival Strategies; Moyenda Black Families Talking, An Exploring Parenthood Project.* York: Joseph Rowntree Foundation.

This study of minority ethnic community members, involving interviews carried out between 1994 and 1996 by a team of eleven people from Exploring Parenthood who were predominantly of African-Caribbean and South Asian descents, provides background data of relevance to child welfare services. The research involved 230 people, interviewed individually and in groups, from London and Luton who were of African, African-Caribbean or South Asian descent. The 25 groups involved in the interviews had been set up by women's organisations, refugees, senior citizens, and people involved in group counselling. Five group interviews were with young people between the ages of 8 and 18. In addition, there were eight case studies looking at the lives of particular individuals in greater detail, including one conducted in India. The author identifies a strong sense of spirituality within these communities which helped to define each group's identity and solidarity. Interviewees felt that individual and family strengths and the ability to overcome problems were in part based on the individual's ability to maintain a vision that opposed the perceived materialism and individualism of UK society. Some interviewees from all ethnic groups also spoke of widespread concern that professionals, including teachers and social workers, take away or undermine their parental authority.

Ince, L. (1998) *Making it Alone: A Study of the Care Experiences of Young Black People.* London: British Agencies for Adoption and Fostering.

A qualitative study which aimed to understand the experiences of a small 'volunteer' sample comprising ten young people who had been in care and the preparation they had received for the process and transition of leaving care. The data were collected from two shire counties in 1995. All participants had either one or two parents who had been born in the Caribbean. They were aged 16–19 (four male and six female) and all had been on care orders lasting between 13 and 18 years. All had lived for most of their time in care with white families or white residential workers and most had had disrupted care careers. Social work professionals were also interviewed. The young people expressed the view that living with white carers had had a negative impact on their own identity and culture. All of the young people spoke of feelings of rejection and loss for themselves and for their own parents and community. Racial problems within education were experienced, along with a lack of support from professionals in regard to racism and bullying. Some had experienced abuse in their foster families, but none had been returned to their birth families. The earlier they entered the care system and the longer they remained there, the less likely were they to have any contact with their birth family. This contributed to the fact that, on leaving care, most found it difficult to reclaim their identity as black young people or feel comfortable and accepted within the black community. These young people spoke of many painful and distressing experiences in care and in the process of leaving care. As well as strongly arguing for strenuous attempts to place children with families of a similar heritage, the author emphasises the need for early preparation for leaving care to include work on understanding and valuing the culture and identity of the communities into which they were born.

Ivaldi, G. (2000) *Surveying Adoption: A Comprehensive Analysis of Local Authority Adoptions.* London: British Agencies for Adoption and Fostering.

An analysis of children adopted from English local authorities in 1998–9 using data from BAAF and local authority statistical returns as well as surveys of local authority policies. 172 children (10% of those adopted) were of minority ethnic origin. There is a section on consideration given to ethnic matching of child with adopters based on a sub-group of 120 mixed-parentage and 48 Black children. Twenty-eight per cent of the mixed-parentage children but only one of those with two minority ethnic parents were placed with a single or two White parents. A partial explanation for this is that children of mixed-parentage were more likely than the other groups to be adopted by their foster parents, who were often white.

This in part related to a longer time taken over the assessment of these children and reaching a 'best interest-adoption' decision.

Jones, A., Jeyasingham, D. and Rajasooriya, S. (2002) *Invisible Families: The Strengths and Needs of Black Families in which Young People have Caring Responsibilities.* London: Policy Press.

Over a 12-month period, the researchers interviewed 17 young people and 15 family members from 20 families. Completed questionnaires were received in respect of 40 agencies and discussions were held with 15 practice managers. There was a high level of unmet social and medical need amongst black parents who were disabled. Young people's work ranged over chores, personal and medical care and interpreting. There was no consistent assessment of the support needs for parents and young people and none of the parents or young people received regular or adequate support services. There was a strong need for health-based services, good quality home care services, counselling and social activity services for children and also for parents. The researchers identified a number of reasons for this low level of responses from social care agencies. Parents were often reluctant to approach local authorities fearing they would be assessed as unable to look after their children and that they may be taken into care. When help was requested the responses from local authorities were mostly inadequate or inappropriate, especially in relation to cultural and religious needs. Some of the services offered were considered by family members to be of poor quality with the result that they turned them down or opted out.

Jones, L., Atkin. K. and Ahmad, W.I.U. (2001) 'Supporting Asian Deaf Young People and their Families: The Role of Professionals and Services.' *Disability and Society 16*, 1, 51–70.

This qualitative research study looked at how Asian deaf young people (average age 15) and their families engage with welfare provision. Twenty-seven interviews were conducted with young deaf people and there were 14 group interviews involving 43 young people. The young people were contacted through community groups, schools, colleges and social groups in the north of England and Scotland. Most of the young people lived at home with their parents, 15 of whom were also interviewed. The lack of British Sign Language (BSL) interpreters caused particular problems when the families were trying to access services. It was common for the young people to be accompanied to interviews with health, social care and education professionals by their parents who acted as interpreters and brokers of services. However, parental involvement could be more intrusive as they got older. Confidentiality and lack of privacy emerged as specific problems. Generally, parents in the study felt that services offered them little support, especially in coming to terms with their child's deafness. Parents expressed concern that deafness limited their ability to socialise their children into cultural and religious values. The study concluded that the effectiveness of the services provided by social workers and health professionals was diminished by stereotypes and myths, both about deafness and about ethnic and faith communities. The authors argue that state services exert a form of social control where professional 'help' disempowers Asian deaf people by privileging 'oralism' over sign language.

Kirton, D., Feast, J. and Howe, D. (2000) 'Searching, Reunion and Transracial Adoption.' *Adoption and Fostering* 24, 3, 6–18.

Aims, methods and sample characteristics

The study was a reanalysis of data from a larger study of 472 adopted adults (Howe, Feast and Coster 2000). There were survey responses from 35 adopted adults (mean age 33) and interviews with 13 (2 male, 11 female). The aim was to learn more about their growing up experience and their attitudes towards and experience of linking up again with their birth parents or seeking out information about them. A particular focus of this report was on the experience of growing up in a family from a different ethnic background.

Main findings/Conclusions

- Transracially adopted respondents had in one respect done better than white respondents in that they were more likely than white respondents to describe their adoptive parents as open to discussion about adoption and more satisfied with the information received. However, there was little mention of any attempts by the adopters 'to positively promote a sense of racial or cultural identity for the children' (p.17).

- Roughly two-thirds of adopted adults, across the ethnic groups, felt close to and loved by their adoptive parents during childhood. However, ethnic minority respondents adopted by white parents were more likely than the white interviewees to say that they felt different from their adoptive family and less likely to say they felt that they belonged to the adoptive family. As a consequence, 45 per cent of ethnic minority adopted people responding to the larger survey were classified by the researchers as 'alienated' and only 21 per cent as 'integrated' into their adoptive families and communities. The corresponding figures for white adopted people were 29 per cent and 48 per cent. From interviews, reasons identified included being treated differently by members of the adoptive extended family and by neighbours.

- Most were brought up in largely white communities and several described meeting or knowing very few other black people. 'Some interviewees spoke of a sharp contrast between a warm, caring environment within the family and a cold, hostile one beyond' (p.8).

- Only one of the thirteen interviewees 'conveyed a strong sense of black minority ethnic identity (p.10) and four attached little importance to their black heritage. More than half of the adopted people interviewed reported 'wrestling with the effects of racial stereotypes, isolation in "white" communities and ambivalence towards black people' (p.10). A very small number described racist attitudes on the part of their adopters and others expressed a sense of shame that they themselves had internalised racist attitudes. Some described how teachers and family members refused to take seriously their reports of racial harassment or abuse.

- Many of those interviewed expressed reservations about transracial adoption owing to the potential for increased identity confusion (over and above that for all adopted children) and the inherent limitations on the capacity of white adoptive parents to empathise with their child's experiences of racism.

- Issues of racial and ethnic identity figured strongly amongst the reasons why these adopted adults sought out birth relatives but their hopes were often unrealised.

- Transracially adopted people were more likely than their white counterparts to search for birth fathers. Those adopted transracially were less likely than white counterparts to say they felt at home with birth relatives or that reunion had made them more complete as a person (23% compared with 54% of the white respondents).

This article is rich in detailed quotes from the young people. From their qualitative and quantitative data the researchers conclude that '…while transracial adoption has many successful elements, usually including strong loving relationships with adoptive parents, it also frequently gives rise to feelings of difference or even alienation from the family' (p.17).

Kohli, R. (2000) 'Breaking the Silence: Social Work with Unaccompanied Asylum Seeking Children.' *Professional Social Work*, June 2000.

The article provides interim findings from qualitative research on the nature of social work practice with unaccompanied asylum-seeking young people who are or were at some point 'looked after' under the Children Act 1989. Data on 34 young people, their social workers and the service provided were obtained through interviews with their social workers from four local authorities. The young people came from 12 countries but Eritrea and Kosovo accounted for 18 of the 34 in the sample. The majority of the young people were Black African (22 of the 34). About half had declared their religious origins to be Muslim (16), and the rest Christian. There were 23 boys/young men and 11 girls/young women. At the time of the study the young were aged between 11 and 19 years and the majority (21) had arrived within the preceding 12 months. Just over 10 per cent of the sample came to the UK as part of a sibling group. The young people came into the UK with minimal identification – no mementos, photographs, keepsakes, or any links with their past lives. Some were assisted by an agent and others were 'trafficked' with the intention of abuse or exploitation. About 10 per cent were deeply distressed after being subject to torture and physical and sexual assaults, usually by non-family members. Specialist therapeutic services were used for a minority and there was little use of mainstream child and adolescent mental health services. Many of the young people resisted same 'race' placements or placements with families of ethnic communities other than white British and some exhibited racism. Some found comfort in church and mosque based communities. Social workers reported that many were worried about opening up and talking about their past and their feelings because it might jeopardise their asylum claims. They were deeply committed to getting a good education, and many were high academic achievers. Ten per cent arrived with at least one sibling and all sibling groups were placed together. The researcher concludes that many aspects of this work are common to all child placement social work. The young people needed and wanted a reliable and trusting relationship that combined practical help and emotional support. The majority also turned to their field social workers as well as, or instead of, their carers for elements of surrogate parenting. The workers also have to develop new knowledge and acquire skills in networking with communities and with bodies such as the Home Office and Immigration Service.

Lees, S. (2002) 'Gender, Ethnicity and Vulnerability in Young Women in Local Authority Care.' British Journal of Social Work 32, 7, 907–922.

Aims, methods and sample characteristics

This research aimed to explore issues of ethnicity and gender for 124 young women who started to be looked after in one outer London Borough between 1990 and 1999. Only 24 (19%) were white; 34 (27%) (including most of the 24 unaccompanied asylum seekers) were African; 33 (27%) were African-Caribbean; 21 (17%) were of mixed heritage; and 10 (8%) were 'Asian or other nationalities'. The ethnic origin of 2 was not known. All those who were over 16 at the time of the research were invited to take part in the interview study. Of the 8 who responded, 4 were African-Caribbean, 2 were of mixed heritage and 2 were White.

Main findings/Conclusions

- Young women of African and African-Caribbean heritage (including those of mixed heritage) were over-represented amongst those coming into care in this borough.

- Forty per cent of the social workers in the borough were of African-Caribbean or mixed African-Caribbean/White heritage, suggesting that racism amongst social workers is unlikely to have played a big part in the reasons why Black young women were over-represented in the care population for the borough.

- The young women in the cohort as a whole had a higher incidence of physical and mental health problems than their peers who were not in care, but Black young women were less likely to self-harm (16% did so) than the White young women (25%).

- Substantial proportions of the young women in the whole cohort had experienced the death of a parent (16%); lived with parental mental illness (25%); been physically abused (two-thirds); been sexually abused (half). (These data are not analysed by ethnic group.) Despite the extent of abuse, mainly by fathers and step-fathers, it was rare for the offender to be prosecuted. Young women who ran away because they were being assaulted by a parent were often described as 'beyond control'.

- Of those who ran away in response to stresses at home, 81 per cent were black compared with only 16 per cent who were white.

- The authors conclude that explanations for over-representation are complex and interacting. They include the lack of extended family members, with single-parent families having fewer relatives to turn to for practical help and emotional support and some grandparents being in the home country; a higher level of material disadvantage; a higher tendency for black young women to be more autonomous and therefore more likely to run away from abusive situations at home. They note that the young women were 'often subjected to particularly strict forms of discipline and restrictions on their autonomy' (p. 921). The young women interviewed gave examples of positive social work practice but there were many complaints about change of worker, workers not listening when they complained about parental abusive behaviour, the lack of resources for children in care, and inadequate attention to their educational needs, which increases the likelihood of future social exclusion.

Lindblad, F., Hjern, A. and Vinnerljung, B. (2003) 'Intercountry Adopted Children as Young Adults: A Swedish Cohort Study.' American Journal of Orthopsychiatry 72, 2, 190–202.

This national cohort study of the long-term outcomes for 5942 Swedish adults who were adopted as infants from overseas is important because of the size of sample and because, although numbers are still comparatively small, the cumulative numbers of inter-country adopted adults in the UK population are increasing. It also has more general relevance both as a long-term outcome study of transracial adoption and a study of the long-term impact of early privation during the early months after birth. National data sets are used to provide information about family circumstances, employment, health problems and educational attainment for this group of young adults whose well-being is then compared with that of their non-adopted siblings (1884); the general population (723,154); non-adopted immigrants (of whom 3544 were non-European and 8834 were European). The adopted adults were all born between 1968 and 1975 and entered Sweden before the age of seven. Fifty-four per cent were or East Asian heritage – mostly Korean; 24 per cent were of South Asian heritage; 15 per cent were adopted from South America and 7 per cent from Africa. Seventy-seven per cent joined their adoptive families within three months of their birth. Logistic regression was used to control for a range of possible intervening variables. Adopted people were more often long-term recipients of social welfare payments than the other groups. In terms of employment, they did less well than the indigenous young people and were similar to the non-adopted immigrants. The authors comment, 'A conceivable explanation for our results is that adoptees – because of their non-Swedish appearance – may have been rejected because of discrimination by employers in their decisions about whom to hire' (p.199). The level of education of the adoptees was similar to that of their peers in the general population, but lower when adjusted for the socio-economic status of the adoptive families in which they grew up. More of the adopted women were single parents, and more of the adopted men who were parents did not live with their children, than was the case for the comparison groups. There was also a higher risk of the adopted young people developing psychiatric symptoms including substance abuse. Amongst the adopted group, there were better results for the South Koreans, which the authors consider may be related to the better pre- and post-natal care in Korea for infants who will be adopted overseas. The outcome for adopted women was better than for adopted men. The authors emphasise that the majority of the adopted adults progressed satisfactorily into adult life but conclude that the data on psychiatric problems imply that specific measures have to be taken as these children grow up, including access to psychiatric counselling.

Lowe, N., Murch, M., Borkowski, M., Weaver, A., Beckford, V. and Thomas, C. (1999) *Supporting Adoption: Reframing the Approach.* London: British Agencies for Adoption and Fostering.

Basic data were provided by 115 adoption agencies (a 72% response rate) providing basic data on the 1539 placements made in 1993–4. Forty-one per cent were over the age of five at placement. Fifteen per cent were of minority ethnic origin (9% of mixed race parentage; 3% African-Caribbean; 2% Asian and 1% from another minority ethnic group). A small number was placed transracially, including some White children placed in families where at least one adopter was of a different ethnic background. Data were available on 1932 approved families of whom 180 (less than 10%) were of minority ethnic origin. There is information on 219 children, 6 per cent of whom were of minority ethnic origin. Interviews were conducted with purposive samples of adopters from 48 families, included some where the placement had disrupted. In seven of these families either the child or one or both adopters were of minority ethnic origin.

Lowe, N. and Murch, M. (2002) *The Plan for the Child: Adoption and Long-term Fostering*. London: British Agencies for Adoption and Fostering.

This study was commissioned to inform the Choice Protects debate on the respective roles of adoption and long-term foster care in providing permanence and stability for looked after children. Using data from files and interviews with social workers and managers the researchers explore the reasons why plans were made for either adoption or long-term fostering for 220 children aged under 12 in 1999 who had been looked after for at least 12 months. Eleven per cent of the children were of minority ethnic origin (3% of mixed heritage, 2% Caribbean, 1% African, 3% Asian, 2% 'black other') but this information was missing in respect of 19 per cent of cases. The original plan for the child was long-term foster care in 40 per cent of cases, adoption in 29 per cent of cases and 'other' (including return home) in 31 per cent of cases. Twelve months later, some plans had changed and long-term fostering was the plan in 47 per cent of cases, adoption in 23 per cent of cases and 'other' in 29 per cent of cases. Of the 22 children whose parents were of minority ethnic origin, 65 per cent were the subject of a plan for long-term fostering compared with 53 per cent of the white children. As with other studies, children of mixed ethnicity were more likely than those with two black or Asian parents to be placed for adoption rather than long-term foster care.

Messent, P. and Murrell, M. (2003) 'Research leading to action: A Study of Accessibility of a CAMH Service to Ethnic Minority Families.' *Child and Adolescent Mental Health 8*, 3, 118–124.

This 'in-house' action research was carried out by the Child and Adolescent Mental Health Service (CAMHS) teams in Tower Hamlets with the aim of identifying any differences in referral rates and services provided to the borough's main ethnic groups. In Tower Hamlets the majority group is Bangladeshi (54% of the child population) but they represent only 19 per cent of CAMHS referrals. African and Black British/Caribbean each make up 4 per cent of the population and 3 per cent of referrals for a service. White children are 28 per cent of the child population but make up 32 per cent of referrals. The ethnicity of 30 per cent of the children was not known, despite the fact that an ethnic monitoring form should have been in use for all referrals. A purposive sample of 116 referrals was explored in more detail to identify differences between ethnic groups. African-Caribbean families were more likely than Bangladeshi families to refer themselves, and their children were more likely to be referred in an emergency. Focus groups were convened with Bangladeshi parents who had used the service and Bangladeshi workers in the voluntary and statutory sector. The parents all agreed that the low rate of referral was not due to Bangladeshi children having fewer problems, but rather resulted from a low level of awareness of the service and how it might help.

Mullender, A. Hague, G., Imam, U., Kelly, L., Malos, E. and Regan, L. (2002) *Children's Perspectives on Domestic Violence*. London: Sage.

Aims, methods and characteristics of sample

A questionnaire was completed by 1395 children aged 8–16 in school settings in three areas in England providing information on their knowledge of and attitudes towards domestic violence. Twenty-four per cent were of minority ethnicity. This was followed by a two-stage interview process with 45 children who had experience of domestic violence. Nine others were interviewed in groups. Twenty-nine per cent of those interviewed were of minority ethnic backgrounds, including 12 of South Asian and 2 of East Asian descent. Twenty-two of their non-abusing mothers were also interviewed, as were 14 professionals involved in providing assistance. It proved difficult to identify a sample of Asian mothers willing to take part in the study. The interview study provides detailed information on how children make sense of male violence towards their mother in South Asian households.

Main findings/Conclusions

- No significant differences were found between the attitudes of the different ethnic groups responding to the survey towards domestic violence, nor on their reports of knowing someone who had experienced domestic violence.

- From their interviews with the Asian young people who had experienced domestic violence (only half of whose mothers were UK-born), the researchers found that confidentiality emerged as a distinctive theme for Asian women and children when compared to the wider sample.

- One notable difference identified in the South Asian sample was the potential contribution of other members of the extended family to their mother's abuse.

- Some of the South Asian children interviewed were influenced in their understanding of domestic violence and the likelihood of seeking help by considerations of family honour ('izzat'). There was a tendency for them to differ from the other children interviewed in that they were more likely to refer to cultural expectations that they must continue to show respect to their fathers, irrespective of their behaviour towards their mothers.

- For all the children in the study, moving away from their familiar surroundings, friends and family was very difficult, but for South Asian children the problem was compounded by a greater vulnerability and exposure to racism in new communities and schools. For those who had to move from their communities, specialist refuges were valued for their ability to provide effective help.

The researchers report concerns that unsympathetic treatment from white people or organisations could further restrict the likelihood of seeking help for some minority ethnic parents and children. They stress the competence of the young people, their ability to look for creative ways forward and the importance of their perspective being taken on board when policies are developed to meet the special needs of South Asian women and children.

Neil, E. (2000) 'The Reasons Why Young Children are Placed for Adoption: Findings from a Recently Placed Sample and a Discussion of Implications for Subsequent Identity Development.' Child and Family Social Work 5, 4, 303–316.

Neil, E. (2002a) 'Contact After Adoption: The Role of Agencies in Making and Supporting Plans.' Adoption and Fostering 26, 1, 25–38.

Neil, E. (2003) 'Accepting the Reality of Adoption: Birth Relatives' Experiences of Face-to-face Contact.' Adoption and Fostering 27, 2, 32–43.

Aims, methods and sample characteristics

This is a prospective longitudinal study of a cohort of 168 children, placed for adoption by ten local authority or voluntary adoption ages during 1996–7. Social workers provided detailed non-identifying information by means of a postal questionnaire. The main aims were to determine current practice in relation to openness in adoption and to consider whether contact arrangements bore any relationship to other characteristics of the cases. There were 136 white children (81% of the sample), 21 children of mixed parentage (12.5%) and 11 children (6.5%) with two parents of the same minority group (seven of Indian descent, one African-Caribbean, two Filipino and two Korean children). There was an intensive interview sample of 36 children whose birth or adoptive families were involved in face-to-face contact arrangements. This is a longitudinal study and the sample has been added to by the inclusion of children placed at the same time who were planned to have indirect contact. The intention is to follow these children through into adulthood.

Main findings/Conclusions

- It was more likely that children from minority ethnic groups would be placed for adoption at their parents' request than was the case for white children. From the comments of the social workers, this appeared to be linked to the status of single parenthood within particular cultures.

- Children of ethnic minority origin, especially those with two black or Asian birth parents, tended to be placed for adoption at a younger age than white children, although numbers were not statistically significant.

- There was no significant difference between the children from different ethnic groups in terms of the delay from plan to placement. On average, adoption was planned for white and mixed parentage children at about 13–14 months of age and for black and Asian children at about 8 months. The difference was not statistically significant and was affected by the fact that these children were younger on starting to be looked after and more likely to be placed at the request of their parents.

- There were 24 adoptive families where one or both parents were of minority ethnic origin. The main motivation for all ethnic groups was infertility. Unlike the birth parents, few adopters of either gender were of mixed parentage. Fewer adoptive fathers than mothers were of minority ethnic origin.

- All the white children were placed with white adopters as were six of the minority ethnic children (all of mixed heritage). Half of these had face-to-face contact arranged to maintain links with the child's ethnic, cultural or religious background. All the children whose parents were of the same minority ethnic origin were placed with adopters of the same ethnicity and religion. However, because of the complex interaction of ethnic group, country of origin, religion and language 10 (31%) of the 32 children from minority ethnic groups – mainly those of mixed heritage – had elements of their culture missing from their new adoptive families.

- Children of minority ethnic origin were more likely than white children to have no contact at all with a birth relative after adoption (7 out of 22–32% compared with 9% of the white children). This is partly explained by more of the minority ethnic children being placed at their parents' request and not requesting even indirect contact. As explained by the social workers, in some cases young women felt unable to make use of a 'letter box' service because family members did not know of their pregnancy and they were either physically afraid or fearful of the shame to themselves or their families if this became known. More generally, whether or not there was ongoing contact after placement was more related to the policy and practice of the agency than to the characteristics of the case or the wishes of the birth relatives.

O'Neale, V. (2000) *Excellence not Excuses: Inspection of Services for Ethnic Minority Children and Families*. London: Social Services Inspectorate.

This report summarises the key findings from a national inspection of local authority child and family services to minority ethnic families. The inspections were carried out in eight English authorities in 1998–1999, with the aim of evaluating the quality and appraising the appropriateness of the services provided to ethnic minority children in need (including those looked after) and their parents and carers. Particular attention was paid to the adequacy of the systems for collecting data on ethnicity and using this to monitor the appropriateness and quality of services. Attention was also paid to mechanisms for liaising with minority communities and consulting family members. Position statements were analysed and 80 case records were read and the social workers interviewed. Meetings were held with a cross-section of staff and with ethnic minority voluntary groups. A survey was undertaken of the opinions of parents who had been assessed for a service or following a child protection referral. The findings are presented in summary form using percentages but there is no information on the size of sample or response rate, making it difficult to interpret this part of the report. Examples of good practice are reported.

Quinton, D., Rushton, A., Dance, C. and Mayes, D. (1998) *Joining New Families: A Study of Adoption and Fostering in Middle Childhood*. Chichester: Wiley.

Rushton, A., Dance, C. and Quinton, D. (2000) 'Findings from a UK Based Study of Late Permanent Placements.' *Adoption Quarterly 3*, 3, 51–71.

These publications report on the first stages of a prospective longitudinal study of the placement of sixty-one children aged between five and nine who joined unrelated foster or adoptive families during middle childhood. Twelve of the children were of minority ethnic origin (seven of African-Caribbean heritage – including three who also had a white parent; four of South Asian and white heritage; one of White and Middle Eastern heritage). Half were placed with parents of a similar ethnic background and half were placed with white parents. The study involved in-depth interviews with new parents (at one month, six months and twelve months after placement) and social workers (one month into placement). Standardised tests were used to assess the well-being of the children at the start of the placement and one year later. The researchers found that the age of placement, sex, ethnicity, number of placement moves, type of permanent placement all had no influence on predicting the interim outcome one year after placement. When the characteristics of the new parents were considered, a lower level of responsiveness was associated with less positive outcomes but neither age nor ethnicity appeared to make a difference. The best predictors of placement instability were overactive/restless behaviours, being placed alone, and being 'singled out for rejection' by the birth parents.

Qureshi, J., Berridge, D. and Wenman, H. (2000) *Where to Turn: Family Support for South Asian Communities.* London: National Children's Bureau/Joseph Rowntree Foundation.

Aims, methods and sample characteristics

Six focus groups were convened in 1999 drawing their membership from the four main ethnic and linguistic South Asian communities in Luton. The groups were attended by 53 parents and were facilitated by researchers of the same gender and community background. Case vignettes were used to tease out how members of these communities understood the role of social services departments and their partner agencies. Key themes emerging from these and from interviews with managers fed into a study of a purposive sample of 20 cases of Asian families open to child and family social work teams. Eleven social workers were interviewed about their work with Asian families. Two were from Asian communities, two were of African or African-Caribbean ethnic origin and seven were White. Four cases were analysed in more detail and in these cases one or both parents were interviewed in their preferred language. No children were interviewed as they either declined to be interviewed or their parents refused permission for them to take part.

Main findings/Conclusions

- Most South Asian parents interviewed expressed the view that family stress and breakdown in their communities was more common than perceived by professionals and the wider public.

- There was a lack of knowledge about the welfare system and understanding about the role of social workers. Families experiencing problems would first seek help from family and friends due to the 'embarrassment' and 'stigma' about the use of social services. Focus group members had more confidence in the police than in social services as agencies able to deal with sensitive issues.

- South Asian women were more positive about initiatives and programmes to reduce domestic stress and to prevent family breakdown than men (who were more suspicious of interventions into family life). This was seen to be particularly important for policy and practice as men held particular powers as religious and community leaders.

- There was a low level of formal family support services provided in this area specifically for South Asian families. The Social Services Department employed few Asian staff and no South Asian managers. There were no specific policies concerning South Asian families and no specific training for staff.

The researchers concluded that professionals' misunderstandings about family circumstances sometimes led to negative assumptions about caring. Most of the social workers interviewed felt impeded by not having sufficient understanding of the lives of the children and parents. Interpreting services were much used and valued, but problems were also identified. This is a very detailed analytical study generating recommendations for policy across the local authority as well as for social work practice and future research.

Richards, A. (2001) *Second Time Around: A Survey of Grandparents Raising their Grandchildren*. London: Family Rights Group.

A survey was distributed in 2000–2001 to 251 grandparents who were caring for a grandchild, identified through a wide range of sources from self-help and advocacy groups to women's magazines. One hundred and sixty-nine questionnaires were completed and verbal responses given by a further 11 Bangladeshi grandparents. One hundred and nineteen were interviewed either face-to-face or over the phone or as attendees at a series of focus groups or day workshops. Of the 180 who provided details, 42 (23%) were of minority ethnic origin (4 African-Caribbean, 21 Sikh, 10 Chinese, 11 Pakistani and 2 of mixed parentage). Partly because of the different ways in which the grandparents were contacted, there were differences between the East and South Asian kinship carers and the rest of the sample. All the South Asian and Chinese grandparents with caring responsibilities lived in the same household as one or both of the child's parents. Whilst all of the white, Caribbean and dual heritage grandparents had stepped in as carers after a family crisis, the Asian carers were doing this as part of their culturally expected role as grandparents. Whilst 38 per cent of the whole sample said that they were involved to some extent with social services this applied to none of the Asian grandparents.

Richards, A. and Ince, L. (2000) *Overcoming the Obstacles*. London: Family Rights Group.

The research aimed to build on earlier research in order to identify ways in which services for looked after children of minority ethnic origin could be improved and to disseminate examples of good practice. A questionnaire seeking detailed information about employment policies, ethnic monitoring and services to ethnic minority families was distributed to all (157) local authorities in 1997 and 52 were returned. There were follow-up telephone or face-to-face interviews with 85 representatives of statutory and voluntary agencies and advocacy projects. There were group discussions and some individual interviews involving 19 young people, 11 foster carers and 17 parents. The low response rate detracts from the quantitative analysis but the report is particularly useful for its examples of good practice and the ideas about how improvements could be made.

Robinson, L. (2000) 'Racial Identity, Attitudes and Self-esteem of Black Adolescents in Residential Care: An Exploratory Study.' *British Journal of Social Work 30*, 3–24.

A quantitative study comparing the self esteem and racial identity attitudes of 40 African-Caribbean young people aged 13–16 living in residential care with 40 African-Caribbean young people matched in terms of age, sex and educational attainment, who were not in care and attended a comprehensive school in the same city. The author first explores the psychology literature on self esteem and identity and summarises the research on black identity development. She found that the two groups had relatively high levels of self-esteem and of internalisation of their identity as black young people. Self-esteem was most likely to be high for those who strongly identified themselves as belonging to the black community. She concluded that 'these findings are encouraging because a negative racial identity and low self-esteem have been the characteristics traditionally attributed to young black people in residential care' (p.16). The author suggests that this may be because these second generation British African-Caribbeans have grown up in a less overtly racist environment than that which surrounded their parents and also because they were in residential care near to their home communities and families. Many of their care workers were black and had strategies to reinforce a positive black identity and counteract the impact of racism.

Rowe, J., Hundleby, M. and Garnett, L. (1989) *Child Care Now: A Survey of Placement Patterns.* London: British Adoption and Fostering Agencies.

Aims, methods and sample characteristics

This large-scale pre-Children Act 1989 survey aimed to provide information on the number and characteristics of children in different placements and the outcome of those placements. Information was obtained via questionnaires completed by social workers on nearly 10,000 placements of 3748 children admitted to care in 1984–1985 in six contrasting authorities, and any changes of placement for children already in care. There is a chapter analysing the placements of the 19 per cent of the sample who were of minority ethnic origin.

Main findings/Conclusions

- African-Caribbean children were disproportionately represented in admissions to care, but this was largely due to the large numbers of young (mainly African-Caribbean) children being admitted for temporary care during family emergencies. Six per cent of the full sample (36% of the minority ethnic children) were African-Caribbean. Mixed-parentage children (8% of the full sample and 44% of the minority ethnic children) had a particularly high admission rate but their in-care patterns were more like those of white children and they stayed longer than African-Caribbean, African or Asian children. African children made up 2 per cent of the sample and 12 per cent of the minority ethnic children. South Asian children were under-represented amongst those coming into care (1% of the sample and 8% of the ethnic minority children in the sample areas).

- Adoption or a long-term foster placement was planned for about 10 per cent of mixed parentage children, but for hardly any children from other minority ethnic groups.

- Placements of black and mixed-parentage children broke down slightly less often than those of white children.

This research is now dated but the size of the sample and analysis by different types of placement for different ethnic groups makes it an important study especially allowing for an examination of changes over time. In 2003 the DH commissioned a study to replicate the Rowe *et al.* (1989) study as part of its Quality Protects research programme.

Rushton A., Treseder, J. and Quinton, D. (1995) 'An 8 Year Prospective Study of Older Boys Placed in Permanent Substitute Families.' *Journal of Child Psychology and Psychiatry 36, 4, 687–695.*

A detailed prospective study of 18 boys placed for adoption or permanent fostering between 1983 and 1986. The study emphasises the importance of selecting samples of children who are broadly similar (in this case boys aged between five and nine at placement). Five were British-born of African-Caribbean origin and two were of mixed parentage. In all except one of the placements (a mixed-parentage boy with a white family) the ethnic origin of the new family was the same as that of the child. Four of the placements of black or mixed-parentage children disrupted within the follow-up period and only one was rated as 'good'. The poor results were due to a range of factors not necessarily associated with ethnic origin, including previous adverse placement histories, over-activity and poor peer relationships in the boys, and 'less positive parenting' as assessed by the researchers in the first year after placement. The numbers are small, but the study is important in highlighting the importance of focusing on the adopters' approach to parenting an older child and on ways of providing them with advice, support and therapy.

Rushton, A., Dance, C., Quinton, D. and Mayes, D. (2001) *Siblings in Late Permanent Placements.* London: British Agencies for Adoption and Fostering.

A mixed methods prospective research study of 133 members of sibling groups placed from care with 77 adoptive or permanent foster families when at least 1 sibling was aged between 5 and 11. The study aimed to provide information on the children, their relationships with each other and with siblings in the new families, and contact arrangements when they were not placed together. It compared the well-being of children placed with a sibling with those separated from siblings (at 3 months and 12 months after placement) and described the nature of the social work and other support services. Only 4 of the substitute families taking part were of minority ethnic background, all 4 being dual heritage families. Ten of the children in the interview sample were of dual heritage. Four of the 5 placed singly and 1 of the sibling groups were placed with white parents and 2 white children were placed with a dual heritage family. Four-fifths of the children settled well during the first year but 7 of the placements disrupted, including 2 sibling groups and 5 singly placed children. Numbers are too small for analysis in terms of ethnicity of either the new parents or the children. The researchers conclude that there appear to be advantages in following the guidance in the Children Act to place children together with siblings but that on occasions, after careful assessment, a child will benefit from being placed separately from a sibling. There will be further follow-ups of these children (as a combined sample with those in the Quinton *et al.* 1998 study).

Sellick, C. and Connolly, J. (2001) *National Survey of Independent Fostering Agencies*. Norwich: University of East Anglia.

A survey providing information on independent foster care agencies, their foster carers and the children for whom they were providing placements in 1999–2000. There was a 60 per cent response rate with over 55 completing questionnaires and providing data on the last 10 children placed by each of them (513 children and young people). Out of the 2260 individual foster carers, 82 per cent were described as 'White' (n=1880), with 8 per cent (n=179) described as Black-Caribbean. During the 12-month study period 3211 children were fostered by these IFA carers. Of the children 2624 (78%) were described as UK White and 22 per cent as either White (other) or of minority ethnic origin.

Sinclair, I. and Gibbs, I. (1998) *Children's Homes: A Study in Diversity*. Chichester: Wiley.

Gibbs, I. and Sinclair, I. (1998) 'Treatment and Treatment Outcomes in Children's Homes.' *Child and Family Social Work 4*, 1, 1–8.

Gibbs, I. and Sinclair, I. (2000) 'Bullying, Sexual Harassment and Happiness in Residential Children's Homes.' *Child Abuse Review 9*, 247–256.

Aims, methods and sample characteristics

Quantitative and qualitative data were gathered from looked after children in 48 children's homes across 5 English local authorities between 1993 and 1996. Minority ethnic young people made up about 7 per cent of residents, although this varied by local authority. The sample included African-Caribbean (n=19), Asian (n=13), mixed African-Caribbean and white (n=35), mixed Asian and White (n=11) and other (n=3). A census of current staff and of current and past residents was carried out. Postal questionnaires were sent to the social workers of the young people and to the staff in the 48 homes. Follow-up questionnaires were sent to the young people and their social workers six months later. There were face-to-face interviews with 223 young people, 99 parents and 47 heads of home. Eighteen of the young people interviewed were of minority ethnic origin. As well as providing information about the ethnic minority children in the body of the report, the authors provide an appendix looking particularly at issues of ethnicity.

Main findings/Conclusions

- Around 7 per cent of staff were of minority ethnic origin. More than two-thirds of these were of African-Caribbean descent and the others were of mixed heritage. Although the overall proportions of ethnic minority staff and ethnic minority children were similar, neither ethnic minority staff nor young people were evenly distributed across the homes.

- Eighty per cent of the ethnic minority young people responded that 'black and Asian residents get a fair deal' and 20 per cent said this was 'sometimes true'. However 50 per cent felt that the home was a better place 'for white residents than black'.

- Along with other parents, those of minority ethnic origin felt a lack of power in relation to staff in homes. However their difficulties in approaching children's homes were increased by fears of cultural differences and racist responses.

The researchers found no direct evidence of racism in the children's homes. However they reported that staff in the homes had difficulty in providing an environment that embraced diversity so that children of minority ethnic origin were at ease. Difficulties were reported over food, dress and general distrust with the police (who checked on people with whom they wished to stay). Overall the researchers conclude that 'the black and minority ethnic young people did not feel particularly victimised but did find the homes an uneasy and uncomfortable place in which to be' (p.267). More generally, the researchers concluded that, irrespective of ethnicity of the child, the results on residential care were not encouraging. Four out of ten of the young people interviewed said that they had thought of killing themselves in the previous month; four out of ten of those who stayed six months and had no previous conviction acquired one; half said that someone had tried to bully them or sexually harass them since they arrived. After allowing for differences in intake, these differences were not related to staffing ratios or proportions of qualified staff. Rather, they were related to the degree to which staff agreed with each other and with the head of home on how the home should be run, and the head's sense of his or her role and autonomy.

Sinclair, I. and Wilson, K. (2003) 'Matches and Mismatches: The Contribution of Carers and Children to the Success of Foster Placements.' British Journal of Social Work 33, 871–874.

Sinclair, I., Gibbs, I. and Wilson, K. (2004) Foster Carers: Why They Stay and Why They Leave. London: Jessica Kingsley Publishers.

Sinclair, I., Wilson, K. and Gibbs, I. (2004) Foster Placements: Why They Succeed and Why They Fail. London: Jessica Kingsley Publishers.

Aims, methods and sample characteristics of

These two linked studies provide quantitative and qualitative data on foster care practice in the late 1990s in seven English local authorities. The quantitative component in the first study included a census of all (1528) foster carers currently registered. Nine hundred and forty-four carers responded to a postal questionnaire (62%). The full cohort was followed up to see which foster carers ceased fostering. For the second study questionnaires were completed by 495 of the foster carers of 596 children who had been placed with foster carers for at least a month (an 83% response rate), 416 social workers and 492 family placement workers. According to the foster carers 84.2 per cent of the foster children were white and of English, Welsh, Irish or Scots origin. The remaining foster children included: 1.7 per cent Caribbean, 1.9 per cent African, 8.9 per cent mixed parentage, 2.2 per cent Asian, and 0.2 per cent 'other'. Nine out of ten of these foster children's carers described themselves as white and of English, Irish, Scottish or Welsh origin. Follow-up questionnaires were sent 12 months later to foster carers, social workers, family placement workers and to 250 children aged 8 or over (resulting in 150 usable responses from the children). There were also 23 detailed case studies, selected to include cases that had gone well and less well and based on interviews with carers and social workers, including some ethnic minority carers and children. For a further follow-up study three years after the first contact, questionnaires were sent to social workers, young people and carers (including new carers or birth parents if the child had returned home or moved on). There were interviews with 87 social workers, children and carers from a purposive sample of 30 cases. Six children of minority ethnic origin were in this interview sample. This is a 'cross-sectional' study involving recent entrants but also children who had been looked after for many years.

Main findings/Conclusions

- Although a quarter had spent 6 months or less in their current placement, 18 per cent had spent 3 years or longer. Half of the sample children first came into care when less than 6 years old.

- At the three-year follow-up, 28 per cent were with the same foster family (including 3% adopted by that family) and 12 per cent had been adopted by other families. Seventeen per cent were with birth parents and 15 per cent with other foster carers. Four per cent were in residential care and 18 per cent were living independently (6% were lost to the sample).

- The studies suggested that placement breakdown was largely explained by characteristics in the child (their wish or otherwise to be fostered and their tendency to behave in difficult ways), the parenting approach of the carers, and the developing interaction between the foster family and the child. Other key influences were the child's happiness at school and the approach of the birth family.

- A key difficulty was that for most children longer-term foster care did not provide a long-term alternative family but it was not consciously seen as a preparation for the next stage in the child's life. With the exception of adoption, these next stages were seen by both foster carers and social workers as much less satisfactory for the child. Children who returned home were more likely to be re-abused and had worse outcomes in terms of behaviour and ratings of school performance, differences that were not apparently explained by their characteristics. Children and young people returning home or moving into independent living nevertheless appeared to attract less support than those who remained in foster care.

- Social workers reported that they sought to place children with families which were as far as possible matched in terms of ethnicity, culture and language.

Outcomes for white children of UK origins were routinely compared with outcomes for children of other ethnicities (grouped together because of lack of numbers). There were no apparent differences although there was a tendency for children in ethnically 'matched' placements to do better in terms of breakdown if they were girls and worse if they were boys. Case studies suggested that close and sensitive matching (e.g. including religion and country of origin) could be very important to the child, and that simple matching in terms of 'Black' could not override the importance of having a 'good' carer. Some of the data from interviews refer to ethnicity, especially to questions around differences between the child and the carers, and some of these refer to racist attitudes on the part of carers (including in at least one case a relative).

Sinclair, R. and Hai, N. (2003) *Children of Mixed Heritage in Need in Islington*. London: National Children's Bureau.

Aims, methods and sample characteristics

The research focused on the backgrounds and specific needs of children of mixed heritage who were on the caseloads of Islington child and family social work teams. It aimed to assess the quality of information available; to look at how families perceived their ethnicity, and whether they considered that their needs had been met. Children of mixed heritage made up 34 per cent of the teams' caseloads and 60 per cent of those of minority ethnic origin. A purposive sample of 12 mixed-heritage families was identified and a detailed case study methodology was adopted. In six of these cases the mother was identified as 'white' and in six cases the father was identified as 'white'. Eight were looked after, three were on the child protection register and one was a family support case. Eight of the social workers for these children were of minority ethnic origin and four were white. Of the foster carers and key workers, two were white and the others of minority ethnic origin. There is also a discussion of the adequacy or otherwise of government and local authority statistics and records on children of mixed heritage.

Main findings/Conclusions

- The study was impeded by the poor quality of recording of information on the ethnic background of the birth parents (available for only 66% of mothers and 57% of fathers). Information on religion was recorded for only 51 per cent of children, 18 per cent of mothers and 17 per cent of fathers.

- The diversity of the borough's population is emphasised by the fact that almost half the sample were in the 'other mixed' group. Twenty-two (45%) of the mothers were white UK and seven (26%) were white European. Four mothers were of Caribbean origin, two African, three Asian and three of mixed heritage.

- Amongst the seventeen ethnic minority fathers whose ethnicity was recorded, nine were of Caribbean descent, three were African, three were Asian and two were recorded as of 'other or mixed' ethnicity.

- Given this complexity, the researchers comment on the difficulty of 'ethnic matching' whether in terms of placement or social worker. 'Matching by broad ethnic category (especially where this focuses on "race" and excludes culture and religion) is unlikely to adequately reflect actual backgrounds' (p.35).

The report on the quantitative part of the study is a rich source of information on the attitudes of parents and young people towards being a member of a mixed heritage family, and their satisfaction or otherwise with the services provided. This is complemented by the views of the social workers and carers about the services they were able (or not able) to provide and the extent to which they were able to help the young people develop a positive identity, incorporating pride in the different aspects of their heritage, culture and religion.

Smith, M. A., Heverin, A., Nobes, G. and Upton, P. (1995) *Punishment and Control of Children in the Home: Parental Actions and Strategies: Report to the Department of Health*. London: Thomas Coram Research Unit.

Nobes, G. and Smith, M. (1997) 'Physical Punishment of Children in Two Parent Families.' *Clinical Child Psychology and Psychiatry 2*, 271–281.

Nobes, G., Smith, M., Upton, P. and Heverin, A. (1999) 'Physical Punishment by Mothers and Fathers in British Homes.' *Journal of Interpersonal Violence 14*, 8, 887–902.

This is a normative study using a carefully piloted survey instrument to seek self-report details on control strategies. The survey was administered via interviews with parents and carers of 'indigenous children', randomly selected from Health Authority lists. Since the 'indigenous English' definition included all children whose grandparents were born in the UK, the sample included some African-Caribbean and South Asian children but data on these were not analysed separately in these publications. There was a response rate from primary carers of 81 per cent. A further analysis (Nobes *et al.* 1999) compared punishments used by 362 mothers and by 103 fathers in the 366 two-parent families. All except 20 mothers and 9 fathers in the two-parent sample were white. The study provides background data on how UK families discipline and control their children. In common with earlier researchers whose work they discuss, the authors find that physical punishment of children (usually by way of smacking, and spanking, pushing and shoving) is a common occurrence in family life in England. Only 7 per cent of mothers and 9 per cent of fathers reported having never used a physical punishment and just over a quarter of mothers and 17 per cent of fathers reported smacking or hitting a child at least weekly. Fathers were more likely than mothers to use physical restraint (including pushing, throwing and holding). Sixteen per cent of mothers and 21 per cent of fathers had used punishments rated by the researchers as 'severe'. Ten per cent of mothers and 15 per cent of fathers said they had used an implement to smack a child – most usually a slipper or wooden spoon. Although the data are not analysed by ethnic group this study can provide baseline data for other researchers when the relationship between physical punishment and significant harm is being discussed in respect of different patterns of family life in different cultural groups.

Thoburn, J., Wilding, J. and Watson, J. (2000) *Family Support in Cases of Emotional Maltreatment and Neglect*. London: The Stationery Office.

Aims, methods and sample characteristics

The fieldwork for this research took place in 1994–5 in two inner city areas with diverse ethnic populations and a rural county. The main reasons for referral to social services child and family teams were analysed for a total cohort of 712 children under the age of 8. In the 2 city areas the majority of the referred were of minority ethnic origin (61% and 77% respectively). Thirty-seven per cent of the half of the sample that involved concerns about child maltreatment involved physical or sexual abuse. For phase two (intensive sample) 180 randomly selected families involving referrals for family support and cases involving emotional maltreatment or neglect were contacted and the main parent/carer in 122 cases agreed to be interviewed. There were 40 'service request' cases and 82 'neglect' or 'emotional maltreatment' cases. Of these parents, 108 were re-interviewed approximately 12 months later. Records of all 180 cases were scrutinised.

Main findings/Conclusions

• Of the 263 children of minority ethnic origin 114 (43%) were of South Asian origin; 66 (25%) were black African; 45 (17%) were of African-Caribbean origin and 38 (14%) were of mixed parentage or recorded as 'other' ethnic origin.

• Ethnic minority children were more likely than white children to be referred when under the age of 12 months (24% were under 1 compared with 11 per cent of the white children).

• Around half each of the Asian, African and African-Caribbean children were referred for a service rather than for child protection reasons, as were 65 per cent of those in the 'other' group (the proportion for the white children was 43%). More of the South Asian children than the African-Caribbean, African or white children were referred because of neglect or child safety concerns. More of the white children or those in the 'other' group (including children if mixed heritage) were referred because of concerns about physical or sexual abuse.

• Twenty-eight of the 45 ethnic minority parents in the interview sample came to England fairly recently, in 19 cases as immigrants and in 9 cases as refugees or asylum seekers. For 25 per cent of the ethnic minority parents interviewed in one City area and 45 per cent in the other the first language was not English and interviews were conducted in the language of their choice.

• When comparisons were made on indicators of economic and social disadvantage, few differences were found between those referred for family support services and those referred because of child protection concerns. In this respect white families and those of minority ethnic origin were similar. Overall levels of informal social and emotional support were similar between service request cases and those referred because of child protection concerns, and between ethnic minority families and white families.

- The social service response to ethnic minority families was less likely to be a Section 47 (child protection) investigation than was the case with white families, even when the referral mentioned child protection concerns. This was especially the case when concerns were expressed about inadequate supervision leading to child safety concerns.

- There was a trend towards white families being more likely than those of minority ethnic origin to receive a long-term service and for the service to ethnic minority families to have ended within four weeks of referral.

- More of the white than the ethnic minority families were provided with a service rated by the researchers as 'generally good' (68% compared with 48%). More of the services to ethnic minority families were rated as 'inappropriate to their needs'.

- More of the white families showed either overall improvement or deterioration and more of the ethnic minority families were in the 'little change' or 'mixed' outcome groups. Whilst 60 per cent of the white parents interviewed considered that their own well-being had improved, this applied to only 44 per cent of the ethnic minority parents interviewed on both occasions. On the other hand, whilst 27 per cent of the white parents considered that their well-being had deteriorated, this applied to only 19 per cent of the parents of minority ethnic origin.

This is a detailed study of day-to-day work of child and family teams in areas of ethnic and cultural diversity and with families living in highly stressful circum-stances. A majority of the social workers and team managers was of south Asian or African-Caribbean descent and the agency managers had given much thought to how to provide an ethnically sensitive service. When ethnic minority families received a longer-term social work service (whether initiated as part of a child pro-tection or a family support inquiry) most found it helpful. Only a small minority of those who actually received a social work service of more than a week's duration were dissatisfied with it. More of them were 'unsatisfied' because they were refused services to meet their own needs for help and services and those of their children.

Thoburn, J., Norford, L. and Rashid, S. P. (2000) *Permanent Family Placement for Children of Minority Ethnic Origin*. London: Jessica Kingsley.

Charles, M., Rashid, S.P. and Thoburn, J. (1992) 'The Placement of Black Children with Permanent New Families.' *Adoption and Fostering* 16, 3, 13–19.

Moffatt, P. G. and Thoburn, J. (2001) 'Outcomes of permanent family placement for children of minority ethnic origin.' *Child and Family Social Work* 6, 13–21.

Rashid, S. P. (2000) 'The Strengths of Black Families.' *Adoption and Fostering* 24, 1, 15–22.

Aims, methods and characteristics of sample

This is a long-term follow-up study of ethnic minority children placed from care by 24 voluntary adoption agencies with adoptive or permanent foster families not previously known to them in the early 1980s. Baseline data were obtained from records shortly after the children were placed and after between 6 and 10 years for the full sample, and between 10 and 14 years for the interview sample of 51. The aim was to learn more about longer term outcomes and to provide a descriptive account of the children's lives before they joined their new families, as they grew up and as young adults. Fratter *et al.* (1991) reported on the outcomes for the full cohort of 1165 children, approximately two-thirds of whom were placed for adoption and one-third as permanent foster children. Of these 1165 placements, 246 (21%) were of children of minority ethnic origin (half of them of mixed-race parentage). For the Thoburn, Norford and Rashid (2000) study, this sample was enhanced by additional ethnic minority children placed at the same time in order to increase the numbers placed with families of similar ethnic origin. The age range at the time of follow-up was between 14 and 30. There was a purposive sample of 51 children including roughly half placed with white families and half with families where there was at least one minority ethnic parent. Half of these children were of mixed-race parentage and half had two birth parents of the same minority ethnic background. One or both adoptive or foster parents was interviewed as were 28 of the young people. For the full sample, whether or not the placement lasted or disrupted was the only outcome measure, though data were also available on whether there was any face-to-face birth family contact after placement. For the full sample numbers were large enough for the use of *logit* analysis to control for variables (Moffatt and Thoburn 2001). For the small sample a range of outcome measures was used, including standardised measures of well-being, employment and education, ethnic and adoptive identity and overall satisfaction of parents and young people.

Main findings/Conclusions

- Forty-two per cent of the children both of whose parents were of minority ethnic origin were placed as permanent foster children compared with 17 per cent of children of mixed ethnicity and 16 per cent of white children. This is to some extent explained by the younger age at placement of the children of mixed-race parentage in the sample.

- Children with two black or Asian parents were more likely to be placed with black or Asian families, and these parents were more likely to foster than adopt, to have older children and sibling groups placed with them, and to facilitate birth family contact.

- Twenty-four per cent of the placements of minority ethnic children disrupted in the sense that they returned to care or relationships with the family broke down irretrievably before they reached adulthood. When other differences between the children were taken into account, there was no difference in breakdown rates between those with two minority ethnic parents and white children. But there was a slightly higher disruption rate for children of mixed parentage (Fratter *et al.* 1991)

- There was no difference in disruption rates between those placed as foster children and those placed for adoption. Some of the young people in the interview sample (mostly those who were adopted) gave reasons for preferring adoption; some (mostly those who remained as foster children) gave reasons for preferring not to be adopted.

- A history of deprivation or abuse prior to placement was independently associated with placement breakdown as was having emotional or behavioural problems at the time of placement.

- There was no statistically significant difference in rates of disruption, when other variables such as age and behavioural difficulties were held constant, between those placed with white families and those with families in which at least one of the parents was of minority ethnic origin.

- There are detailed accounts, using the words of parents and young people, of the satisfactions and stresses of the experience of growing up in foster or adoptive families and in families with similar and different cultures, including a chapter on experiences of racism and strategies for dealing with it.

The authors conclude that permanent family placement for children of minority origin who cannot be brought up by their birth parents can be highly satisfactory for the children and parents. However, it is not without risks, both in terms of breakdown and children's well-being. With careful selection and support, the evidence from this study indicates that some white families can successfully parent ethnic minority children, including encouraging in them a sense of pride as a member of a particular ethnic and cultural group. However, after a careful review of the interview data, the researchers conclude that transracial placement brings with it additional tasks and pressures on top of those already inherent in adoption or foster placement, and that wherever possible it is desirable to place children with families who are ethnically and culturally similar.

Tizard, B. and Phoenix, A. (1993) *Black, White or Mixed Race? Race and Racism in the Lives of Young People of Mixed Parentage.* London: Routledge.

A normative study involving in-depth interviews with 58 teenagers who had one white and one minority ethnic parent. The study explores social identities and their complexity within families. It also explores racism and racial abuse within mixed-heritage families and notes that many of the parents were unaware of the extent of racism and racial abuse experienced by their children. The sample is atypical in that 61 per cent came from social classes 1 and 2 and 55 per cent attended independent schools. The authors conclude from these interviews that, at the time of their research, there were several contemporary British black lifestyles and that the notion of a 'positive black identity' was oversimplified and prescriptive, reifying 'race' and neglecting other social identities such as gender, class, occupation, peer and neighbourhood groupings. They conclude by relating their findings to the debate on transracial adoption, hypothesising that transracially adopted children of mixed heritage are likely to have a different sense of identity from those growing up in a black family.

Tunstill, J. and Aldgate, J. (2000) *Services for Children in Need: From Policy to Practice.* London: The Stationery Office.

This mixed methods research provides a detailed account and interim evaluation of family support services to 93 'middle years' children 'in need'. Twelve (13%) were of minority ethnic origin. As with similar studies including small numbers of children, the authors did not consider it appropriate to analyse the data in terms of ethnicity. Families in all ethnic groups were concerned about their children's behaviour and wanted advice and practical help to improve the situation. A wide range of practical, advocacy and social casework services was provided to these parents and children, sometimes in family centres and sometimes in their own homes. The response of the parents and children interviewed who received a support service was generally positive. Families referred by professionals were more likely to feel stigmatised than those who sought help on their own behalf, but the number feeling stigmatised as a result of receiving services had dropped when the family members were re-interviewed.

Tunstill, J. and Aldgate, J. with Hughes, M. and Peel, M. (2004)
*Family Support at the Centre: The Role of Family Centres in the Local
Service Network.* London: Royal Holloway College, University of
London.

This study reports on a national survey of 559 family centres in 1999, repeated two
years later. Descriptive data are provided from 415 centres and there were detailed
interviews with staff, parents and children involved with 40 of them. The study
focused particularly on the role of family centres in co-ordinating formal and
informal support. Although not specifically focusing on services to minority ethnic
families, many of the centres were in areas in which substantial proportions of black
and Asian families live. Of the 83 parents interviewed 17 per cent were of minority
ethnic origin. Survey respondents and interviewees were asked about policies and
resources specifically designed to make the centres more accessible and appropriate
for the different ethnic groups in their communities. The study also looks at
barriers to attendance. The detailed picture of family centres provides helpful
pointers to those looking for research studies that will assist them in making their
services more appropriate to minority ethnic families. The researchers conclude
that the 'mixed model' of referral and service provision is most likely to reach the
families most in need of help whilst minimising the risk of stigma, and with it community disapproval. However, the researchers identified a trend towards either
closure or a reduced role for family centres and changes of referral systems towards
more 'referral only' models.

Wade, J. and Biehal, N. with Clayden, J. and Stein, M. (1998) *Going
Missing. Young People Absent from Care.* Chichester: Wiley.

In this study of 210 young people who went missing from their placement at least
once during 1995–6, a fifth of the full sample and a quarter of those running away
from residential care were Black or Asian, or were of mixed heritage. However,
when they took into consideration the over-representation of African-Caribbean
young people in the children's homes in their sample, this group were no more
likely to run away than the White young people in residential care. Eight young
people of African-Caribbean or mixed heritage were included in the interview
sample. Most went missing from residential care but just over a third did so from
foster care and 2 per cent from a placement in care but living with parents.

Wade, J. (2003) 'Children on the Edge – Patterns of Running Away in the UK.' *Child and Family Law Quarterly* 15, 4, 343–352.

Mitchell, F., Rees, G. and Wade, J. (2002) *Young Runaways in Wales: Patterns, Needs and Services.* Cardiff: National Assembly for Wales.

Raws, P. (2001) *Lost Youth: Young Runaways in Northern Ireland.* London: The Children's Society.

Wade, J. (2002) *Missing Out: Young Runaways in Scotland.* Aberlour Child Care Trust.

These linked studies report on children under 16 in the general community who run away or are forced to leave home throughout the UK. Large representative samples of school pupils aged 14 and 15 were asked to complete survey schedules giving information of any incidents of 'running away' and being away at least overnight. In-depth interviews were conducted with around 300 young runaways and there were interviews with the professionals involved in seeking to provide them with services. In terms of ethnic background, white young people are the most likely to run away (the researchers estimate that ten per cent of white children do so before the age of 16) followed by 7.5 per cent of young people of African-Caribbean origin and 5.5 per cent of those of Indian/Pakistani/Bangladeshi origin. The main reasons young people gave included family conflict and instability, violence, emotional abuse and neglect. Half of those who had run away more than three times had first run away before the age of 11. Although young people across cultures run away for broadly similar reasons, ethnic minority children appear less likely than white children to access mainstream city centre-based services and are thus even more exposed to danger and trauma. The researchers conclude that services for young runaways of minority ethnic origin should be better targeted and delivered with greater sensitivity to the different cultures of the young people who go missing.

Waterhouse, S. and Brocklesby, E. (1999) 'Placement Choices for Children – Giving More Priority to Kinship Placements?' In R. Greef (ed.) *Fostering Kinship.* Aldershot: Ashgate.

The fieldwork for this research was done in 1996–7. Questionnaires and interviews with the foster carers, the child's worker and the foster carers' link worker were used to explore the organisational processes involved in 50 consecutive temporary foster placements (involving 71 children) made by 5 UK local authorities. Forty-four per cent of the children were of minority ethnic origin. Of the 47 carer households interviewed, 12 (26%) were Black Caribbean; 3 were Indian, 3 Black African, one Pakistani, and 3 were mixed-heritage households. Fifteen carer households were active members of a religious faith. Forty-five per cent of carers were single parents. Sixty-six per cent of placements were made in an emergency even though the majority of the children's cases were open and already well known to the agency. In only four cases (8%) did the social worker consider that they had been given a choice of placement. The poorer 'matches' were mostly related to the perceived inability of the carers to meet the full range of a child's needs rather than specifically related to ethnicity. There were only four placements in which children were placed transracially, two of white children placed with minority ethnic carers and two of minority ethnic children placed with white carers. There were more examples (nine) of children being placed with families who spoke a different language or practised a different religion or, although of the same ethnic background and religion, were from a totally different social class and culture. None of the six mixed-parentage children in the sample was placed in a foster home that reflected their particular ethnic origin, although these placements were only regarded as a poor match if the carer household comprised a single or two white parents. All these children had come into care from the care of a white parent and the plan was for them to return to that household. Nine of the 50 placements raised sibling separation issues but more of the African-Caribbean, African and dual heritage children than the white or South Asian children were placed with at least one sibling. Children of mixed-heritage parents were more likely than the other groups to be placed with kinship carers.

Ethnicity and faith group membership as reported to the Census 2001

Table A.1 Ethnic composition for total UK population, April 2001			
	Population count	*Percentage of total population*	*Minority ethnic population (%)*
White	54153898	92.12	n/a
Mixed	677117	1.15	14.6
Asian or Asian British			
Indian	1053411	1.79	22.7
Pakistani	747285	1.27	16.1
Bangladeshi	283063	0.48	6.1
Other Asian	247664	0.42	5.3
Black or Black British			
Black Caribbean	565876	0.96	12.2
Black African	485277	0.83	10.5
Black Other	97585	0.17	2.1
Chinese	247403	0.42	5.3
Other	230615	0.39	5.0
All minority ethnic population	4635296	7.88	100
All population	58789194	100	n/a

Source: National Statistics 2003, *Census, April 2001.*

Table A.2 The UK population: by ethnic group, April 2001

	England	Wales	Scotland	Northern Ireland	UK total	UK %
White	44679361	2841505	4960334	1672698 [1]	54153898	92.12
British	42747136	2786605	*	*	n/a	n/a
Scottish	*	*	4459071	*	n/a	n/a
Irish	624115	17689	49428	*	n/a	n/a
Other British	*	*	373685	*	n/a	n/a
Other White	1308110	37211	78150	*	n/a	n/a
Mixed	643373	17661	12764	3319	677117	1.15
White and Black Caribbean	231424	5996	*	*	n/a	n/a
White and Black African	76498	2413	*	*	n/a	n/a
White and Asian	184014	5001	*	*	n/a	n/a
Other Mixed	151437	4251	*	*	n/a	n/a
Asian or Asian British/Scottish	2248289	25448	55007	2679	2331423	3.97
Indian	1028546	8261	15037	1567	1053411	1.79
Pakistani	706539	8287	31793	666	747285	1.27
Bangladeshi	275394	5436	1981	252	283063	0.48
Other Asian	237810	3464	6196	194	247664	0.42
Black or Black British/Scottish	1132508	7069	8025	1136	1148738	1.95
Black Caribbean	561246	2597	1778	255	565876	0.96
Black African	475938	3727	5118	494	485277	0.83
Black Other	95324	745	1129	387	97585	0.17

Chinese or other ethnic group	435300	11402	25881	5435	478018	0.81
Chinese	220681	6267	16310	4145	247403	0.42
Other	214619	5135	9571	1290	230615	0.39
All minority ethnic population	4459470	61580	101677	12569	4635296	7.88
All population	49138831	2903085	5062011	1685267	58789194	100

Source: National Statistics 2003, *Census, April 2001*.

1 Includes 1170 people who ticked 'White Irish Traveller' box.

* Answer category not provided as a tick-box option in this country.

Table A.3 Religion in Britain, April 2001		
	Thousands	*Percentage of total*
Christian	42079	71.6
Buddhist	152	0.3
Hindu	559	1.0
Jewish	267	0.5
Muslim	1591	2.7
Sikh	336	0.6
Other religion	179	0.3
All religions	**45163**	**76.8**
No religion	9104	15.5
Not stated	4289	7.3
All no religion/not stated	**13626**	**23.2**
Total	**58789**	**100**

Source: National Statistics 2003, *Census, April 2001.*

Template for research summaries

1. Name(s) of researchers and organisations.

2. Dates of research data collection.

3. Part/s of UK where research data were collected.

4. Title of study.

5. Source of funding.

6. Publications/reports from study.

7. Aim(s) of study.

8. Did the study focus on minority ethnic children or families or were these families included as part of a general population?

9. Which ethnic groups were included in your study and were numbers large enough to report on each group separately?

10. If you are able to do so, please give approximate numbers in the different ethnic groups in your research population?

11. How were children/families identified for inclusion in the research?

12. What were the broad characteristics of the children, e.g. all under 18 or specific age groups; gender; children with disabilities; sibling groups; children who have been abused?

13. Were families identified on the basis of particular characteristics, e.g. living in areas of deprivation, involved in child protection processes?

14. Brief description of methodology.

15. What were the quantitative methods used and response rates?

16. What were the qualitative methods used and how was information analysed?

17. Main findings (with particular reference to children and families of minority ethnic origin).

18. The conclusions which you draw from the study about child welfare interventions with minority ethnic children and their families. Please say how 'robust' you consider the evidence to be on which you base those conclusions and where any areas of uncertainty/ambiguity lie.

19. What questions did your research leave unanswered?

The approach to the research review

The review included research and evaluation reports, and a small number of studies in progress where first-stage data analysis had been completed, as well as published research and statistics. Researchers known to be working in the fields of child welfare were asked to provide summaries, focusing particularly on the dimensions of ethnicity and culture in their work. Some summaries were already available (as with the Joseph Rowntree research programme on ethnicity and disability). Three workshops were held bringing together researchers and statisticians to debate the evidence. The emphasis of the workshops was on research methodology and the 'robustness' of the data currently available, with the aim of teasing out explanations for any inconsistencies and of debating the validity and generalisability of their studies. Discrepancies of fact and differences of interpretation were explored. Areas of ambiguity and gaps in the research were identified, leading to suggestions for a future research agenda. Before each of the workshops a draft research overview was circulated for comments to all those participating or who provided research summaries but were unable to attend. Thirty-one researchers came to one or more of the workshops and 61 were invited. There have been two national seminars involving policy makers, practitioners and a small number of service users prior to the completion of this manuscript.

Web-based searches used a combination of keywords: families, children, adolescents, family support, placement, protection, in need, intervention, social work, social care, social workers, social services, social welfare, provision of services, voluntary organisations, ethnicity, ethnic minority, minorities, race, religion, language, culture, cultural identity, identity, race relations, racism, multiculturalism, African, Caribbean, black, Asian, Bangladesh*, Pakistan*, White, black and ethnic children, Muslim, disability, perceptions of disability, asylum, refugees, in care, foster care, kinship care, child care, adopt*, child adoption, child welfare, transracial adoption, interracial families, carer*, abuse*, care leavers, health, mental health, mental illness, self harm, community care, interpreters, children act, parenting, family centres, single-parent families, sure start, children's fund, mediation, protection, risk*, Statistics, SSI, Censuses. These turned up a large volume of work which had to be sifted for its relevance to UK child welfare services in the UK. In the body of the publication we have concentrated on research conducted in the UK or that was transferable to child welfare services in the UK.

The following E-Journal collections, databases and search engines were used: SOSIG, IBSS (BIDS), DOH, Regard, EBSCO, Google, CareData, CHILDDATA, National Statistics Online, UEA Catalogue (OPAC), PsychINFO, Science Direct,

Zetoc (Brit. Lib.), Social Sciences Citation Index, Web of Knowledge, CareDataWeb. Searches were conducted for published work and grey literature at University of East Anglia Libraries.

An asterisk after a word results in a search for similar words. For example, adopt will result in a search for 'adoption', 'adoptee', 'adopted', etc.

References

Adelman, L., Middleton, S. and Ashworth, K. (2003) *Britain's Poorest Children: Severe and Persistent Poverty and Social Exclusion.* London: Centre for Research on Social Policy and Save the Children.

Adoption Register for England and Wales (2003) *Annual Report.* London.

Africans Unite Against Child Abuse (2002) *The Challenges of Migration: The Experiences of the African Child in the UK.* London: AFRUCA.

Ahmed, S., Cheetham, J. and Small, J. (1986) *Social Work with Black Children and their Families.* London: Batsford, British Agencies for Adoption and Fostering.

Aldgate, J. and Bradley, M. (1999) *Supporting Families Through Short Term Fostering.* London: The Stationery Office.

Aldgate, J. and Tunstill, J. (1996) *Making Sense of Section 17: Implementing Services for Children in Need within the 1989 Children Act.* London: HMSO.

Ali, Z., Fazil, Q., Bywaters, P., Wallace, L. and Singh, G. (2001) 'Disability, Ethnicity and Childhood: A Critical Review of Research.' *Disability and Society 16,* 7, 949–968.

Anane-Agyei, A., Hobatto, W. and Messent, P. (2002) 'The African Families Project: A Black and White Issue.' In B. Mason and A. Sawyer (eds) *Exploring the Unsaid: Creativity, risks and dilemmas in working cross-culturally.* London: Karnac Books.

Anderson, A. (1997) 'Servants and Slaves: Europe's Domestic Workers.' *Race and Class 39,* 1, 37–49.

Armstrong, S. and Slaytor, P. (eds) (2001) *The Colour of Difference: Journeys in Transracial Adoption.* Sydney: The Federation Press.

Arnold, E. and James, M. (1989) 'Finding Black Families for Black Children in Care: A Case Study.' *New Community 15,* 3, 417–425.

Aspinall, P. (2000) 'The Challenges of Measuring the Ethno-cultural Diversity of Britain in the New Millennium.' *Policy and Politics 28,* 1, 109–118.

Axford, N., Little, M. and Morpeth, L. (in preparation) *Children Supported and Unsupported in the Community.* Totnes: Dartington Social Research Unit.

Aymer, C. and Okitikpi, T. (2001) *Young Black Men and the Connexions Service.* London: Department for Education and Skills.

Ballard, R. (1999) *Britain's Visible Minorities: A Demographic Overview.* Manchester: Centre for Applied South Asian Studies. www.art.man.ac.uk/CASAs

Banks, N. (1995) 'Children of Black Mixed Parentage and their Placement Needs.' *Adoption and Fostering 19,* 2, 19–24.

Barker, C. (1999) *Protecting Children from Racism and Racial Abuse: A Research Review.* London: National Society for the Prevention of Cruelty to Children.

Barlow, J., Shaw, R. and Stewart-Brown, S. (2003) *Parenting Programmes and Minority Ethnic Parents.* York: Joseph Rowntree Foundation.

Barn, R. (1993) *Black Children in the Public Care System.* London: Batsford.

Barn, R. (1999a) 'White Mothers, Mixed-Parentage Children, and Child Welfare.' *British Journal of Social Work 29,* 2, 269–284.

Barn, R. (ed) (1999b) *Working with Black Children and Adolescents in Need.* London: British Agencies for Adoption and Fostering.

Barn, R. (2001) *Black Youth on the Margins: A Research Review*. York: Joseph Rowntree Foundation.

Barn, R., Sinclair, R. and Ferdinand, D. (1997) *Acting on Principle: An Examination of Race and Ethnicity in Social Services Provision for Children and Families*. London: British Agencies for Adoption and Fostering.

Barnardos (forthcoming) *Organizational factors which promote or impede effective service provision to black and ethnic minority communities – a review of recent literature*. London: Barnardos.

Barnes, J. and the NESS Research Team (2003) 'Characteristics of Sure Start local programme areas. Rounds 1 to 4 National Evaluation of Sure Start Report No. 3.' http://www.ness.bbk.ac.uk/documents/Activities/LCA/FinalLCAReportJuly2003.pdf

Barrett, D. (ed) (1997) *Child Prostitution in Britain*. London: The Children's Society.

Barrett, D. (ed) (2000) *Youth Prostitution in the New Europe*. London: Russell House.

Barrett, D. and Melrose, M. (2003) 'Courting Controversy – Children Sexually Abused through Prostitution.' *Child and Family Law Quarterly 15*, 4, 371–382.

Barter, C. (1999) *Protecting Children from Racism and Racial Abuse: A research review*. London: NSPCC.

Barth, R. P. (1997) 'Effects of Age and Race on the Odds of Adoption Versus Remaining in Long-term Out-of-home Care.' *Child Welfare 76*, 2, 285–308.

Barth, R. and Berry, M. (1988) *Adoption and Disruption: Rates, Risks and Responses*. New York: Aldine de Gruyter.

Battacharya, G., Ison, L. and Blair, M. (2003) *Minority Ethnic Attainment and Participation in Education and Training*. London: Department for Education and Skills.

Bebbington, A. and Miles, J. C. (1989) 'The Background of Children who Enter Local Authority Care.' *British Journal of Social Work 19*, 349–368.

Becher, H. and Husain, F. (2003) *Supporting Minority Ethnic Families: South Asian Hindus and Muslims in Britain: Developments in Family Support*. London: National Family and Parenting Institute.

Beek, M. and Schofield, G. (2004) *Providing a Secure Base in Long-term Foster Care*. London: British Agencies for Adoption and Fostering.

Beishon, S., Modood, T. and Virdee, S. (1998) *Ethnic Minority Families*. London: Policy Studies Institute.

Berridge, D. and Brodie, I. (1998) *Children's Homes Revisited*. London: Jessica Kingsley Publishers.

Berridge, D. and Cleaver, H. (1987) *Foster Home Breakdown*. Oxford: Basil Blackwell.

Berridge, D. and Smith, P. (1993) *Ethnicity and Child Care Placements*. London: National Children's Bureau.

Berridge, D., Beecham, J., Brodie, I. Coles, T., Daniels, H., Knapp, M. and MacNeill, V. (2003) 'Services for Troubled Adolescents: Exploring User Variation.' *Child and Family Social Work 8*, 4, 269–280.

Berthoud, R. (2000) *Family Formation in Multi-cultural Britain: Three Patterns of Diversity*. Colchester: Institute for Social and Economic Research, University of Essex.

Bhabra, S., and Ghate, D. with Brazier, L. (2002) *Consultation Analysis: Raising the Educational Attainment of Children in Care. Final Report to the Social Exclusion Unit*. London: Policy Research Bureau.

Bhardwaj, A. (2001) 'Growing Up Young, Asian and Female in Britain: A Report on Self-harm and Suicide.' *Feminist Review 68*, 52–67.

Biehal, N., Clayden, J., Stein, M. and Wade, J. (1992) *Prepared for Living?* London: National Children's Bureau.

Biehal, N., Wade, J., Clayden, J. and Stein, M. (1995) *Moving On. Young People and Leaving Care Schemes.* London: HMSO.

Bignall, T. and Butt, J. (2000) *Between Ambition and Achievement: Young Black Disabled People's Views and Experiences of Independence and Independent Living.* London: Policy Press.

Blofield, J. (2004) *The Bennett Inquiry.* Cambridge: Norfolk, Suffolk and Cambridgeshire Strategic Health Authority, HSG9427.

Bohmann, M. and Sigvardsson, S. (1990) 'Outcome in Adoption: Lessons from Longitudinal Studies.' In D.M. Brozinsky and M.D. Schechter (eds) *The Psychology of Adoption.* New York: Oxford University Press.

Brah, A. (1992) 'Difference, Diversity and Differentiation.' In J. Rouald and A. Rattansi (eds) *Race Culture and Difference.* London: Sage.

Brandon, M. and Lewis, A. (1996a) 'The Children Act Definition of Significant Harm – Interpretations in Practice.' *Health and Social Care in the Community 4*, 1, 11–20.

Brandon, M. and Lewis, A. (1996b) 'Significant Harm and Children's Experiences of Domestic Violence.' *Child and Family Social Work l*, 1, 33–42.

Brandon, M., Thoburn, J., Lewis, A. and Way, A. (1999) *Safeguarding Children with the Children Act 1989.* London: The Stationery Office.

British Agencies for Adoption and Fostering (1998) *Exchanging Visions: Papers on Best Practice in Europe for Children Separated from their Birth Parents.* London: BAAF.

British Agencies for Adoption and Fostering (2000) *Linking Children with Adoptive Parents.* London: BAAF.

British Crime Survey (2000) London: Home Office.

Broad, B. (1998), 'Kinship care: Children Placed with Extended Families and Friends.' *Childright 155*, 16–17.

Broad, B. (2001a) (ed) *Kinship Care: The Placement Choice for Children and Young People.* Lyme Regis: Russell House.

Broad, B. (2001b) 'Kinship Care: Supporting Children in Placements with Extended Family and Friends.' *Adoption and Fostering 25*, 2, 33–42.

Broad, B., Hayes, R. and Rushforth, C. (2001) *Kith and Kin: Kinship Care for Vulnerable Young People.* London: National Children's Bureau.

Brooks, D and Barth, R. (1999) 'Adult Trans-racial and Inter-racial Adoptees: Effects of Race, Gender, Adoptive Family Structure and Placement History on Adjustment Outcomes.' *American Journal of Orthopsychiatry 691*, 89–99.

Brophy, J. (2000a) '"Race" and Ethnicity in Care Proceedings: Implications from a National Survey of Cases Containing Expert Evidence.' *Adoption and Fostering 24*, 2, 70–72.

Brophy, J. (2000b) '"Race" and Ethnicity in Public Law Proceedings.' *Family Law 30*, 740–743.

Brophy, J. (2003) 'Diversity and Child Protection.' *Family Law 33*, 674–678.

Brophy, J. with Bates, P., Brown, L., Cohen, S., Radcliffe, P. and Wale, C.J. (1999) *Expert Evidence in Child Protection Litigation: Where Do We Go From Here?* London: The Stationery Office.

Brophy, J., Jhutti-Johal, J. and Owen, C. (2003a) *Significant Harm: Child Protection Litigation in a Multi-cultural Setting.* London: Department of Constitutional Affairs.

Brophy, J., Jhutti-Johal, J. and Owen, C. (2003b) 'Assessing and Documenting Child Ill-treatment in Ethnic Minority Households.' *Family Law 33*, 756–764.

Brown, L. (2003) 'Mainstream or Margin? The Current Use of Family Group Conferences in Child Welfare Practice in the UK.' *Child and Family Social Work 8*, 4, 331–340.

Butt, J. (1994) *Same Service or Equal Service? The Second Report on Social Services Departments' Development, Implementation and Monitoring of Services for the Black and Minority Ethnic Community.* London: HMSO/National Institute for Social Work.

Butt, J. (2000) *Black and Minority Ethnic Children and their Families, a Literature Review for the Social Services Inspectorate.* London: Racial Equality Unit.

Butt, J. and Box, L. (1998) *Family Centres: A Study of the Use of Family Centres by Black Families.* London: Racial Equality Unit.

Butt, J. and Mirza, K. (1996) *Social Care and Black Communities: A review of recent research studies.* London: HMSO.

Cabinet Office Strategy Unit (2003) *Ethnic Minorities and the Labour Market: Final Report.* London: The Cabinet Office.

Caesar, G., Parchment, M. and Berridge, D. (1994) *Black Perspectives on Services for Children in Need.* Barkingside: Barnardo's/National Children's Bureau.

Candappa, M. (2004) *Improving Services to Black and Ethnic Minority Children and their Families: Four Demonstration Projects under Quality Protects Initiative.* Understanding Children's Social Care Series, No. 6. London: Institute of Education/Department of Health.

Carstens, C. A. (2001) 'Defining the Boundaries: Social Worker Assessment of Sexual Abuse in a Cultural Context – Multivariate Analysis of Workers' Labelling of Intimacy Behaviour.' *Child and Family Social Work 6,* 4, 315–325.

Cawson, P., Wattam, C., Brooker, S. and Kelly, G. (2000) *Child Maltreatment in the United Kingdom: A Study of the Prevalence of Child Abuse and Neglect.* London: National Society for the Prevention of Cruelty to Children.

Cemlyn, S and Briskman, L. (2003) 'Asylum, Children's Rights and Social Work.' *Child and Family Social Work 8,* 3, 163–178.

Chahal, K. and Julienne, L. (1999) *'We Can't All Be White!': Racist Victimisation in the UK.* York: Joseph Rowntree Foundation. www.jrf.org.uk/knowledge/findings/housing/679.asp

Chamba, R., Ahmad, W., Hirst, M., Lawton, D. and Beresford, B. (1999) *On the Edge: Minority Ethnic Families Caring for a Severely Disabled Child.* Bristol: The Policy Press.

Chamba, R., Ahmad, W. and Jones, L. (1998) 'Improving Services for Asian Deaf Children: Parents' and Professionals' Perspectives.' York: Joseph Rowntree Foundation.

Chand, A. (2000) 'The Over-representation of Black Children in the Child Protection System: Possible Causes, Consequences and Solutions.' *Child and Family Social Work 5,* 67–77.

Charles, M., Rashid, S.P. and Thoburn, J. (1992) 'The Placement of Black Children with Permanent New Families.' *Adoption and Fostering 16,* 3, 13–19.

Charlton, L., Crank, M., Kansara, K. and Oliver, C. (1998) *Still Screaming: Birth Parents Compulsorily Separated from their Children.* Manchester: After Adoption.

Cleaver, H. (2000) *Fostering Family Contact. Studies in Evaluating the Children Act 1989.* London: The Stationery Office.

Cleaver, H. and Freeman, P. (1995) *Parental Perspectives in Cases of Suspected Child Abuse.* London: HMSO.

Cline, T., de Abreu, G., Fihosy, C., Gray, H., Lambert, H. and Neale, J. (2002) *Minority Ethnic Pupils in Mainly White School.* London: Department for Education and Skills.

Commission for Racial Equality (1998) *Stereotyping and Racism: Findings from Two Attitude Surveys.* London: CRE.

Cross, M. (1991) 'Editorial.' *New Community 17,* 3 307–311.

Court Service Civil Business Branch (2003) *Guidance: Arranging interpreters for people with a hearing impairment and for foreign languages.* London: Department for Constitutional Affairs.

Dennis, J. (2002) *A Case for Change: How Refugee Children in England are Missing Out.* London: Refugee Council.

Department for Constitutional Affairs (2003) *Judicial Statistics.* London: TSO.

Department for Education and Employment (1999a) *Sure Start: A Guide to Evidence Based Practice.* London: DfEE.

Department for Education and Employment (1999b) *Sure Start for All: Guidance on Involving Minority Ethnic Children and Families.* London: DfEE.

Department for Education and Skills (2003) *Every Child Matters.* London: The Stationery Office.

Department of Health (1995) *Child Protection: Messages from Research.* London: HMSO.

Department of Health (1999a) *Working Together to Safeguard Children.* London: HMSO.

Department of Health (1999b) *Adoption Now: Messages from Research.* Chichester: Wiley.

Department of Health (2000) *Assessing Children in Need and their Families.* London: The Stationery Office.

Department of Health (2001) *The Children Act Now: Messages from Research.* London: HMSO.

Department of Health and Social Security (1985) *Social Work Decisions in Child Care.* London: HMSO.

Derbyshire, H. (1994) *Not in Norfolk: A Study of Racial Harassment in Rural Areas.* Norwich: Race Equality Council.

Devon County Council (2003) *Why Does Race Matter in Devon? A Guide for Foster Carers and Social Services Staff on Meeting the Needs of Black and Minority Ethnic Children and Families.* Exeter: Excellence Not Excuses Working Group, Devon County Council.

Dickens, J., Howell, D., Schofield, G., Sellick, C. and Thoburn, J. (2003) *Report on Looked After Children in West Midlands and Eastern Authorities.* Norwich: University of East Anglia Centre for Research on the Child and Family.

Dutt, R. and Phillips, M. (1996) *Report of the National Commission of Inquiry into the Prevention of Child Abuse. Volume 2. Background Papers.* London: The Stationery Office.

Dutt, R. and Phillips, M. (2000) 'Assessing Black Children in Need and their Families.' In K.N. Dwivedi (ed) (2002) *Meeting the Needs of Ethnic Minority Children: Including Refugee, Black and Mixed Parentage Children: A Handbook for Professionals,* 2nd edition. London: Jessica Kingsley Publishers.

Farmer, E. and Owen, M. (1995) *Child Protection Practice: Private Risks and Public Remedies.* London: HMSO.

Farmer, E. and Pollock, S. (1998) *Sexually Abused and Abusing Children in Substitute Care.* Chichester: Wiley.

Farmer, E., Moyers, S. and Lipscombe, J. (2004) *Fostering Adolescents.* London: Jessica Kingsley Publishers.

Fazil, Q., Bywaters, P., Ali, Z., Wallace, L. and Singh, G. (2002) 'Disadvantage and Discrimination Compounded: The Experience of Pakistani and Bangladeshi Parents of Disabled Children in the UK.' *Disability and Society 17,* 3, 237–253.

Fenton, S., Carter, J. and Modood, T. (2000) 'Ethnicity and Academia, Closure Models, Market Models.' *Sociological Research Online 5,* 2.

Fitzgerald, J. (1990) *Understanding Disruption.* London: British Agencies for Adoption and Fostering.

Fitzgerald, M. and Hale, C. (1996) *Ethnic Minorities, Victimisation and Racial Harrassment. Home Office Research Findings. No.39* London: Home Office Records and Statistics Directorate.

Fletcher, B. (1993) *What's in a Name: The Views of Young People in Foster and Residential Care.* London: National Consumer Council.

Flynn, R. (2000) 'Black Carers for White Children.' *Adoption and Fostering 24*, 1, 47–52.

Flynn, R. (2002a) *Short Breaks: Providing Better Access and More Choice for Black Disabled Children and their Parents.* Bristol: The Policy Press.

Flynn, R. (2002b) 'Research Review: Kinship Foster Care'. *Child and Family Social Work 7*, 311–321.

Fonaghy, P., Steel, M., Higgit, H. and Target, M. (1994) 'The theory and practice of resilience.' *Journal of Child Psychology and Psychiatry 35*, 2, 231–257.

Fratter, J. (1996) *Perspectives on Adoption with Contact.* London: British Agencies for Adoption and Fostering.

Fratter, J. Rowe, J., Sapsford, D. and Thoburn, J. (1991) *Permanent Family Placement: A Decade of Experience.* London: British Agencies for Adoption and Fostering.

Freeman, P and Hunt, J. (1998) *Parental Perspectives on Care Proceedings.* London: The Stationery Office.

Frost, N. (1997) 'Delivering Family Support: Issues and Themes in Service Development.' In N. Parton (ed) *Child Protection and Family Support. Tensions, Contradictions and Possibilities.* London: Routledge.

Frost, N., Johnson, L., Stein, M. and Wallis, L. (2000) 'Home Start and the Delivery of Family Support.' *Children and Society 14*, 5, 328–342.

Gallagher, B., Christmann, K., Fraser, C. and Hodgson, B. (2003) 'International and Internet Child Sexual Abuse and Exploitation – Issues Emerging from Research.' *Child and Family Law Quarterly 15*, 4, 353–370.

Garbarino, J. (1982) *Children and Families in Social Environments.* New York: Aldine de Gruyter.

Gardner, R. (2003) *Supporting Families: Child Protection in the Community.* London: Wiley.

Garnett, L. (1992) *Leaving Care and After Care.* London: National Children's Bureau.

Ghate, D. and Hazel, N. (2002) *Parenting in Poor Environments: Stress, Support and Coping.* London: Jessica Kingsley Publishers.

Gibbs, I. and Sinclair, I. (1998) 'Treatment and Treatment Outcomes in Children's Homes.' *Child and Family Social Work 4*, 1, 1–8.

Gibbs, I. and Sinclair, I. (2000) 'Bullying, Sexual Harassment and Happiness in Residential Children's Homes.' *Child Abuse Review 9*, 247–256.

Gibbons, J. (ed) (1992) *The Children Act 1989 and Family Support – Principles into Practice.* London: HMSO.

Gibbons, J., Conroy, S. and Bell, C. (1995) *Operating the Child Protection System.* London: HMSO.

Gill, O. and Jackson, B. (1983) *Adoption and Race: Black, Asian and Mixed Race Children in White Families.* London: British Agencies for Adoption and Fostering.

Gilligan, R. (1998) 'Beyond Permanence? The importance of rescilience in child permanency planning.' In M. Hill and M. Shaw (eds) *Signposts in Adoption.* London: BAAF.

Gilroy, P. (1993) *Small Acts.* London: Serpent's Tail.

Goodman, R. and Richards, H. (1995) 'Child and Adolescent Psychiatric Presentations in Second-Generation Afro-Caribbeans in Britain.' *British Journal of Psychiatry 167*, 362–369.

Gray, B. (2002a) 'Emotional Labour and Befriending in Family Support and Child Protection in Tower Hamlets.' *Child and Family Social Work 7*, 13–22.

Gray, B. (2002b) 'Working with Families in Tower Hamlets: An Evaluation of the Family Welfare Association's Family Support Services.' *Health and Social Care in the Community 10*, 2, 112–122.

Grotevant, H. D. and McRoy, R. G. (1998) *Openness in Adoption.* Thousand Oaks, CA: Sage.

Halpern, D. and Nazroo, J. (2000) 'The Ethnic Density Effect: Results from a National Community Survey of England and Wales.' *International Journal of Social Psychiatry 46*, 1, 34–46.

Hamilton, C., Daly, C. and Fiddy, A. (2003) *Mapping the Provision of Education and Social Services for Refugees and Asylum Seeking Children: Lessons from the Eastern Region.* Colchester: Children's Legal Centre.

Hardiker, P., Exton, K. and Barker, M. (1991) 'The Social Policy Context of Prevention in Child Care.' *British Journal of Social Work 21*, 4, 341–59.

Harwin, J. and Forrester, D. (2002) *Parental Substance Misuse and Child Welfare: A Study of Social Work with Families in which Parents Misuse Drugs or Alcohol: Interim Report to Nuffield Foundation.* London: Brunel University.

Harwin, J., Owen, M., Locke, R. and Forrester, D. (2003) *Making Care Orders Work: A Study of Care Plans and their Implementation.* London: The Stationery Office.

Haskey, J. (1997) 'Population Review: (8) The Ethnic Minority and Overseas-born Populations of Great Britain.' *Population Trends 88*, 13–30.

Hatton, C., Akram, Y., Shah, R., Robertson, J. and Emerson, E. (2004) *Supporting South Asian Families with a Child with Severe Disabilities.* London: Jessica Kingsley Publishers.

Heath, A. and McMahon, D. (1997) 'Educational and Occupational Attainments: The Impact of Ethnic Origins.' In V. Karn (ed) *Employment and Housing among Ethnic Minorities.* London: The Stationery Office.

Henricson, C., Katz, I., Mesie, J., Sandison, M. and Tunstill, J. (2001) *National Mapping of Family Services in England and Wales: A Consultation Document.* London: National Family and Parenting Institute.

Hodges, J. and Tizard, B. (1989) 'Social and Family Relationships of Ex-institutional Adolescents.' *Journal of Child Psychology and Psychiatry 30*, 1, 77–97.

hooks, B. (1991) *Yearning.* London: Turnaround.

Howe, D. (1997a) *Patterns of Adoption: Nature, Nurture and Psychosocial Development.* Oxford: Blackwell Science.

Howe, D. (1997b) 'Parent-reported Problems in 211 Adopted Children.' *Journal of Child Psychology and Psychiatry 38*, 4, 401–411.

Howe, D., Feast, J. with Coster, D. (2000) *Adoption Search and Reunion: The Long Term Experience of Adopted Adults.* London: Children's Society.

Humphreys, C., Atkar, S. and Baldwin, N. (1999) 'Discrimination in Child Protection Work: Recurring themes in work with Asian Families.' *Child and Family Social Work 4*, 283–291.

Hunt, J. and Macleod, A. (1999) *The Best-Laid Plans: Outcomes in Judicial Decisions in Child Protection Proceedings.* London: The Stationery Office.

Hunt, J., MacLeod, A. and Thomas, C. (1999) *The Last Resort: Child Protection, the Courts and the 1989 Children Act.* London: The Stationery Office.

Husain, F. and O'Brien, M. (1999) *Muslim Families in Europe: Social Existence and Social Care.* London: University of North London.

Hylton, C. (1997) *Family Survival Strategies; Moyenda Black Families Talking, An Exploring Parenthood Project.* York: Joseph Rowntree Foundation.

Ince, L. (1998) *Making it Alone: A Study of the Care Experiences of Young Black People.* London: British Agencies for Adoption and Fostering.

Ivaldi, G. (2000) *Surveying Adoption: A Comprehensive Analysis of Local Authority Adoptions.* London: British Agencies for Adoption and Fostering.

Iwaniec, D. (1995) *The Emotionally Abused and Neglected Child: Identification, Assessment, and Intervention.* Chichester: Wiley.

Jones, A. (2001) 'Child Asylum Seekers and Refugees: Rights and Responsibilities.' *Journal of Social Work 1*, 3, 253–271.

Jones, A. and Butt, J. (1995) *Taking the Initiative.* London: National Society for the Prevention of Cruelty to Children.

Jones, A., Jeyasingham, D. and Rajasooriya, S. (2002) *Invisible Families: The Strengths and Needs of Black Families in which Young People have Caring Responsibilities.* London: Policy Press. www.jrf.org.uk/knowledge/findings/socialcare/412.asp

Jones, D. and Ramchandani, P. (1999) *Child Sexual Abuse: Informing Practice from Research.* London: The Stationery Office.

Jones, L., Atkin. K. and Ahmad, W.I.U. (2001) 'Supporting Asian Deaf Young People and their Families: The Role of Professionals and Services.' *Disability and Society 16*, 1, 51–70.

Kemp, S. P. and Bodonyi J. M. (2000) 'Infants Who Stay in Foster Care: Child Characteristics and Permanency Outcomes of Legally Free Children First Placed as Infants.' *Child and Family Social Work 5*, 2, 95–106.

Kershaw, S. (1999) 'Sex for Sale: A Profile of Young Male Sex Workers.' *Youth and Policy 63*, 26–37.

Khalique, R. and Skidmore, P. (2001) *Tower Hamlets Young People's Sexual Health Peer Research Survey, Autumn 2000–Spring 2001.* London: Docklands Outreach.

Kirton, D. (1999) 'Perspectives on "Race" and Adoption: The Views of Student Social Workers.' *British Journal of Social Work 29*, 779–796.

Kirton, D. (2000) *'Race', Ethnicity and Adoption.* Buckingham: Open University Press.

Kirton, D., Feast, J. and Howe, D. (2000) 'Searching, Reunion and Transracial Adoption.' *Adoption and Fostering 24*, 3, 6–18.

Kohli, R. (2000) 'Breaking the Silence: Social Work with Unaccompanied Asylum Seeking Children.' *Professional Social Work*, June 2000.

Kohli, R. (2003) 'Editorial.' *Child and Family Social Work 8*, 3, p.161.

Kohli, R. and Mather, R. (2003) 'Promoting Psychosocial Well-being in Unaccompanied Asylum Seeking Young People in the United Kingdom.' *Child and Family Social Work 8*, 3, 201–212.

Kurtz, Z., Thomas, R. and Wolkind, S. (1994) *Services for the Mental Health of Children and Young People in England: A national review.* London: South West Thames Regional Health Authority and Department of Health.

Laming, H. (2003) *The Victoria Climbié Inquiry.* London: The Stationery Office.

Lees, S. (2002) 'Gender, Ethnicity and Vulnerability in Young Women in Local Authority Care.' *British Journal of Social Work 32*, 7, 907–922.

Lewis, G. (2000) *Race, Gender and Social Welfare.* Cambridge: Polity Press.

Lindblad, F., Hjern, A. and Vinnerljung, B. (2003) 'Intercountry Adopted Children as Young Adults: A Swedish Cohort Study.' *American Journal of Orthopsychiatry 72*, 2, 190–202.

Little, M. (1997) 'The Re-focusing of Children's Services: The Contribution of Research.' In N. Parton (ed) *Child Protection and Family Support. Tensions, Contradictions and Possibilities.* London: Routledge.

Lloyd, E. (1999) *What Works in Parenting Education*. Barkingside: Barnardos.

Logan. J. (1999) 'Exchanging Information Post-adoption: Views of Adoptive Parents and Birth Parents.' *Adoption and Fostering 23*, 4, 27–37.

London Borough of Lambeth (1987) *Whose Child? The report of the panel of inquiry into the death of Tyra Henry 1987*. London: London Borough of Lambeth.

London Research Centre (1993) *First Findings, London Housing Survey, 1992*. London: London Research Centre.

Lowe, N. and Murch, M. (2002) *The Plan for the Child: Adoption and Long-term Fostering*. London: British Agencies for Adoption and Fostering.

Lowe, N., Murch, M., Borkowski, M., Weaver, A., Beckford, V. and Thomas, C. (1999) *Supporting Adoption: Reframing the Approach*. London: British Agencies for Adoption and Fostering.

Lupton, C. and Stevens, M. (1997) *Family Outcomes: Following through on Family Group Conferences*. Portsmouth: Social Services Information Unit.

MacLeod, M. (1996) *Children and Racism*. London: ChildLine.

MacLeod, M. and Morris, S. (1996) *Why Me? Children talking to Childline about Bullying*. London: Childline.

MacPherson, W. (1999) *The Stephen Lawrence Inquiry*. London: The Stationery Office.

McRoy, R. G., Zurchev, L. A., Lauderdale, M. L. and Anderson, R. N. (1982) 'Self-esteem and Racial Identity in Transracial and Inracial Adoption.' *Social Work 27*, 522–526.

Maitra, B. (1996) 'A Universal "Diagnostic" Category? The Implication of Culture in Definition and Assessment.' *International Journal of Social Psychiatry 42*, 4, 287–304.

Malek, M. and Joughin, C. (eds) (2004) *Mental Health Services for Minority Ethnic Children and Adolescents*. London: Jessica Kingsley Publishers.

Mama, A. (1995) *Beyond the Masks: Race, Gender and Subjectivity*. London: Routledge.

Marsh, P. and Crow, G. (1998) *Family Group Conferences in Child Welfare*. Oxford: Blackwell Science.

Masson, J., Harrison, C. and Pavlovic, A. (1997) *Working with Children and 'Lost' Parents*. York: York Publishing Services.

Melrose, M., Barrett, I. and Brodie, I. (1999) *One Way Street*. London: The Children's Society.

Meltzer, H., Gatward, R., Goodman, R. and Ford, T. (2000) *The Mental Health of Children and Adolescents in Great Britain*. London: The Stationery Office.

Meltzer, H., Gatward, R., Corbin, T., Goodman, R. and Ford, T. (2003) *Persistence, Onset, Risk Factors and Outcomes of Childhood Mental Disorders*. London: The Stationery Office.

Messent, P. and Murrell, M. (2003) 'Research Leading to Action: A Study of Accessibility of a CAMH Service to Ethnic Minority Families.' *Child and Adolescent Mental Health 8*, 3, 118–124.

Mitchell, F. (2003) 'The Social Services Response to Unaccompanied Children in England.' *Child and Family Social Work 8*, 3, 179–189.

Mitchell, F., Rees, G. and Wade, J. (2002) *Young Runaways in Wales: Patterns, Needs and Services*. Cardiff: National Assembly for Wales.

Modood, T., Beishon, S. and Virdee, S. (1994) *Changing Ethnic Identities*. London: Policy Studies Institute.

Modood, T., Berthoud, R., Lakey, J., Nazroo, J., Smith, P., Virdee, S. and Bershon, S. (1997) *Fourth National Survey of Ethnic Minorities in Britain: Diversity and Disadvantage*. London: Policy Studies Institute.

Moffatt, P. G. and Thoburn, J. (2001), 'Outcomes of Permanent Family Placement for Children of Minority Ethnic Origin.' *Child and Family Social Work 6*, 13–21.

Morris, S. and Wheatley, H. (1994) *Time to Listen. The Experiences of Young People in Foster and Residential Care*. London: ChildLine.

Mullender, A., Hague, G., Imam, U., Kelly, L., Malos, E. and Regan, L. (2002) *Children's Perspectives on Domestic Violence*. London: Sage.

Nanton, P. (1992), 'Official Statistics and Problems of Inappropriate Ethnic Categorisation.' *Policy and Politics 20*, 4.

National Evaluation of Sure Start Research Team (NESS) (2003) *Report on Implementation*. London: Department for Education and Skills.

National Statistics (2002) *Labour Force Survey*. London: The Stationery Office.

National Statistics (2003) *Census, April 2001*. London: The Stationery Office.

National Statistics and Department for Education and Skills (2003) *Educational Qualifications of Care Leavers Year Ending 31 March 2002: England*. London: Department for Education and Skills.

National Statistics and Department for Education and Skills (2004) *Children in Need in England. Results of a Survey of Activity and Expenditure as Reported by Local Authority Social Services' Children and Families Teams for a Survey Week in February 2003*. London: Department for Education and Skills.

National Statistics and Department of Health (2001) *Children in Need in England September/October 2001*. London: Department of Health.

National Statistics and Department of Health (2003a) *Referrals, Assessments and Children and Young People on Child Protection Registers*. London: Department of Health.

National Statistics and Department of Health (2003b) *Children Looked After by Local Authorities, Year Ending 31 March 2002, England*. London: Department of Health.

National Statistics Online *Ethnicity, Labour Market*. www.statistics.gov.uk

Nazroo, J. (1997) 'Health and Health Services.' In T. Modood and R. Berthould (eds) *Ethnic Minorities in Britain: Diversity and Disadvantage. The Fourth National Survey of Ethnic Minorities*. London: Policy Studies Institute.

NCH Action for Children (1997) *Family Forum: Family Life – The Age of Anxiety*. London: NCH Action for Children.

Neil, E. (2000) 'The Reasons Why Young Children are Placed for Adoption: Findings from a Recently Placed Sample and a Discussion of Implications for Subsequent Identity Development.' *Child and Family Social Work 5*, 4, 303–316.

Neil, E. (2002a) 'Contact after Adoption: The Role of Agencies in Making and Supporting Plans.' *Adoption and Fostering 26*, 1, 25–38.

Neil, E. (2002b) 'Managing Face to Face Contact for Young Adopted Children.' In H. Argent (ed) *Staying Connected: Managing Contact Arrangements In Adoption*. London: British Agencies for Adoption and Fostering.

Neil, E. (2003) 'Accepting the Reality of Adoption: Birth Relatives' Experiences of Face-to-face Contact.' *Adoption and Fostering 27*, 2, 32–43.

Nobes, G. and Smith, M. (1997) 'Physical Punishment of Children in Two Parent Families.' *Clinical Child Psychology and Psychiatry 2*, 271–281.

Nobes, G., Smith, M., Upton, P. and Heverin, A. (1999) 'Physical Punishment by Mothers and Fathers in British Homes.' *Journal of Interpersonal Violence 14*, 8, 887–902.

Office of Population Censuses and Surveys (1995–97) *Ethnicity in the 1991 Census*, vols 1–4, London: HMSO.

O'Neale, V. (2000) *Excellence Not Excuses: Inspection of Services for Ethnic Minority Children and Families*. London: Social Services Inspectorate.

Okitikpi, T. and Aymer, C. (2003) 'Social Work with African Refugee Children and their Families.' *Child and Family Social Work 8*, 3, 213–222.

Owen, D. (1996) 'Black-Other: The melting pot.' In C. Peach (ed) *Ethnicity in the 1991 Census 2.* London: OPCS.

Owen, M. (1999) *Novices, Old Hands and Professionals: A Study of Adoption by Single People.* London: British Agencies for Adoption and Fostering.

Owen, M. and Farmer, E. (1996) 'Child Protection in a Multi-racial Context.' *Policy and Politics 24,* 3, 299–313.

Oxfam and The Refugee Council (2002) *Poverty and Asylum in the UK.* London: The Refugee Council.

Oxford English Dictionary (2002) Oxford: Oxford University Press.

Packman, J. and Hall, C. (1998) *From Care to Accommodation: Support, Protection and Control in Child Care Services.* London: The Stationery Office.

Packman, J., Randall, J. and Jacques, N. (1986) *Who Needs Care?* Oxford: Blackwell.

Palmer, T. and Stacey, L. (2002) *Stolen Children: Barnardos' Work with Children Abused through Prostitution.* Barkingside: Barnardos.

Pankaj, V. (2000) *Family Mediation Services for Minority Ethnic Families in Scotland.* Edinburgh: The Scottish Executive Central Research Unit.www.scotland.gov.uk/cru/kd01/purple/mediation-01.pdf

Parekh, B. (2000) *The Future of Multi-Ethnic Britain, Report of the Commission on the Future of Multi-Ethnic Britain.* London: Profile Books.

ParentlinePlus Nottingham (2002) *Helpline Ethnic Monitoring Pilot Discussion Document.* London: ParentlinePlus.

ParentlinePlus (2003) *National Call Data Report April 03–September 03.* London: ParentlinePlus.

Parker, D. (1995) *Through Different Eyes: The cultural identities of young Chinese people in Britain.* Aldershott: Avebury.

Parton, N. (ed) (1997) *Child Protection and Family Support. Tensions, Contradictions and Possibilities.* London: Routledge.

Performance and Innovations Unit (2000) *Prime Minister's Review: Adoption.* London: The Cabinet Office.

Phillips, C. and Bowling, B. (2002) 'Racism, Ethnicity, Crime and Criminal Justice.' In M. Maguire, R. Morgan and R. Reiner (eds) *The Oxford Handbook of Criminology,* 3rd edition. Oxford: Oxford University Press.

Philpot, T. (2001) *A Very Private Practice: An Investigation into Private Fostering.* London: British Agencies for Adoption and Fostering.

Prevatt Goldstein, B. (1999) 'Black, with a White Parent, a Positive and Achievable Identity.' *British Journal of Social Work 29,* 2, 285–301.

Prevatt Goldstein, B. (2002) 'Catch 22 – Black Workers' Role in Equal Opportunities for Black Service Users.' *British Journal of Social Work 32,* 765–778.

Prevatt Goldstein, B. and Small, J. (2000) 'Ethnicity and Placement: Beginning the Debate.' *Adoption and Fostering 24,* 1, 9–15.

Prevatt Goldstein, B. and Spencer, M. (2000) *'Race' and Ethnicity: A Consideration of Issues for Black, Minority Ethnic and White Children in Family Placement.* London: British Agencies for Adoption and Fostering.

Prevatt Goldstein, B. (2003) 'Black Families and Survival.' In S. Cunningham-Burley and J. Jamieson (eds) *Families and the State, Changing Relationships.* Basingstoke: Palgrave MacMillan.

Quinton, D. (2004) *Supporting Parents: Messages from Research.* London: Jessica Kingsley Publishers.

Quinton, D. and Selwyn, J. (1998) 'Contact with Birth Parents in Adoption – A Response to Ryburn.' *Child and Family Law Quarterly 10*, 4, 349–61.

Quinton, D., Rushton, A., Dance, C. and Mayes, D. (1997) 'Contact Between Children Placed Away from Home and their Birth Parents: Research Issues and Evidence.' *Clinical Child Psychology and Psychiatry 2*, 3, 393–413.

Quinton, D., Rushton, A., Dance, C. and Mayes, D. (1998) *Joining New Families: A Study of Adoption and Fostering in Middle Childhood.* Chichester: Wiley.

Qureshi, J., Berridge, D. and Wenman, H. (2000) *Where to Turn: Family Support for South Asian Communities.* London: National Children's Bureau/Joseph Rowntree Foundation.

Radford, K. (2004) *Count Me In.* Belfast: Save the Children.

Rashid, S. P. (2000) 'The Strengths of Black Families.' *Adoption and Fostering 24*, 1, 15–22.

Raws, P. (2001) *Lost Youth: Young Runaways in Northern Ireland.* London: The Children's Society.

Raynor, L. (1970) *Adoption of Non-white Children: The Experience of a British Adoption Project.* London: Allen and Unwin.

Razarch, S. (1998) *Looking White People in the Eye.* Toronto: University of Toronto Press.

Refugee Council and British Agencies for Adoption and Fostering (2001) *Where Are the Children?* London: Refugee Council.

Rhodes, P. J. (1992) *Racial Matching in Fostering – The Challenge to Social Work Practice.* Aldershot: Avebury.

Richards, A. (2001) *Second Time Around: A Survey of Grandparents Raising their Grandchildren.* London: Family Rights Group.

Richards, A. and Ince, L. (2000) *Overcoming the Obstacles.* London: Family Rights Group.

Robinson, L. (2000), 'Racial Identity, Attitudes and Self-Esteem of Black Adolescents in Residential Care: An Exploratory Study.' *British Journal of Social Work 30*, 3–24.

Robinson, L. (2001) 'A Conceptual Framework for Social Work Practice with Black Children and Adolescents in the United Kingdom.' *Journal of Social Work 1*, 2, 165–185.

Rowe, J., Hundleby, M. and Garnett, L. (1989) *Child Care Now: A Survey of Placement Patterns.* London: BAAF.

Rowe, J., Hundleby, M. and Keane, A. (1984) *Long-term Foster Care.* London: Batsford.

Rushton, A. (2004) *The Adoption of Looked After Children. A Scoping Review.* London: SCIE.

Rushton, A. and Dance, C. (2003) 'Preferentially Rejected Children and their Development in Permanent Family Placement.' *Child and Family Social Work 8*, 4, 257–268.

Rushton, A. and Minnis, H. (1997) 'Annotation: Transracial Family Placements.' *Journal of Child Psychology and Psychiatry 38*, 147–59.

Rushton, A. and Minnis, H. (2000) 'Transracial Placements: A Commentary on a New Adult Outcome Study.' *Adoption and Fostering 24*, 1, 53–58.

Rushton, A., Dance, C. and Quinton, D. (2000) 'Findings from a UK Based Study of Late Permanent Placements.' *Adoption Quarterly 3*, 3, 51–71.

Rushton, A., Dance, C., Quinton, D. and Mayes, D. (2001) *Siblings in Late Permanent Placements.* London: British Agencies for Adoption and Fostering.

Rushton A., Treseder, J. and Quinton, D. (1995) 'An 8 Year Prospective Study of Older Boys Placed in Permanent Substitute Families.' *Journal of Child Psychology and Psychiatry 36*, 4, 687–695.

Rutter, M. (1987) 'Psychosocial resilience and protective mechanisms.' *American Journal of Orthopsychiatry 57*, 316–331.

Rutter, M. and the English and Romanian adoptees study team (1997) 'Developmental Catch-up and Deficit Following Adoption after Marked Early Privation.' *Journal of Child Psychology and Psychiatry 339*, 4, 465–476.

Rutter, M. and Tienda, M. (submitted) 'The Multiple Facets of Ethnicity.' In M. Rutter and M. Tienda (eds) *Ethnicity and Causal Mechanisms.* New York: Cambridge University Press.

Rutter, M., Andersen-Wood, L., Beckett, C., Bredenkamp, D., Castle, J., Groothues, C., Kreppner, J., Keaveney, L., Lord, C. and O'Connor, T.G. (1999) 'Quasi-autistic Patterns Following Marked Early Global Privation.' *Journal of Child Psychology and Psychiatry 40*, 4, 437–449.

Rutter, M., Giller, M. and Hagell, A. (1998) *Anti-Social Behaviour by Young People.* Oxford: Blackwell.

Ryan, M. (2000) *Working With Fathers.* Abingdon: Radcliffe Medical Press.

Ryburn, M. (1997) 'In whose best interests? Post-adoption contact with the birth family.' *Child and Family Law Quarterly 53*, 53–70.

Safe on the Streets Research Team (1999) *Still Running: Children on the Streets in the UK.* Barkingside: Barnardos.

Schofield, G. (2002) *Part of the Family: Pathways through Foster Care.* London: British Agencies for Adoption and Fostering.

Schofield, G., Beek, M., Sargent, K. with Thoburn, J. (2000) *Growing up in Foster Care.* London: British Agencies for Adoption and Fostering.

Scourfield, J., Evans, J., Shah, W. and Beynon, H. (2002) 'Responding to the Experiences of Minority Ethnic Children in Virtually All-white Communities.' *Child and Family Social Work 7*, 3, 161–176.

Sellick, C. and Connolly, J. (2001) *National Survey of Independent Fostering Agencies.* Norwich: University of East Anglia.

Sellick, C. and Thoburn, J. (2002) 'Family Placement Services.' In D. McNeish *et al.* (eds) *What Works? Effective Social Care Services for Children and Families.* Milton Keynes: Open University Press/Barnardos.

Sellick, C., Thoburn, J. and Philpot, T. (2004) *What Works in Adoption and Foster Care?* Barkingside: Barnardos.

Selman, P. (ed) (2000) *Intercountry Adoption: Developments, Trends and Perspectives.* London: British Agencies for Adoption and Fostering.

Selwyn, J and Sturgess, W. (2001) *International Overview of Adoption – Policy and Practice.* Bristol: School of Policy Studies.

Sheldon, B. (2001) 'The validity of evidence based practice in social work.' *British Journal of Social Work 31*, 5, 801–810.

Sheppard, M. and Kelly, N. (2001) *Social Work Practice with Depressed Mothers in Child and Family Care.* London: The Stationery Office.

Simmonds, J. (2001) *First Steps in Becoming an Adoptive Parent: An Evaluation of National Adoption Week 1989.* London: British Agencies for Adoption and Fostering.

Simmonds, J., Bull, H. and Martin, H. (1998) *Family Group Conferences in Greenwich Social Services.* London: Goldsmiths College.

Sinclair, I. and Gibbs, I. (1998) *Children's Homes: A Study in Diversity.* Chichester: Wiley.

Sinclair, I. and Gibbs, I. (1999a) 'Measuring the Turbulence of English Children's Homes.' *Children and Youth Services Review 21*, 1, 57–64.

Sinclair, I. and Gibbs, I. (1999b) 'Staff Qualifications and Ratios in Children's Homes: Are They the Key to the Outcomes of Care?' *Policy and Politics 27*, 4, 187–197.

Sinclair, R. and Hai, N. (2003) *Children of Mixed Heritage in Need in Islington.* London: National Children's Bureau.

Sinclair, I. and Wilson, K. (2003) 'Matches and Mismatches: The Contribution of Carers and Children to the Success of Foster Placements.' *British Journal of Social Work,* 871–874.

Sinclair, I., Gibbs, I. and Wilson, K. (2004) *Foster Carers: Why They Stay and Why They Leave.* London: Jessica Kingsley Publishers.

Sinclair, I., Wilson, K. and Gibbs, I. (2004) *Foster Placements: Why They Succeed and Why They Fail.* London: Jessica Kingsley Publishers.

Small, J. (1982) 'New Black Families.' *Adoption and Fostering 6,* 3, 35–39.

Smith, C. and Carlson, B.E. (1997) 'Stress, coping and resilience in children and youth.' *Social Studies Review 7,* 2, 231–236.

Smith, C. and Logan J. (2004) *After Adoption: Direct Contact and Relationships.* London: Routledge.

Smith, L. (1998) *Essex Family Group Conference Project Summary Report.* Chelmsford: Essex Social Services Department.

Smith, M. A., Heverin, A., Nobes, G., and Upton, P. (1995) *Punishment and Control of Children in the Home: Parental Actions and Strategies: Report to the Department of Health.* London: Thomas Coram Research Unit.

Smith, T. (1996) *Family Centres.* London: HMSO.

Social Exclusion Unit (2003) *Minority Ethnic Issues in Social Exclusion and Neighbourhood Renewal.* London: Office of the Deputy Prime Minister.

Sonuga-Barke, E. J. S. and Mistry, M. (2000) 'The Effect of Extended Family Living on the Mental Health of Three Generations within Two Asian Communities.' *British Journal of Clinical Psychology 39,* 129–141.

Statham, J., Dillon, J. and Moss, P. (2001) *Placed and Paid For: Supporting Families through Sponsored Day Care.* London: The Stationery Office.

The Stephen Lawrence Inquiry (2000) *The Report of the Inquiry (CM 4262-1).* London: The Stationery Office.

Stevenson, O. (1998) *Neglected Children: Issues and Dilemmas.* Oxford: Blackwell Science.

Strachan, R. and Patel, K. (1996) *Anti-Racist Practice or Heuristics.* Preston: University of Central Lancashire Racism and Welfare Conference.

Swann Report (1985) *Education for All: The Report of the Committee of Inquiry into the Education of Children from Ethnic Minority Groups.* London: HMSO.

Thoburn, J. (1990) *Success and Failure in Permanent Family Placement.* Aldershot: Avebury.

Thoburn, J. (2002a) 'Outcomes of Permanent Substitute Family Placement for Children in Care.' In T. Vecciato, A. N. Maluccio and C. Canali (eds) *Evaluation in Child and Family Services.* New York: Aldine de Gruyter.

Thoburn, J. (2002b) *Adoption and Permanence for Children who Cannot Live Safely with Birth Parents or Relatives. Quality Protects Briefing 5.* London: Department of Health.

Thoburn, J., Lewis, A. and Shemmings, D. (1995) *Paternalism or Partnership? Family Involvement in the Child Protection Process.* London: HMSO.

Thoburn, J., Murdoch, A. and O'Brien, A. (1986) *Permanence in Child Care.* Oxford: Blackwell.

Thoburn, J., Norford, L. and Rashid, S. P. (2000) *Permanent Family Placement for Children of Minority Ethnic Origin.* London: Jessica Kingsley Publishers.

Thoburn, J., Wilding, J. and Watson, J. (2000) *Family Support in Cases of Emotional Maltreatment and Neglect.* London: The Stationery Office.

Thomas, C., Beckford, V., Lowe, N. and Murch, M. (1999) *Adopted Children Speaking.* London: British Agencies for Adoption and Fostering.

Thomas, N. (1994) *In the Driving Seat: A Study of the Family Group Meetings Project in Hereford.* Swansea: University of Wales Department of Social Policy.

Tilbury, C. (2004) 'The influence of performance measurement on child welfare and practice.' *British Journal of Social Work 34,* 214–225.

Timms, J. and Thoburn, J. (2003) *Your Shout!* London: National Society for the Prevention of Cruelty to Children.

Tizard, B. and Phoenix, A. (1993) *Black, White or Mixed Race? Race and Racism in the Lives of Young People of Mixed Parentage.* London: Routledge.

Triseliotis, J., Shireman, J. and Hundleby, M. (1997) *Adoption: Theory, Policy and Practice.* London: Cassell.

Tunstill, J. and Aldgate, J. (2000) *Services for Children in Need: From Policy to Practice.* London: The Stationery Office.

Tunstill, J. and Aldgate, J. with Hughes, M. and Peel, M. (2004) *Family Support at the Centre: The Role of Family Centres in the Local Service Network.* London: Royal Holloway College, University of London.

Virdee, S. (1997) 'Racial Harassment.' In T. Modood and R. Berthould (eds) *Ethnic Minorities in Britain: Diversity and Disadvantage, the Fourth National Survey of Ethnic Minorities.* London: Policy Studies Institute.

Vonk, M. E. (2001) 'Cultural Competence for Transracial Adoptive Parents.' *Social Work 46,* 3, 246–255.

Wade, J. (2002) *Missing Out: Young Runaways in Scotland.* Aberlour Child Care Trust.

Wade, J. (2003) 'Children on the Edge – Patterns of Running Away in the UK.' *Child and Family Law Quarterly 15,* 4, 343–352.

Wade, J. and Biehal, N. with Clayden, J. and Stein, M. (1998) *Going Missing. Young People Absent from Care.* Chichester: Wiley.

Warman, A. and Roberts, C. (2003) *Adoption and Looked after Children: An International Comparison.* Oxford: Oxford Centre for Family Law and Policy.

Waterhouse, S. and Brocklesby, E. (1999) 'Placement Choices for Children – Giving More Priority to Kinship Placements?' In R. Greef (ed) *Fostering Kinship.* Aldershot: Ashgate.

Webb, S. (2001) 'Some considerations on the validity of evidence based practice in social work.' *British Journal of Social Work 31,* 1, 57–80.

Webster, C. (1995) *Youth Crime, Victimisation and Racial Harassment: The Keighley Crime Survey.* Bradford: Bradford and Ilkley College, Centre for Research in Applied Community Studies.

Werner, P. and Modood, T. (1999) *Debating Cultural Hybridity.* London: Zed Books.

Wilson, A. (1987) *Mixed Race Children: A Study of Identity.* London: Allen and Unwin.

Wimmer, A. (2004) 'Does Ethnicity Matter? Everyday group formation in three Swiss immigrant neighbourhoods.' *Ethnic and Racial Studies 27,* 1, 1–36.

Youth Justice Board (2003) *Youth Survey 2003: A Research Study Conducted for the Youth Justice Board by MORI January–March 2003.* London: Youth Justice Board.

Subject Index

Author Index